MW01291789

The
Last Bake Sale

The Fight for Fair School Funding

Andru Volinsky

Change can happen.

Andru

Peter E. Randall Publisher
Portsmouth, New Hampshire
2025

© 2025 Andru Volinsky

All rights reserved. No part of this publication may be reproduced, distributed, or transmitted in any form or by any means, including photocopying, recording, or other electronic or mechanical methods, without the prior written permission of the publisher, except in the case of brief quotations embodied in critical reviews and certain other noncommercial uses permitted by copyright law.

ISBN: 978-1-942155-90-4 print
ISBN: 978-1-942155-91-1 eBook
Library of Congress Control Number: 2024923920

Published by
Peter E. Randall Publisher LLC
5 Greenleaf Woods Drive, U102
Portsmouth, NH 03801
www.PERPublisher.com

Book Design: Tim Holtz
Cover Design: Trevor Bartlett

Printed in the United States of America

This book is dedicated to my loving wife, Amy, who has taken much more blame, and not enough credit, for my conduct than she deserves. It will continue to be a very interesting adventure for quite a while. It is also dedicated to our children Joshua, Mollie and Bekah of whom we are very proud and to whom I apologize for always being late to pick you up. Now you know why I wasn't there on time.

Contents

Introduction

Dr. José Cárdenas was the superintendent of the Edgewood Independent School District, one of nine school districts in the city of San Antonio, Texas. It was the poorest district of the nine and was located in the hot and gritty lower part of the city. Its children were mostly Mexican American. High above was the Alamo Heights Independent School District, sitting on the bluffs looking down on Edgewood. Its school population was overwhelmingly Anglo.

The educational differences between the well-funded Alamo Heights school district and the poorly funded Edgewood school district set the scene for school funding fights that occurred across the nation over the next fifty years. Forty-five states have hosted efforts by litigants, community organizers, parents, and educators to fight for needed resources for schoolchildren living in poverty and a modicum of equity for taxpayers who foot the bill. New Hampshire, where I was lead litigation counsel for more than a decade, was part of this fight. New Hampshire has one of the least equitable funding systems in the nation, where the poorest taxpayers pay the highest school taxes and the wealthiest pay the least. Even though they pay the lowest taxes, the wealthiest taxpayers are able to provide the most resources for their children, at times ignoring the needs of others.

Dr. Cárdenas, who became a national leader in the fair-school-funding movement, found that resources in Edgewood were so limited that students in high school typing classes drew keyboards on pieces of cardboard because the school could not afford typewriters. He also learned the absence of resources was not the Edgewood community's fault. Residents of Edgewood worked hard for their children and paid higher taxes than residents of Alamo Heights.

Two factors conspire against school districts with high poverty levels in America. The first factor is simply the math of school funding. In school districts with low property wealth, like Edgewood, even higher taxes are not enough to raise revenues sufficient to meet local needs.

Second, even though states could make up the difference in funding, they almost never do. Some states, in fact, give more state money to the wealthy districts than to the neediest.

New Hampshire takes this failing paradigm to an extreme,[1] as its state funds constitute the lowest percentage of school funding in America. New Hampshire relies more heavily on local property taxes to fund its schools than any other state, and this extreme reliance on local school property taxes accentuates the differences in property wealth. Communities with high property wealth really do have an advantage and pass that advantage on to their children.

Litigators and organizers have brought to light not only the schools that could not afford typewriters but also the impact of school buildings that are old, cold and ill-suited to educational purposes, and that are also unsafe and unsanitary.

These conditions have lifelong effects on the children without privilege who attend these schools. These children are often Black or Brown. As one leader in the fair-funding movement has said, "It is almost always about race."

New Hampshire's unique tax structure, without a broad income or sales tax, protects those with wealth and privilege. While New Hampshire has the wealth to fix its school funding problems, it resists necessary changes. Leaders in other states do not all have the wealth to address needed improvements in funding.

Like many states, New Hampshire has two school systems: one is well-financed and achieves high academic standards. The other is failing. Both are financed primarily by local property taxes. Like Texas and other states across the country, New Hampshire's best schools are often in the school districts with the lowest taxes. In these well-funded districts, property values are very high and, as a result, taxes can be kept very low.

It's just the math.

If two districts plan to raise the same amount of revenue to fund their schools, the one with higher property values achieves its goal with lower taxes. The higher property values are often not a result of the residents being more industrious. They result from the community's ability to wrangle state resources for economic development, or are the result of a desirable location on a lake, near a ski area, or overlooking the ocean. In the poorer school districts, property values are limited and, even with high tax rates, schools cannot keep up.

Newport, New Hampshire, is a poor community in the western part of the state. An active machining industry once thrived there, as did woolen mills. Both are now long shuttered. Newport's students achieve among the lowest scores on standardized tests in the state. Almost half are eligible for free or reduced-price lunch, which indicates a high level of poverty.

Adjacent Sunapee, New Hampshire, is located on a beautiful lake. It has eight times the property value of Newport. Newport's school tax rates are much higher than Sunapee's even though Newport spends less on its schoolchildren. The cost of homes is high in Sunapee on the lake. There is, in effect, a price of admission to attend good schools and have lower taxes.

As one attendee at a school funding seminar in Newport aptly put it, "If the glacier cut left instead of right, we'd have the lake and Sunapee would have the school funding problem."

States across the country maintain similarly regressive school funding schemes, where children who are most in need of public schools are provided the fewest resources while their parents pay the highest taxes. Children in wealthy districts attend well-funded schools with substantial resources, while their parents pay low taxes. Worse, wealthy districts receive state aid that has been commandeered to favor the most privileged. Lawyers and school advocates have challenged these funding schemes, which deprive children of adequate resources and impose inequitable burdens on taxpayers.

The first part of this book looks at the national scene, explaining how the law and complementary public and political engagement strategies developed. The school funding story is intertwined with the story of race in our country and of privilege protecting privilege. The story begins with the 1954 *Brown v. Board of Education* desegregation case and runs into a brick wall erected by a seemingly hospitable and genteel son of the South, Justice Lewis Powell Jr.

The second part focuses on the shortcomings and unfairness of the New Hampshire school funding system, with an eye towards sharing lessons learned. New Hampshire's most inhospitable counterpart to Lewis Powell was William Loeb, the former publisher of New Hampshire's only statewide newspaper, the *Union Leader* of Manchester. Loeb used his front pages to bludgeon politicians, race bait, and make First-in-the-Nation presidential candidates miserable.

The third part of the book provides a prescription for what we need to do to fund and support public education based on New Hampshire's example.

Throughout, this book describes how to leverage school funding litigation, and other forms of public-policy-oriented litigation, to complement grassroots organizing and political efforts. Engaging in litigation to shape public policy is a very difficult proposition, especially when the clients are poor or otherwise disadvantaged. Sometimes, however, there are few alternatives. Our litigation that spanned 1990 through 2003 occurred in the context of a judiciary that was not liberal. The chief justice of the New Hampshire Supreme Court during much of our litigation, David Brock, was a former Marine who was appointed by Meldrim Thomson Jr., a skinflinty governor who hated communists and ran on a platform of "Ax the Tax."

School funding is the story of how we treat our children. It is also about how we treat our democracy. Both aspects are poignant, with lots of twists, turns, and intrigue. My hope in writing this book was not only to record our history but to move the reader to action. Although the focus here is on school funding, the lessons learned can be applied to other seemingly intractable problems, like housing, climate and income inequality. Organizers reinforced by lawyers who are committed to making change can make a difference.

Good luck to you who are working to make change happen.

PART ONE

Why a National Movement Became Necessary

Chapter 1

Plessy to *Brown*
The End of Legal Segregation

The case of *Brown v. Board of Education* outlawed segregation in public schools.[2] It is among the most important cases ever decided by the United States Supreme Court.

Brown put the lie to the concept of "separate but equal" and established education as an important constitutional right. In the court's 1954 decision, Chief Justice Earl Warren famously wrote for a unanimous court that education is

> a principal instrument in awakening the child to cultural values, in preparing him for later professional training, and in helping him to adjust normally to his environment. In these days, it is doubtful that any child may reasonably be expected to succeed in life if he is denied the opportunity of an education. Such an opportunity, where the state has undertaken to provide it, is a right which must be made available to all on equal terms.[3]

The lawyers who represented school districts in the South were surprised by the *Brown* decision. They counted on the Supreme Court to continue to apply the separate-but-equal doctrine that existed prior to *Brown*, perhaps with some rigor. The decision to outlaw segregation was game-changing.

The prior law, established in *Plessy v. Ferguson*,[4] upheld segregation if there were equal accommodations for those who were disenfranchised. For Homer Plessy, a light-skinned Black man, it was train travel that was at issue. If Mr. Plessy could get a decent train ride in Louisiana—outside of the Whites-only cars—that was good enough. But the law applied to all public accommodations, including housing and public schools and, as we saw with public schools, "equal" was often a misnomer. *Plessy*, decided in 1896, was this country's governing law until 1954. Truman's order desegregating the military during World War II and revolutions in manufacturing, communications, and public transportation were no match for the staying power of *Plessy*. Its discriminatory decree persevered.

Thurgood Marshall founded the Legal Defense Fund, Inc. (LDF), the legal advocacy arm of the National Association for the Advancement of Colored People (NAACP), to challenge the principle of separate but equal, and spent decades working to overturn *Plessy*'s scurrilous precedent. Marshall's team included three lawyers who went on to become federal judges: Constance Baker Motley, Robert Carter, and Spottswood Robinson III. (And President Lyndon B. Johnson appointed Marshall to become a Supreme Court justice.) Despite all of this firepower, and support from local lawyers and parents of disadvantaged children, Marshall's team made little progress for years.

Marshall's team failed to overturn *Plessy* in two prior efforts at the US Supreme Court before *Brown*. In *Sweatt v. Painter*, law school was at issue. In *McLaurin v. Oklahoma State Regents*, it was graduate school education. The US Supreme Court decided both cases on the same day in 1950.[5]

Heman Marion Sweatt was a postal worker in Houston, Texas, who organized his colleagues to improve their working conditions. He had an undergraduate degree from Wiley College in Marshall, Texas, an historically Black college started in the 1880s and affiliated with the United Methodist Church. Sweatt worked as a teacher and principal before joining the post office. His work with lawyers to organize fellow workers and his interest in civil rights led him to apply to the University of Texas School of Law to challenge the state's constitutional prohibition against integrated public schools and universities. At the time, Texas did not have a public law school for Black students.

George W. McLaurin sued the state of Oklahoma so he could pursue a doctorate in education at the University of Oklahoma. McLaurin already had a master's degree in education. Oklahoma did not have a doctoral program in education for Black students. The state admitted

McLaurin to the doctoral program but made him sit at desks located out-side classrooms or in closets. Eventually, the US Supreme Court ordered McLaurin's admission to the University of Oklahoma's doctoral program on an equal status with the White students. The main library at the University of Oklahoma is designated a US Historic Landmark to commemorate McLaurin's efforts.

The Supreme Court, led by Chief Justice Fred Vinson, overturned losses at the trial level by Sweatt and McLaurin, but refused to tackle the larger issue of segregation, ruling, "Broader issues have been urged for our consideration, but we adhere to the principle of deciding constitutional questions only in the context of the particular case before the Court." Perhaps it was the conservative nature of the justices on the Court in 1950 or a failure of Chief Justice Vinson's leadership that kept the Court's focus on equality of facilities and away from segregation. The fact that both challenges were initiated by adult plaintiffs seeking admission to graduate programs may also have influenced the Court.

The Supreme Court findings for Marshall's clients in *Sweatt* and *McLaurin* aside, most of the challenges to equality took place in front of judges who were locally elected and close to the people for whom Jim Crow and segregation were a way of life, if not a right. Many of these judges benefited from Jim Crow. Today, according to the Brennan Center for Justice, thirty-eight states elect their highest court judges. In eight of these states, the election is overtly partisan.[6]

A fight to determine the quality of facilities or curricula for Black and Brown students was the fight that the lawyers defending segregation wanted because the concept of segregation was not put on trial. Compliance with court-decreed improvements could also be the subject of excuses and foot-dragging by school officials. The playing field in these cases was far from level.

The legal world really did shift with the *Brown* decision in 1954. The case required two different Supreme Court arguments, and the Court issued two formal opinions. Chief Justice Vinson retired and was replaced by Chief Justice Earl Warren, a former California governor, after the first oral argument. It was Warren's leadership that led to the unanimous

1954 decision that outlawed segregation in *Brown* I, the first decision in the Brown case. A year later, in *Brown* II, the Court compromised on a timetable, finding that desegregation should happen "with all deliberate speed."[7]

Five cases were consolidated by the Court to make up the *Brown* docket because they all focused on challenges to the legality of segregation. All five cases required the Court to decide if segregation was legal. The five cases originated in Kansas (*Brown*), Virginia (*Davis v. County School Board of Prince Edward County)*, Delaware (*Gebhart v. Belton*), the District of Columbia (*Bolling v. Sharpe*), and South Carolina (*Briggs v. Elliott*). The five cases allowed Marshall's team to show the Court that segregation was a widespread problem throughout the South, in cities and in rural areas, and that it affected the youngest schoolchildren.

The Virginia case began with a student-led walkout to protest conditions at the high school for Black students in Prince Edward County. The lead organizer was Barbara Johns, the niece of Vernon Johns, pastor of the Dexter Avenue Baptist Church in Montgomery, Alabama. (Martin Luther King Jr. succeeded Reverend Johns at the pulpit.) A three-judge panel of the federal court in Virginia upheld segregation but found that the schools for Black children were demonstrably inferior, lacking a gym or cafeteria and with a curriculum that was extremely limited when compared to the local high school for White children. The court did not order remedial action because the county, in response to the suit, appropriated money for a new high school for the county's Black children.

The Delaware case was a combination of two cases that were consolidated by the state courts. In both cases, Black children were barred from attending local all-White schools. In one case, the school district refused to bus the Black children to the distant schools they were forced to attend. Perhaps most galling, a bus for White children passed the eight-year-old plaintiff's home twice a day.[8]

The Bolling case involved Black students' request to attend the all-White John Phillip Sousa Junior High School in DC. James Nabrit Jr. and George E. C. Hayes, both Howard University School of Law professors, represented the students. Although the decision was released on the same day as *Brown*, *Bolling* was separately decided under the Fifth Amendment's due process clause because the Fourteenth Amendment ("No State shall . . . deny to any person within its jurisdiction the equal protection of the laws.") doesn't apply to the District of Columbia, since it is not a state.[9]

In *Briggs v. Elliott*, parents in rural Clarendon County, South Carolina, between Myrtle Beach and Columbia, initially petitioned for busing for their students, as in the Delaware case. When their request was denied, they challenged segregation of the schools itself. A three-judge panel of federal judges heard the case. Two of the judges upheld segregation but acknowledged that the Black children's schools and access to busing were unequal to that of White students and should be improved. One judge voted to outlaw segregation. In a dissenting passage that forecast the *Brown* decision, Judge Waties Waring wrote, "Segregation in education can never produce equality. It is an evil that must be eradicated."[10]

Even though Chief Justice Warren brought together a unanimous court to issue a powerful opinion condemning segregation, the Court pulled a punch when it came to ordering a remedy. Rather than issuing a specific directive to the state boards of education that included concrete timetables to desegregate, or appointing a judicial master to oversee an orderly process of desegregation, its remedy was to order desegregation "with all deliberate speed." This compromise delayed desegregation and, many believe, undermined the Court's moral authority.

The country did not abandon its slow walk to desegregation until 1969, when the Court finally ordered desegregation to occur at once.[11] However, by the 1970s there was at least progress in terms of the Court's clarity of purpose. That's when families in Los Angeles County challenged the California system of funding its schools—the next logical step in making the right to a high-quality public education a full-fledged constitutional right. If *Brown v. Board* decreed segregation illegal, the *Serrano v. Priest* case in California took the next step by focusing on equalizing resources for both poor and wealthy, White and minority students.

Chapter 2

Brown to *San Antonio* Desegregation Runs into a Roadblock

Serrano v. Priest I (1971) and *Rodriguez v. San Antonio Independent School District* (1973)

By the late 1960s, America finally had a clear directive from the US Supreme Court to desegregate its public schools—now. "With all deliberate speed" was no longer good enough. The problem was that the US Supreme Court did not order an equalizing of public resources. Public schools in property-poor communities faced huge disadvantages when compared to schools in wealthy communities, because the value of the property determined the relative ease with which revenue could be raised. Wealthy communities captured a private advantage over communities with lesser property values. All it took to enjoy the advantage was being able to afford the price of an expensive home in one of the wealthier communities. Then, as a member of this exclusive club, the homeowner's children could attend a better-resourced school while the homeowner enjoyed lower taxes.

Two cases filed in 1968 challenged this system of school funding, which was built on local financial wealth and disregarded the needs of children. *Serrano v. Priest* was the first of these cases. It was filed in state court in Los Angeles County. The second was *Rodriguez v. San Antonio Independent School District,* filed in federal court in Texas.

John Serrano, a social worker, became the lead plaintiff in the California case as the result of a chance encounter with lawyers from the Western Center on Law and Poverty. At a restaurant in east LA, the lawyers overheard Serrano mention that he was shocked by the advice he was given by his son's elementary school principal. The principal told Serrano he should move the family to a higher-wealth community to get better resources for his bright second-grade son.[12]

Sid Wolinsky led the plaintiffs' legal team. Wolinsky's team chose to downplay race-based concerns to avoid complications his team considered unnecessary in litigating the case before an all-White supreme court.[13] They focused solely on the financial disparities that existed in a school funding system based on local property wealth. Also, school funding challenges in Chicago and Virginia that focused on racial animus were failing.[14]

In the Serrano case, Baldwin Park in heavily Mexican American east LA was compared to Beverly Hills for purposes of the trial. Although Baldwin had two and a half times more students than Beverly Hills, its school budget was one million dollars less. Baldwin Park's per-pupil spending was $577, while the Beverly Hills school district spent $1,232.

Beverly Hills real estate was characterized by mansions with swimming pools. Wilshire Boulevard, with its high-end offices and luxury retail stores, was in Beverly Hills. Beverly Hills High School had an oil well on its land. Baldwin Park was mostly one-story stucco homes, mom-and-pop grocery stores, and food truck stands. The available property to tax for education was $3,706 per student in the Baldwin Park school district versus $50,885 in the Beverly Hills district.[15]

Demetrio Rodriguez was the lead plaintiff in the Texas challenge. Court procedures required the Texas case that was filed in his name be assigned to a panel of three judges, who quickly stayed the case. The judges delayed consideration of the case in order to afford the Texas legislature one last opportunity to fix a very broken school funding system before the court stepped in.

Courts should exercise judicial restraint and defer to legislatures in cases that impact public policy, as these federal judges did. The judges' deference to the legislature in the Rodriguez case, however, was likely unwarranted as a commission appointed by Governor Connally just a few years earlier had found grave injustices in how Texas schools were funded, yet the legislature ignored the problem as it had for decades. The legislature held true to form and did not take advantage of the delay in the court proceedings to fix anything, and two years later the judges allowed the case to move forward. By now, the Serrano case had been decided by the California Supreme Court.

Both the Texas and California school funding systems relied heavily on local property taxes to fund public education. The problem caused by this heavy reliance was that the distribution of property wealth has little to do with the funding needs of particular school districts and the children in them.

In Texas, the difference between the two target districts compared and contrasted at trial was $5,960 in local taxable property per child in the Edgewood Independent School District and $49,000 per child in affluent Alamo Heights. Both school districts were located in the city of San Antonio. Ninety percent of the children in the Edgewood district were Mexican American, and 6 percent were Black. The student population of Alamo Heights was 92 percent White. Both districts were the same geographic size, but Edgewood had twenty-two thousand students spread over twenty-five elementary and secondary schools and Alamo Heights had five thousand students and six schools.

At best, a funding system based on local boundaries is arbitrary. School district boundaries are often established for purposes unrelated to funding needs. A land grant from a long-dead king may determine the boundaries of a town or school district. The value of property also changes over time. Direct government action—such as the siting of interstate highways, the failure to regulate environmentally hazardous activities, or permitting banks to refuse mortgages to Black and Brown applicants seeking to purchase homes (a process called "redlining")—also creates funding problems in the communities where minority families live because all these actions lead to lower property values.

School funding cases often report property wealth on a per-student basis rather than on a district basis because the per-pupil number allows comparison of the relative financial strengths of school districts regardless of their size. A school district with a million dollars in property wealth per student has a lot more financial strength than a school district with a thousand dollars in property wealth per student. Greater property wealth means local school boards have more choice in how they govern their school districts. In a funding system based on local property taxes, local property wealth enhances local control.

As mentioned in the Introduction, education funding is just a math problem. The value of taxable property multiplied by the tax rate determines the revenue available to be spent.

Spending by school districts at the time of the Serrano and Rodriguez cases varied just as widely as property wealth. The two are obviously related: regardless of need, you can't spend what you don't have. Without property wealth, the ability to raise revenues for schools is limited.

In both California and Texas, the disparity in local property values could have been offset by state funds, but it wasn't. It never is.

State aid in California at the time included a flat grant of $125 per pupil given to every school district and a very modest equalization grant for poorer districts. The flat grants were not intended to reduce inequality in funding. The equalization program was far too limited to make a difference. In Texas, the state gave more aid to Alamo Heights than it did to Edgewood as a result of a preference in the funding laws for certified teachers. Edgewood could not afford to hire as many certified teachers, and so the funding law made the funding inequities worse.

The trial judge in the Serrano case dismissed the lawsuit and the plaintiffs appealed. The California Supreme Court considered its job on appeal to be "to determine whether the California public school financing system, with its substantial dependence on local property taxes and resultant wide disparities in school revenue, violates the equal protection clause of the Fourteenth Amendment." The Fourteenth Amendment was adopted in 1868, in part to give equal rights to formerly enslaved people.

The California court concluded "that this funding scheme invidiously discriminates against the poor because it makes the quality of a child's education a function of the wealth of his parents and neighbors." The court also found that education was a fundamental right of the school-children involved in the case, and ruled against California.[16] The court ordered the case be returned to the trial court and the plaintiffs be given a full trial to prove their allegations.

Declaring a right to be "fundamental," as the California Supreme Court did, is a big deal. Fundamental rights are carefully protected by courts. State action that affects a fundamental right is subject to the most searching analysis, called "strict scrutiny." New Hampshire's contribution to the United States Supreme Court, Justice David Souter, has described strict scrutiny analysis as being almost always fatal to the government; its application "leav[es] few survivors."[17] State action that infringes upon a fundamental right is only justified by a compelling state purpose, which the California Supreme Court concluded did not exist.

At the other end of the spectrum, the "rational basis" test is highly deferential to state decisions that affect constitutional rights that are not considered fundamental. Economic issues and social welfare concerns are not considered fundamental rights. Rational basis review almost always allows the challenged action to continue. A law professor and judge important to this story, J. Harvie Wilkinson III, has described rational basis review as "supine," much like the review a doormat offers a trespasser.

The characterization of a constitutional right as fundamental or not determines the test that courts will use to examine challenged state action. The test selected likely determines the outcome of the case.

The California Supreme Court found that education is a fundamental right because "education is the lifeline of both the individual and society."[18] The court considered the role of education as "indispensable" in the "modern industrial state," as "a major determinant of an individual's chances for economic and social success in our competitive society [and] . . . [as] a unique influence on a child's development as a citizen and his participation in political and community life."[19] These sentiments echoed what Chief Justice Earl Warren had written in the *Brown* decision almost twenty years earlier.

The California court concluded that "education also supports each and every other value of a democratic society—participation, communication, and social mobility, to name but a few."[20] For this last proposition, the court cited the work of three law professors who were also social scientists and leading thinkers on the topic of equitable education funding. Professors John Coons and Stephen Sugarman taught at the

University of California at Berkeley School of Law, and William Clune taught at the University of Wisconsin Law School.[21] They wrote *Private Wealth and Public Education* (Harvard University Press, 1970). Coons and Sugarman also filed a friend-of-the-court (amicus) brief on behalf of the appellants, as did two lawyers who would later become mayors of San Francisco, George Moscone and Willie Brown.

The California Supreme Court also tackled the question of whether state conduct conditioned on a person's "wealth" should be subjected to strict scrutiny. State action that places people into categories or classes may be subjected to strict scrutiny when the categories are "suspect." Race is a prototypical suspect class. The case of *Loving v. Virginia* (1967) provides a good example of state conduct that infringed on the suspect class of race. In *Loving*, the United States Supreme Court struck down a Virginia statute that criminalized marriage between people of different races.[22]

The California court concluded that wealth was a suspect classification that triggered strict scrutiny. It didn't matter whether the "wealth" at issue was the individual wealth of a person or the collective wealth of a school district. Wealth determined how children were treated in terms of the quality of their education, and that was sufficient to overturn the California funding system. Here, the judges waxed poetic: "[A]ffluent districts can have their cake and eat it too: they can provide a high-quality education for their children while paying lower taxes. Poor districts, by contrast, have no cake at all."[23]

The Serrano case jumped ahead of the Rodriguez case because of the two year stay. The delay allowed the federal judges in Texas to rely on the *Serrano* I rulings in reaching their decision, which struck down the Texas school funding scheme as unconstitutional. Professors Coons, Sugarman, and Clune, who had been pivotal in the California litigation, also testified for the plaintiffs in the Texas litigation.

The three-judge panel in Texas found that the wealthiest communities enjoyed the lowest taxes yet raised and spent more for their children's education than the poorest districts, and that the state's funding system served to worsen the inequities.

Dr. José Cárdenas, the former superintendent of Edgewood, described the Edgewood District as "a pocket of poverty within the city of San Antonio."[24] He also wrote that before he became superintendent, "no special effort had been conducted to alter the instructional program to take into account cultural, language, economic, or other circumstances . . . levels of expectancy were very low . . . poor performance was considered normal and satisfactory."[25] In other words, no one cared.

The three-judge panel procedure provided for direct appeal to the United States Supreme Court, and the state of Texas used this opportunity to appeal its loss and attempt to establish the law of the land. With the losing party's name now going first on appeal, the case became known in the United States Supreme Court as *San Antonio Independent School District v. Rodriguez.*

Prior to the US Supreme Court taking up the appeal in *Rodriguez,* two state courts and two federal courts had all carefully considered state school funding systems based on local property taxes. The California state case and the Texas federal case are discussed above. The case of *Robinson v. Cahill* was organized by the NAACP and brought in state court in New Jersey. A federal case called *Van Dusartz v. Hatfield* was litigated in Minnesota. All four cases found that the funding systems being challenged violated the Equal Protection Clause of the Fourteenth Amendment to the United States Constitution. That clause prevents a state from "deny[ing] to any person within its jurisdiction the equal protection of the laws." The Robinson case in New Jersey also included a court finding that the funding system violated the New Jersey state constitution.

There was a great deal of national interest in the *Rodriguez* appeal because the funding of schools affected taxpayers across the country and because the four cases had already ruled that property-tax-based systems were unconstitutional. Chief Justice Warren Burger assigned Justice Lewis Powell Jr. to write the opinion. Powell was the newest Supreme Court justice at the time. Richard Nixon appointed Powell to fill the seat of Justice Hugo Black, who had become ill and died shortly after leaving the court in the fall of 1971. Nixon appointed Warren Burger to replace Earl Warren as chief justice in 1969.

Burger considered Powell to be the "education justice" because Powell served on and eventually chaired the Richmond, Virginia, school board and later the state of Virginia's Board of Education. Powell's appointments, however, were not without controversy.

When Powell was first appointed to Richmond's school board, the city's Black newspaper, the *Richmond Afro-American*, advocated instead for the appointment of the first Black school board member, as one third of the city was Black.[26] The state's first two Black candidates to the Virginia state board of education were later also passed over by Governor J. Lindsay Almond in 1961, and Powell and Colgate Darden were appointed.[27]

Powell was on the Richmond school board when *Brown* was decided in 1954. Powell thought the Brown case was wrongly decided, and in fact was "shocked" at the decision.[28] He was silent in the face of Virginia's organized effort to fight the public school desegregation ordered by the Supreme Court and dubbed the "Massive Resistance."[29] Ironically, when Powell was president of the American Bar Association (ABA), the thought leader and professional trade association for lawyers, he derided those who engaged in civil disobedience around the Vietnam War as deciding only to obey "just laws . . . [a] philosophy [that when] carried to its logical extreme would lead to anarchy."[30] Powell did not similarly condemn Virginia's effort to reject *Brown*'s order to desegregate.

When Powell left the Richmond School Board to join the Virginia Board of Education seven years after *Brown* was decided, just two of Richmond's twenty-three thousand Black students attended White schools.[31] On the state board of education, in 1964, Powell voted to reimburse White parents for tuition paid to the segregated private academies that replaced public schools that were closed to avoid desegregation.[32] These tuition reimbursements were the precursor of present-day school vouchers.

While Powell was a leader of his law firm, the firm represented the Prince Edward County School Board against Thurgood Marshall and the NAACP team in one of the companion cases to *Brown*. The Virginia case began when sixteen-year-old Barbara Rose Johns led her fellow high school students in a walkout to protest overcrowded conditions and sub-standard facilities at the county's only high school for Black students, the Robert Russa Moton High School. Rather than build a modern new facility, the school board constructed plywood and tar paper structures that lacked heating and plumbing.[33]

The Powell law firm called Powell's colleague on the state board of education, Colgate Darden, as an expert witness at the Johns trial. Darden testified that segregation was "[s]o ingrained and wrought in the texture of [Virginia] life . . . that its involuntary elimination would severely lessen the interest of the people of the State in the public schools, lessen the financial support, and so injure both races."[34]

Darden, a former governor and congressman, was the University of Virginia president who hired James McGill Buchanan to lead the university's economics department. Buchanan, later a Nobel Laureate, created the free market "Virginia School of Economics," which gave rise to the influence of mega-donors such as the Koch brothers.[35]

Justin Moore, Powell's law partner, remained counsel for the Prince Edward County commissioners when they voted to close all of the county's public schools rather than integrate them.[36] Moore also said at the time that he wanted to set a forty-five-year timeline for Virginia schools to desegregate to comply with *Brown*.[37]

At his death, the *New York Times* described Justice Powell as a "crucial centrist justice," a "balancer and compromiser, a political moderate with an aversion to heated rhetoric and doctrinal rigidity."[38] Not all commentators, however, view Justice Powell so benevolently.

Bill Blum of the Constitutional Accountability Center, a nonprofit that views the Constitution as an inherently progressive document, considers Justice Powell to have been a conservative justice who was rivaled only by Antonin Scalia in his conservatism.[39]

Powell was friends with FBI director J. Edgar Hoover, whom he considered a "great American." When Powell ascended to the presidency of the American Bar Association, he consulted Hoover for programming ideas[40] and offered to use the ABA to help the FBI in any way possible.[41] Powell, from his post on the Virginia state board of education, worked to incorporate books written by Hoover into public education curricula in Virginia. FBI documents also indicate Powell was available to secretly inform against those who supported integration in Virginia schools.[42] Hoover and Powell were both avowed anti-communists, a point the Texas brief in the San Antonio case exploited by comparing fair school funding to socialism.

In 1971, two months before his appointment to the Supreme Court, Powell penned the "Powell Memo," a neoconservative pro-business manifesto.[43] Powell's memo did not become public until after his confirmation, when it was leaked to syndicated columnist Jack Anderson.

The Powell memo parallels Buchanan's work at the University of Virginia. Powell wrote his confidential memo at the behest of his friend and neighbor, Eugene Sydnor Jr., then chair of the US Chamber of Commerce. While the *New York Times* proclaimed Powell a moderate, his confidential manifesto showed something else. In it, Powell urged the business community to be "far more aggressive," to engage in "confrontation politics," and to penalize those who opposed business. The memo targeted Ralph Nader, Charles Reich, Herbert Marcuse, William Kunstler, the ACLU, labor and civil rights groups, and public interest law firms.

Powell devoted special attention to social scientists in his memo. He warned against professors who beguiled their students into despising free enterprise. "Social science faculties (the political scientist, economist, sociologist and many of the historians) tend to be liberally oriented, even when leftists are not present. . . . The social science faculties usually include members who are unsympathetic to the enterprise system."[44] Of course, an important element of the plaintiffs' evidence in the San Antonio case came from social scientists.

Despite his preoccupation with college campuses, Powell's six-thousand-word memo never once mentioned the Vietnam War as a source of campus turmoil and distrust, even though the last of four annual "Marches on Washington" to protest the war occurred while he was writing the memo. The May Day Protests of 1971 resulted in more than twelve thousand arrests, the most arrests ever at the time. It was hard not to notice.

Predictably, Powell also expressed antipathy towards organized labor: "We have seen the civil rights movement insist on re-writing many of the textbooks in our universities and schools. The labor unions likewise insist that textbooks be fair to the viewpoints of organized labor." Powell later played out these feelings in writing the *San Antonio* court opinion. His notes reflect that he thought teachers' unions would never be satisfied with any level of expanded funding.[45]

Finally, and most importantly, Powell wrote in his memo that he considered the courts "the most important instrument for social, economic and political change." He noted that left and liberal groups exploited an "activist-minded" Supreme Court, but the business community did not. Powell urged the Chamber to organize legal teams to respond.

Powell did not directly call for the creation of the Federalist Society—now a spawning ground for activist conservative judges and justices—but he trumpeted the need for business to organize, create, and use its political and monetary capital, and to do so through the courts. Professor Buchanan at the University of Virginia did the same thing at virtually the same time.

Any guesses on how Powell's opinion in the San Antonio case came out?

The decision overturned the Texas ruling, reinstated the discriminatory Texas school funding scheme, and thereby thwarted efforts to make desegregation a practical reality.

Powell's thinking in writing the opinion can be gleaned from the notes and memos that circulated among Powell and his law clerks, which are preserved at the Washington and Lee University School of Law, Powell's alma mater. Powell had two clerks. Larry Hammond, the lead law clerk on the San Antonio case, was a University of Texas School of Law graduate and a holdover from Justice Hugo Black's chambers.[46]

Powell's other clerk was J. Harvie Wilkinson III, a recent University of Virginia Law School graduate and the son of one of Powell's best friends, J. Harvie Wilkinson II of Richmond.[47] The younger Wilkinson was the one who later described the rigor of the rational basis test as "supine."

Powell's notes reflect that he feared local school boards would lose control of their schools if the percentage of state funding increased. He distrusted the proposition that money makes a difference in the quality of education and worried that if the Supreme Court carefully scrutinized state funding of education, it would also have to scrutinize other important state issues, such as welfare funding.

Of course, school funding, unlike welfare, is the result of state action in setting school district boundaries for funding purposes—and then exacerbating the problem by distributing more resources to the wealthy and privileged than to the poor. In addition, education, as both an individual right and a democratic necessity, historically and practically enjoys a more important constitutional place than do individual financial support payments. Welfare, as a federal matter, did not begin until the 1930s under FDR, long after the post-Civil-War Fourteenth Amendment was adopted in 1868. Prior to FDR, welfare was either a purely local concern or a charitable one.

John Adams recognized the importance of education as a protected constitutional right when he wrote the Massachusetts Constitution in 1779. Thomas Jefferson of Virginia came to the same conclusion, as evidenced by his published letters and his insistence that the University of Virginia be created.[48] George Washington, too, promoted education in his farewell address.[49]

Powell relied heavily on the brief written for the state of Texas by his friend, Professor Charles Alan Wright. Wright was a distinguished law professor at the University of Texas and author of the preeminent treatise on federal civil procedure. Wright was also Nixon's lawyer during his impeachment, when Wright recommended assertion of executive privilege to keep Nixon's tapes secret. He also supported the firing of the special prosecutor, Archibald Cox.[50]

Wright challenged the argument that money makes a difference in the quality of education. Powell considered the commonsense assertion that better resourced schools provide a higher-quality education, which Professors Coons, Clune, and Sugarman primarily advanced, to be a "facile new theory."[51]

After the ruling, Professor Wright wrote to Powell, characterizing *San Antonio* as a "splendid opinion" that was "exceptionally clear and forceful statement for precisely the right reasons." Wright ended his letter with, "I am glad to say that reform of the Texas system by the Legislature seems very good."[52] It is not clear to what Wright referred in commending the Texas Legislature, as it did not take action for almost eighteen years after the Rodriguez case was decided, and then only after a second, successful suit.

Powell and the lawyers in the case knew that the Texas school funding system could not withstand strict scrutiny. Both the three-judge panel in Texas and the California Supreme Court characterized the right to an education as "fundamental," which triggered "strict scrutiny" of Texas's justification for the funding scheme. The New Jersey court and the federal court in Minnesota had reached the same legal conclusion.

Race also played an obvious role in the Texas funding system. The children in the Edgewood school district were almost exclusively Mexican American or Black. Classifications based on race, a suspect class, are also subject to strict scrutiny and seldom are allowed to stand.

In preparing to write this book, I spoke with Marisa Bono, the executive director of Every Texan, a statewide advocacy organization devoted to fair school funding and other policy initiatives. Marisa also litigated school funding cases in Texas and New Mexico. In her opinion, unfair school funding is almost always about race.

The parties' arguments in the San Antonio case, however, did not focus on the apparent racial underpinning for the Texas funding system. Just as the lawyers in *Serrano* avoided focusing on race, the lawyers in *Rodriguez* avoided race, perhaps because the state statutes did not explicitly rely on race.

The California Supreme Court also considered wealth a suspect class. Powell rejected wealth as a suspect class because the consideration of wealth was on a community basis, and he and the US Supreme Court concluded that no school district was made up 100 percent of poor people.

Showing how out of touch the Court was with reality, the majority opinion written by Powell stated: "The system of alleged discrimination and the class it defines have none of the traditional indicia of suspectness:

the class is not saddled with such disabilities or subjected to such a history of purposeful unequal treatment, or relegated to such a position of political powerlessness as to command extraordinary protection from the majoritarian political process."[53] This passage ignores almost a century of Jim Crow, the treatment of Mexican Americans in Texas, and the inability of minority voters to effect change over decades.

The key legal issue in *San Antonio* boiled down to the question of whether education was a fundamental right. If the right was fundamental, the Texas school funding system would be subject to strict scrutiny and would fail. If the right was determined not to be fundamental, then the "rational basis" test would apply, and Texas's inequitable system would be upheld.

Chief Justice Earl Warren, as the head of a unanimous Supreme Court in *Brown*, concluded that education is a fundamental right. He wrote that education is "a principal instrument in awakening the child to cultural values, in preparing him for later professional training, and in helping him to adjust normally to his environment. In these days, it is doubtful that any child may reasonably be expected to succeed in life if he is denied the opportunity of an education."[54] The California Supreme Court in *Serrano* I, the three-judge panel in Texas, the New Jersey trial court, and the federal court in Minnesota all agreed with this important precedent.

Powell rejected it.

Instead of focusing on the importance of education to the individual, as the *Brown* court did, and while paying lip service to democracy's dependence on an educated populace, as John Adams did, Powell used an "originalist approach." What this means is he put on his wire-rimmed glasses and read the Constitution and the Fourteenth Amendment to see if the word "education" appeared. As the word "education" is not in either the Constitution or the Fourteenth Amendment, Powell concluded the drafters did not intend the right to be considered fundamental. By choosing the test to determine what is fundamental and what is not, Powell determined the analysis and the outcome of the case.

Just twenty years before the San Antonio case, the Supreme Court in *Brown* decided the constitutional history of education was inconclusive and instead focused on the importance of education to a democratic society. By using "originalism," Powell was able to ignore this prior ruling and insert his own opinion that the drafters of the Fourteenth Amendment in 1868 did not intend education to be a fundamental right.

Finding that "education" is not a fundamental right allowed Powell to apply the "rational basis" test and conclude the Texas school funding system should be upheld. Chief Justice Warren Burger and Justices Stewart, Blackmun, and Rehnquist joined Powell's decision. Stewart also wrote a separate concurrence.

Four justices dissented.

Justice Thurgood Marshall wrote the primary dissent. Justice White joined Marshall's dissent, and also wrote an individual dissent that concluded the Texas system would flunk even the rational basis test because it gave more money to those who least needed it.

Marshall did not mince words. He characterized the decision as an "abrupt departure" from recent state and federal court decisions that overturned state funding schemes that relied on local property wealth.[55] More importantly, he considered the decision "as a retreat from our historic commitment to equality of educational opportunity and as unsupportable acquiescence in a system which deprives children in their earliest years of the chance to reach their full potential as citizens."

He castigated the majority's reliance on the political process, "which, contrary to the majority's suggestion, has proved singularly unsuited to the task of providing a remedy for this discrimination."

> I, for one, am unsatisfied with the hope of an ultimate "political" solution sometime in the indefinite future while, in the meantime, countless children unjustifiably receive inferior educations that [citing *Brown v. Board*] may affect their hearts and minds in a way unlikely ever to be undone.

Marshall directly challenged the ridiculous notion that money does not make a difference in education as it does in all other things.

In my view, though, even an unadorned restatement of this contention is sufficient to reveal its absurdity. . . . It is an inescapable fact that, if one district has more funds available per pupil than another district, the former will have greater choice in educational planning than will the latter.

Justice Marshall also gave credit to the child who overcomes adversity.

That a child forced to attend an underfunded school with poorer physical facilities, less experienced teachers, larger classes, and a narrower range of courses than a school with substantially more funds—and thus with greater choice in educational planning—may nevertheless excel is to the credit of the child, not the State. [Marshall pointed out the obvious:] Likewise, it is difficult to believe that, if the children of Texas had a free choice, they would choose to be educated in districts with fewer resources, and hence with more antiquated [physical] plants, less experienced teachers, and a less diversified curriculum. [He noted] if financing variations are so insignificant to educational quality, it is difficult to understand why a number of our country's wealthiest school districts, which have no legal obligation to argue in support of the constitutionality of the Texas legislation, have nevertheless zealously pursued its cause before this Court.

The claim that money doesn't matter strains credulity. But those opposing equalizing funding can raise it because factors outside of school may prevent a particular child from benefitting from more resources, and children living in poverty require more resources than well-off suburban children. Very sophisticated studies must be used to control for these confounding factors, and these studies require very extensive data sets. These studies and data sets were not available at the time Powell's opinion was written.

The proposition that money doesn't matter in education, however, is ridiculous on its face. Think of it. Who would believe that giving a child more and better access to a helpful adult makes no difference? That a colorful, illustrated, and newer book would not better hold the interest of a middle schooler than a black and white, out-of-date book that Suzy's little brother spit up on last year? As we now know through litigation that took place in Arizona long after Powell's time, substandard buildings with poor lighting, mold, asbestos, and inadequate heating and cooling systems can cause lifelong problems with hypertension and related illnesses.[56]

This argument that money doesn't make a difference is the same that Charles Wright made on behalf of the state of Texas, and the argument that Justice Powell accepted for the Supreme Court.

To be fair, the Coleman Report, issued by the federal government in 1966, supported the claim that the amount of resources devoted to education makes little difference. In a 2021 National Bureau of Education Research study, Professor C. Kirabo Jackson of Northwestern's School of Education and Social Policy debunked this claim. His team re-analyzed all thirty-one prior studies on the subject and concluded that, when properly considered, "a policy that increases per-pupil spending for four years will improve test scores and/or educational attainment over 90 percent of the time."

"Coleman's analysis was not only wrong but generated misunderstandings that remain sadly pervasive today," wrote Stanford economics professor Caroline Hoxby in a 2016 retrospective.[57] Those "misunderstandings" fed a racist narrative that slum kids could not learn.[58] Narratives like this were not, and are not, easily overcome. Many people—teachers, administrators, students, parents, professors, lawyers, and legislators—have been vilified while fighting for improved educational opportunities. The data show that money spent on public education does indeed make a difference.

The most legally substantive aspect of Marshall's dissent was his objection to the "rigidified" application of equal protection analysis by Powell and the majority. The analysis used by the majority was like a coin toss: the result favored one side or the other without any middle ground. Marshall's central theme was that the Court should have employed a sliding scale of scrutiny that depended upon the importance of the right at issue, and that the Court had previously done so.

Two years after the decision, Powell's former clerk, J. Harvie Wilkinson III, also criticized the decision's commitment to the rigid two-tiered equal protection analysis. Wilkinson considered the *San Antonio* decision to be a "major setback to constitutional equality."[59]

Powell and his clerk Larry Hammond thought Wilkinson's criticism unfair. Powell wrote a letter to Wilkinson and Hammond dated March 11, 1976, to preserve his recollection of "Powell Chambers history." In this letter, Powell asserted that Hammond and Wilkinson agreed on the rigid two-tiered approach. He noted that he "consider[s] the case one of the most important I have written."[60]

While the thrust of Wilkinson's article was "the Court got it wrong," Powell wanted the record to reflect that Wilkinson got it wrong, too.

Wilkinson's response to the letter was in the form of a second, short law-journal article in which he recounted how Justice Powell ignored the rigid two-tiered approach when he wanted to. Powell strayed from the rigid two-tiered approach in decisions both before and after the San Antonio case.

One of the cases cited by Wilkinson, in which Powell concurred with the result, was *Frontiero v. Richardson*,[61] a case known for its flexible application of the Fourteenth Amendment's equal protection test. Future justice Ruth Bader Ginsburg argued part of the case, famously quoting abolitionist Sarah Grimké: "I ask no favor for my sex. All I ask of our brethren is that they take their feet off our necks." The case became known for recognizing "middle-tier analysis."

Today, there are generally considered to be three tiers of equal protection analysis: "strict scrutiny" and "rational basis" at the two extremes, and the aptly named "middle-tier analysis" in the middle.

Powell could have adopted a less stringent analysis to reject the Texas funding scheme that gave more money to wealthy districts than to poor ones. Powell's misstatement of the history of common schools in America could also have been corrected. Finally, someone could have informed Powell that his ruling wasn't saving large urban districts, like Richmond, as his chambers notes reflect. In fact, the twenty-five largest urban districts in the country wanted a federal financial takeover because state and local resources were too meager to save them from disaster. Philadelphia School Superintendent Mark Shedd made this point to the US Senate's education subcommittee on September 22, 1971,[62] eighteen months before *San Antonio v. Rodriguez* was decided.

Powell's decision received wide attention. It was praised in many circles. The praise was not universal. The Washington and Lee file includes this letter from Professor M. Lea Rudee, who then taught at Rice University in Texas.

> I have visited many schools in both the Edgewood and Alamo Heights districts. The comparison is so profound that any person of goodwill would disagree with your decision. Edgewood High School has offices and rooms lighted by one bare bulb hanging from the ceiling, while Alamo Heights has the most commodious of physical plants. The affluent district has a large staff of counselors, all specialists at getting their students into college. The counseling staff has more receptionists than Edgewood schools have counselors.
>
> Having firsthand knowledge of the bones and sinew on which your façade of legalism was based, I found it very difficult to use the pro forma title of Justice in my salutation. I am glad that I will not be held accountable for the future generations of students that will remain trapped by the continuing reality of unequal opportunity that was sustained by your decision.

Dr. Cárdenas, the Edgewood superintendent, put it this way:

> I believe that the reasons for failure were moot. Civil rights attorneys pointed out that the Powell decision indicated that the five prevailing fundamentalist Supreme Court justices had made up their minds to reverse the decision and then spent considerable time . . . provid[ing] a legal basis for their action.[63]

There was a clear conflict between Powell's decision and that of the California Supreme Court's decision in *Serrano* I. Unfortunately, in interpreting the federal constitution, the United States Supreme Court has the final word.

But—in finding that education did not deserve the status of a fundamental right because the word "education" is absent from the US Constitution and from the Fourteenth Amendment's Equal Protection Clause, Justice Powell neglected to consider state constitutions.

Justice Marshall did not miss this point. Every state has its own constitution, and the state constitutions have education clauses. Although the *San Antonio* decision foreclosed consideration of education as a federal constitutional right, it opened consideration of education as protected by the constitutions of the individual states.

And so, our story begins in earnest.

Chapter 3

The Beginning of a Movement to Fairly Fund Public Schools

Here's what happened after the Supreme Court concluded that education is not a fundamental right protected by the US Constitution.

Texas
Edgewood v. Kirby (1989–1995)

One hopes Justice Powell and Professor Wright were not betting men. Their misplaced wager on the good faith of the Texas legislature condemned another generation of children to dangerous physical facilities and disadvantages that impacted them for the rest of their lives, and set the course for their children. No help came after Justice Powell's decision relieved Texas of the duty to act fairly. Portions of Edgewood's schools remained condemned and the district's reliance on teachers without certification continued.

After more than ten years of waiting for legislative action, a group of eight property-poor school districts representing more than one million of Texas's three and a half million schoolchildren sued the governor, state board of education, and others. Al Kauffman of the Mexican American Legal Defense and Education Fund (MALDEF) led the legal team. Professor Kauffman now teaches at the Saint Mary's University School of Law in San Antonio, Texas.[64]

The Intercultural Development Research Association (IDRA), the advocacy group led by Dr. Cárdenas, was again deeply involved in the litigation. IDRA acted as advocate, provided research support and expert testimony, and engaged in extensive organizing among lawyers and school funding advocates from across the country who brought their collective expertise to bear on Texas.

IDRA has prided itself on its multifaceted approach to changing education policy. Its model includes raising up the voices of the students and families most impacted by discriminatory school funding policies. It also develops partnerships with researchers, policymakers, educators, and lawyers. IDRA is a good example of the three-legged stool approach to changing public policy: public engagement, political lobbying, and the active use of the courts to challenge illegal conditions. IDRA also conducts and disseminates a great deal of research designed to spur legislators to action.[65]

The new suit sought a declaration that the Texas school finance scheme violated the state's constitution, and the plaintiffs requested injunctive relief that would shut down Texas schools absent corrective action. The case became known as *Edgewood Independent School District v. Kirby*.

IDRA helped solve one of the problems encountered in the original *San Antonio* case. In the 1960s, the state of Texas kept very little statewide data about schools. According to Dr. Cárdenas, "*Rodriguez* led to a sustained 10-year research effort by individuals, organizations and institutions which provided the necessary research information for the success of post-*Rodriguez* court cases throughout the country."[66]

Three years after filing suit, Judge Harley Clark presided over an almost three-month-long trial in Austin. Fun fact: Judge Clark was once a Texas cheerleader who invented the "hook 'em horns" hand sign.

Plaintiffs introduced extensive evidence of inequities caused by unequal funding. For example, Edgewood is in south central Texas where it is hot. Edgewood buildings lacked air conditioning, making school buildings intolerable. Financial struggles also made it difficult to hire enough good, certified teachers or offer a well-rounded curriculum. Edgewood could not afford to purchase computers for its students. Wealthy districts, with the ability to offer better pay, hired more teachers who were better qualified. Their buildings were appropriate to Texas and they had computers for student use.[67]

The state of Texas and the wealthy districts that intervened defended by claiming the system was "equitable for a majority of districts," money does not matter, and making the system fair would undermine local control.[68] The defenses were the same as those on which Justice Powell relied and entirely missed the point. A suit that challenges inequality in funding necessarily admits that some school districts do well. It's not that the system fails all students. It's that some children are treated well, and others are not. The children who are shortchanged live in the poorer districts, have higher needs, and are often Black or Brown.

Judge Clark issued a preliminary decision just three weeks after the trial, followed by more formal rulings within a few months. Clark found that financial problems had grown worse since the Rodriguez case. The eight times discrepancy in per-pupil property wealth that existed between Edgewood and Alamo Heights in 1967–68 had grown to almost fifteen times by 1985–86, the tax year that was the subject of the *Edgewood v. Kirby* trial.

Judge Clark found that education was a fundamental right under the state constitution. He concluded that district boundaries, which determined the property wealth available to a school district, were irrational in that they had nothing to do with how much money a school district needed to educate its children.

In the 1985–86 school year, the wealthiest district in Texas had fourteen million dollars in taxable property for every child in the district. The poorest district had twenty thousand dollars per child. Clark found that the children at risk in the poorer districts required more resources, not fewer. Eighty-four percent of the Mexican Americans in the state were concentrated in the poorest districts. Overall, the highest-spending school district in Texas spent more than $19,000 per student. The lowest-spending district spent $2,000 per student.

Judge Clark concluded that the state did not have a compelling justification for its conduct. He dismissed state claims about local control: "Local control is largely meaningless except to the extent that the wealthy districts are empowered to enrich their educational programs through their local property tax base, a power that is not shared equally by the State's property poor districts." Clark also found that a fair and equitable system that helped districts without property wealth would not undermine local control.

Judge Clark granted the plaintiffs' request for an injunction that would shut down the Texas school system but gave the state two years before the injunction took effect. The Texas legislature immediately responded with calls to amend the Texas state constitution to remove the constitutional basis for Judge Clark's order. Texas also appealed Clark's ruling and the state's intermediate appellate court reversed Clark by a 2–1 vote in a decision that tracked Justice Powell's conclusions. Now it was the plaintiffs' turn to appeal, this time to the Supreme Court of Texas.

The Texas Supreme Court, in a surprising, unanimous decision, ruled for the poor districts, incorporating many of the same themes as Judge Clark.[69] The disparities between rich and poor districts were "glaring." The Texas state foundation aid program that was intended to help the poorer districts underestimated most costs, excluded costs for buildings, and did not contribute enough to local school districts to meet even minimum standards. The Texas court concluded that the school funding system flunked constitutional scrutiny because it was not financially "efficient" and did not provide for "a general diffusion of knowledge" across the state, adopting language from the education clause of the state's constitution.

The Texas court noted the downward spiral caused by the Texas system: "Property-poor districts are trapped in a cycle of poverty from which there is no opportunity to free themselves. . . . The location of new industry and development is strongly influenced by tax rates and the quality of local schools . . . the property-poor districts with their high tax rates and inferior schools are unable to attract new industry or development and so have little opportunity to improve their tax base."[70]

The Texas Supreme Court gave the governor and legislature a little more time but made clear that change was long overdue and immediate action was both needed and expected.

The legislature responded to the court's decision with lots of hand-wringing and foot-dragging. Judge Clark retired and was replaced by Judge F. Scott McCown. McCown appointed a group of masters to recommend a remedy before the entire state school system shut down. A master is an expert, or a panel of experts as in this case, with specialized knowledge, who distills technical information for a judge and recommends a particular course of action.

The group appointed by Judge McCown included Dr. Cárdenas as a representative of the plaintiffs. The panel of special masters produced a funding plan within forty-five days. This accomplishment put to rest the legislature's claim that a fair plan could not be designed.

As the masters were about to present their plan to Judge McCown, Governor William Clements hurriedly announced a surprise press conference at the state capitol to draw attention away from McCown. Clements had his own plan. The legislature quickly passed Clements's plan within a week's time. That plan was challenged in *Edgewood* II and shot down by the Texas Supreme Court in January 1991.

Eventually, Texas passed a plan, known as SB 351, that provided for the sharing of tax bases, preferably on a county-by-county basis. Other than sharing the benefit of valuable properties for tax purposes, the administration of wealthy and poor districts remained completely separate. The solution was purely financial and, because the only variable shared in the new school funding equation was property wealth, local control remained intact.

Wealthy districts immediately challenged the plan.

In *Edgewood* III, the third case in the *Edgewood* group of four supreme court decisions, the Texas Supreme Court, to the surprise of some, found the plan unconstitutional on technical grounds. The funding system did not allow for local votes of appropriations, and the plan was considered a state property tax, which was barred by the Texas Constitution.

The Texas legislature responded to *Edgewood* III by passing three constitutional amendments to allow for tax base sharing. All three amendments failed in the required public vote.

Dr. Cárdenas attributed the failure to misinformation, politicking by the most elite, and knee-jerk opposition to taxation. He also was disappointed that educational leaders in the poorer districts failed to speak out.[71]

The Texas legislature then passed a complicated bill known as SB 7, which provided wealthy districts with options for tax base sharing. They could choose to share the financial benefits of their valuable property tax bases through formal consolidation with poor districts, by adopting a kind of voucher approach that accepted students from low-wealth districts, or by sharing property wealth as HB 352 previously required. If the wealthy districts failed to choose, the state was empowered to transfer commercial parcels from wealthy districts to the tax bases of low-wealth districts or to require districts to formally consolidate. Although challenged in *Edgewood* IV, the Texas courts upheld SB 7.

While not perfect, progress resulted from the lawsuits and, absent the lawsuits, there would have been no progress.

As far as lessons learned, Dr. Cárdenas pointed to the difficulty of changing the long-standing inequitable nature of school funding, the buck-passing of elected officials unwilling to do "what decency, justice, common sense and the best interests of the state demand," and the ease with which opposition to new taxes can be energized. He also pointed out that equity in facilities should have been part of the fight from the outset.[72]

Edgewood students and their families celebrated the first *Edgewood* win with a big rally in the high school's football stadium. David Hinojosa was one of the students who attended the rally. He had recently graduated from Edgewood High School.

David Hinojosa would later become an extraordinary lawyer in the school funding context, as he has directly litigated more school funding cases in more places than any other lawyer, as well as having been a member of the plaintiff class of students in the *Edgewood v. Kirby* case in Texas.

David attended school in the Edgewood school district beginning in the fifth grade. He transferred to Edgewood after having attended school on military bases. His father was a master sergeant. David attended classes in San Antonio, Texas, that were without air conditioning and had windows that were painted shut. His books were well out of date. The material taught was years behind what the schools on the military bases covered.

David did not have the assistance of guidance counselors when he graduated near the top of his class. He did not have a plan for college or a job.

After some wandering, David enlisted in the military, following in his father's footsteps. While in the military, David attended community college and then earned a bachelor's degree. After completing his service, David attended the University of Texas School of Law. He told me that he was motivated by Jonathan Kozol's book *Savage Inequalities*, which includes references to the *Edgewood* schools.

Improvements ordered by the court in the Edgewood cases stagnated over time and resulted in further litigation in a case called *Neeley v. West Orange Cove Consolidated ISD*. David Hinojosa, the Edgewood High School graduate, argued the *West Orange Cove* appeal before the Texas Supreme Court in 2005. His opponent was Texas Solicitor General Ted Cruz.

David remembers Cruz had a very receptive all-Republican supreme court. Cruz argued that school funding was purely a political decision and the legislature had the power to conclude it should end at third grade.

This time, unfortunately, the Texas Supreme Court refused to intercede to remedy funding inequities. The best the court would do was warn the legislature that funding inequities were approaching constitutional dimensions, again.

After the Texas court refused to intervene, a disappointed Hinojosa said, "Fifty years after *Brown v. Board*, our undisputed evidence at trial showed that the quality of education for certain Texas children still suffers as a direct result of which side of the tracks they live on. Despite the glaring disparities between the haves and have-nots, the court refused to confront the issues head-on."[73]

David also litigated *Martinez v. New Mexico*, which established the constitutional right to a public education in New Mexico. The Martinez case focused on the 75 percent of the state's students who were low-income, Latino, Native American, Black, or Asian American. Many of the students were learning to speak English or had disabilities that required extra services for them to learn, thrive, and become college- or work-ready. The trial court found for the students, noting that New Mexico had the lowest graduation rate in the country, and issued an injunction.[74] David left the Mexican American Legal Defense and Education Fund during the lengthy proceedings leading up to the *Martinez* trial to become the first attorney hired by IDRA. Marisa Bono, the lawyer my wife and I met in San Antonio as I worked on this book, took over the position of lead counsel for MALDEF in the New Mexico litigation.

After three years with IDRA and a short stint at a private education law firm in Texas, David joined the Lawyers' Committee for Civil Rights Under Law in Washington, DC. The Lawyers' Committee is a nonprofit that organizes pro bono legal efforts across the nation to challenge racial inequities. The Lawyers' Committee was formed in 1963 at the request of John F. Kennedy to participate in the Civil Rights Movement. David continues to litigate school funding cases today. Working with the Lawyers' Committee, he is counsel in the *Leandro* case in North Carolina representing students from the Charlotte-Mecklenburg School District.

Good lawyers like David Hinojosa are experts at the basics of lawyering. They know the court rules and how to argue cases and write pleadings. Good human beings carry around memories of the clients they represent, and David could not help but mention his former client from Pasadena, Texas, when I spoke with him. The client was a single mother of two children who lived in financially difficult conditions in a district almost as poor as Edgewood. Pasadena did not have enough books for students to take home. They also didn't have paper to copy assignments. The mother, who had little money herself, sent paper to school with her children so they could copy assignments and excerpts from their textbooks.

After a few years, the mother remarried and the family moved to a somewhat better-off school district that could afford schoolbooks and paper. After a few more years, the mother's marriage ended and she moved with her two children back to Pasadena. She described her children's return to the Pasadena schools as "re-traumatizing." David describes the children's trauma as the "saddest man-made state of affairs. School funding is not magic; it can be fixed with a pencil eraser. It's the greatest of injustices."

California
Serrano v. Priest II and III (1973–1976)

The *Serrano v. Priest* litigation began in 1971, before Justice Powell's decision in the *San Antonio* case. The California litigants were ahead of the curve, but their success appeared to be undermined by the Supreme Court's *Rodriguez* decision.

Despite Powell's opinion, the parties proceeded to a sixty-day trial in 1974. The case was saved, in the first instance, by a footnote in the *Serrano* I decision in which the California Supreme Court wrote it would have reached the same conclusions based on the California state constitution as it did under the US Constitution's Fourteenth Amendment.[75]

Professors Coons and Sugarman were among the lawyers for the plaintiffs on appeal in *Serrano* II. The court again ruled for the plaintiff class of schoolchildren in underfunded school districts. The court detailed for the benefit of the legislature half a dozen concrete ways in which wealth-based disparities were certain to be reduced. Today, these options are relevant for state legislatures that continue to struggle with fashioning a remedy:

- The state could fully fund all schools with a statewide property tax.
- The state could consolidate its school districts, reducing the number by half.
- School district boundaries could be maintained, but commercial and industrial properties could be removed from school districts' taxing authority and taxed separately by the state, with revenues fairly distributed among all districts.
- The state could implement power equalization, in which state aid would be distributed in a fashion to allow districts to raise equal revenues for equal efforts without an arbitrary cap.
- Student vouchers could be issued by the state.
- More than one of the above could be used.[76]

Later in the opinion, the court pointed out that school districts require resources to address their specific problems. A district may be geographically isolated. It may have older buildings or more long-term teachers entitled to higher pay. The court concluded these were reasons to condemn the current school finance system because it deprived districts of an equal ability to address their needs. The system undermined local control. Relying on local property wealth meant some districts could address their needs and others could not.

On the issue of whether money made a difference, the California Supreme Court was clear:

> The system before the court fails . . . [because] it gives high-wealth districts a substantial advantage in obtaining higher quality staff, program expansion and variety, beneficial teacher-pupil ratios and class sizes, modern equipment and materials, and high-quality buildings. . . . [D]ifferences in dollars do produce differences in pupil achievement.[77]

In what can only be considered a parting shot, the court stated that its analysis of the California Constitution was not constrained by the "original intent" textual analysis Justice Powell performed:

> [W]e shall continue to apply strict and searching judicial scrutiny to legislative classifications which, because of their impact on those individual rights and liberties which lie at the core of our free and representative form of government . . . are properly considered "fundamental."[78]

The *Serrano* II decision gave the state six years to design and implement a constitutional system of public-school funding. In *Serrano* III, the California Supreme Court approved a fee award to the *Serrano* lawyers on the theory that they acted as private attorneys general who worked to uphold the California Constitution when the state's attorney general did not.[79]

In 1978, two years after *Serrano* II, California voters approved Proposition 13, which limited property taxation, capped the amount at which property assessments could increase year to year, and established supermajority requirements to increase other state and local taxes. Some economists and public policy commentators blame the *Serrano* decisions for the voter outrage that led to Prop 13. William Fischel, an economist at Dartmouth College who was one of the experts in the New Hampshire funding litigation, supports this view.[80] Political scientists have challenged opinions like Fischel's and have concluded that voters generally supported the equalization of school funding. They argue that cuts in progressive federal taxes coupled with increases in regressive state and local taxes caused a pocketbook squeeze on lower and middle classes, regardless of race, beginning ten years before Prop 13 was enacted. These researchers also conclude that Presidents Kennedy and Johnson missed the beginnings of the taxpayers' revolt that led to the election of President Ronald Reagan.[81]

New Jersey
Abbott v. Burke (1986–2022)

The New Jersey Supreme Court had the foresight to decide its school funding case, *Robinson v. Cahill* (1973), based on provisions in the New Jersey Constitution and not rely on the federal equal protection clause. The court in *Robinson* found that money makes a difference, the money available to schools was arbitrarily distributed, and the state of New Jersey could do much better.

Rather than fix the problems caused by New Jersey's overreliance on local property taxes, which averaged 67 percent, the legislature and governors dragged their feet. Further litigation became necessary if things were to improve.

In *Abbott v. Burke*, New Jersey advocates and lawyers used the three-legged stool approach to changing public policy, combining litigation, public engagement and legislative lobbying. To go even further, New Jersey added a fourth leg: sustained foundation funding for the lawsuit and the advocacy. They also had a reliable research arm, with a bevy of experts, at Rutgers, the state university.

Using a modern-day state constitutional provision adopted in 1947, the *Abbott* lawyers leveraged language from the Robinson case that focused on the substance of the state constitution's education clause, which required state support for a "thorough and efficient system of free public schools." New Jersey's school funding system, which left out the disadvantaged and overwhelmingly Black and Brown children in New Jersey's thirty-one largest cities, was not "thorough," nor was it "efficient." The system disserved too many children and did not provide resources necessary to operate high-quality schools in all parts of the state.

Among other things, the *Abbott* litigation is known for establishing the right to, and the clear benefits of, preschool for three- and four-year-old children in the thirty-one *Abbott* districts. In fact, the proof regarding the success of preschools was so strong that other districts with more wealth demanded publicly funded preschools, too. This was eventually accomplished by lowering the threshold to make state-funded universal preschool available from districts with 40 percent poverty rates to districts with only 20 percent poverty.

The Education Law Center (ELC) in Newark was the lead counsel for the *Abbott* districts. Marilyn Morheuser, ELC's executive director, was one of the driving forces behind *Abbott* and was a larger-than-life figure. Marilyn was a former nun with the Kentucky-based Sisters of Loretto who went to law school when she was in her fifties. One of her teachers, Professor Paul Trachtenberg of Rutgers Law School, founded the ELC in 1973. Trachtenberg represented the NAACP in the *Robinson* litigation. Marilyn became the ELC's executive director in 1979 and served in that capacity until 1995. Her successor, David Sciarra, who continued ELC's prominence as school-funding litigators, describes Morheuser as "a powerful force in our field." David has recently retired and serves in a consultative capacity on funding cases. Robert Kim is now the director of the ELC, which now has a branch in Philadelphia that is involved in litigation and is discussed towards the end of this book.

Through decades of litigation, in addition to their focus on preschools, the *Abbott* plaintiffs established the paramount importance of good facilities that support and advance the educational activities conducted in them. Lawyers in later litigation in other states have expanded on the importance of good facilities.

Danny Adelman, the executive director of the Arizona Center for Law in the Public Interest, submitted crucial evidence in his litigation that proved that awful conditions of school buildings cause students to suffer lifelong health problems. There is more at stake than overcoming education and attention deficits. Asbestos, poor lighting, and classrooms that are always too hot or too cold or overcrowded lead to hypertension and other physical problems that plague students for the rest of their lives.

In New Jersey, after seven rounds of litigation that occurred through five different gubernatorial administrations, cold, unhealthy, and dangerous facilities finally gave way to an energetic building plan funded entirely by six billion dollars in state bond financing in the thirty-one *Abbott* districts, with another four billion dollars directed to non-*Abbott* districts. The legislature appropriated just shy of another three billion dollars in a second round of bond financing for the *Abbott* districts in 2008, with an additional one billion dollars going to non-*Abbott* districts.

In 2010, Governor Chris Christie suspended the construction funding, and it was not reinstated until 2022, after another round of litigation led by ELC resulted in a specific order from the New Jersey Supreme Court to reinstate the funding. By this time, Christie had left the state on a quixotic run for president. Governor Phil Murphy has overseen the reinstatement of construction projects after this most recent court ruling.

The New Jersey Supreme Court, throughout the *Abbott* litigation, focused on creating a system of state-funded, high quality, rigorous, age-appropriate preschools. Governor Christine Todd Whitman attempted to avoid the command for rigorous preschooling by co-opting daycare centers that were more focused on babysitting children. The New Jersey Supreme Court rejected Whitman's efforts to substitute the more custodial daycare programs after further litigation.

New Jersey's state-funded preschool education programs now include wraparound mental health and social welfare support services and meet rigorous learning and teaching standards. They are entirely state funded and at a high level. Teacher education requirements and salaries are on par with K–3 teachers, and class sizes in the state-funded preschools are capped at fifteen children.

This emphasis on rigorous preschools reduces instances of grade retention in later grades, and the early attention that children receive in good preschools decreases the need for later special education placements. The data also show significant annual reductions in achievement gaps and substantial positive effects in math, language and literacy, and science achievement through high school. All these effects reduce the need for later, costlier interventions, either during a child's school years or after a child has left school.

During the 2019–20 school year, New Jersey's Abbott Preschool Program—now called the Preschool Expansion Program—provided public preschool in 118 of the state's poorest school districts, serving nearly fifty-two thousand three- and four-year-old children. In the 2020–21 school year, the program expanded to 156 districts.

New Jersey would not have accomplished the changes that occurred without the deep and abiding commitment of lawyers, advocates, and funders over decades. Making these life-altering changes takes decades and resources. The Education Law Center, which has already been mentioned, has been pivotal to making these changes. Rutgers, with its nationally renowned early childhood education center, the National Institute for Early Education Research, provides expertise when needed in the courts and in the legislature. Finally, many nonprofit advocacy groups coordinate their efforts under the umbrella of the Advocates for the Children of New Jersey, with the Fund for New Jersey as one of its principal funders.

Minnesota
Skeen v. State of Minnesota (1993)[82]

Minnesota students and taxpayers did not fare so well after the US Supreme Court decided the San Antonio case. The prior success in the federal *Van Dusartz* was wiped out, and the case was dismissed because it relied entirely on the federal equal protection clause that Powell's decision eviscerated. Years later, in the *Skeen* case, the Minnesota Supreme Court concluded that education is a fundamental right, but that this right did not extend to fair funding. The court refused to recognize the connection between the quality of education needed to meet students' needs and the cost of that education. As a result of the *Skeen* decision, lawyers and advocates have been shut out of the ability to go to court to better fund schools in Minnesota.

PART TWO

New Hampshire's Experience

Chapter 4

The Education System Challenged in the Claremont Suit

In 1990, New Hampshire had about one million residents and 194,000 schoolchildren distributed over 154 school districts. Schools were overwhelmingly funded with local tax dollars. Local property taxes paid for 90 percent of education costs. The federal government kicked in about 3 percent of the cost of public education in the state.

New Hampshire was dead last in the nation in terms of state funding for its schools, and if New Hampshire had tripled its state contribution, it would still have been last in the nation. Nebraska was next worst with a 24-percent state contribution.

Poverty in New Hampshire was limited but existed in pockets. Home buyers could write to the New Hampshire Department of Education to request a "Move Packet" that included state reports that revealed a wide variation in levels of school spending per pupil, property values per pupil, and school tax rates. Forewarned, home buyers of means could thus avoid poorly funded school districts and those with high taxes, which were often one and the same.

How did New Hampshire get to this state of regressive funding where the poorest communities paid the most in taxes and got the least for their children?

Satan is always a good place to start.

As a part of the Massachusetts Bay Colony in colonial times, much of what happened in New Hampshire was driven by what happened in Boston. Work by Puritans, who were led by John Winthrop, to promote Bible reading influenced the effort to educate children in the colony. The effort began with directives for parents to educate their children at home. A few communities responded to this new focus on early education by forming schools. The Boston Latin School opened in 1635 and is the nation's oldest publicly funded school. Unlike most schools in England, Boston Latin was not established by a church; it was created by the townspeople of Boston and supported by rents collected on the islands in Boston Harbor.[83]

Later, afraid the directive requiring parents to teach reading was being neglected, the colony adopted the Massachusetts Old Deluder Satan Act of 1647, which required towns with fifty or more families to arrange instruction in basic reading and writing.[84] In communities of one hundred or more families, grammar schools were required that could prepare boys for admission to Harvard College, which was founded in 1636. Forearmed with the teachings of the Bible, the Puritans hoped their followers could better ward off Satan.

Much later, Horace Mann became the first chair of the Massachusetts Board of Education in 1837 and used his position to enact major reforms. Mann led the Common School Movement, which created publicly funded schools throughout Massachusetts. Mann, a lawyer and legislator, believed that education was the key to good citizenship and democratic participation. His belief that education should be publicly funded and universally available spread across New England and the Midwest in the mid-1800s.[85]

The South lagged behind. Indeed, many states in the South passed anti-literacy laws that punished the education of enslaved people. Lewis Powell's Virginia was one of these states, having passed the Anti-Education of Slaves Act of 1819.[86] Over time, however, the theory of Common Schools spread across America, including in the South.

Theory and practice, however, did not always mesh. The goal of Common Schools proponents was to create a somewhat uniform system of practical, functioning schools attended by children of all backgrounds. The quality of these schools, however, waxed and waned in step with funding.

The Creation of a New Hampshire State School System

New Hampshire schools were not organized into a state system until after World War I, when it became clear that many of its young men who went to war could not read. Embarrassed by its failure to prepare its sons,

New Hampshire revamped its locally controlled public schools to create a state system of education. The 1919 laws gave the state board of education the "same powers of management, supervision, and direction over all public schools in this state as the directors of a business corporation have over its business."[87] New Hampshire also invested in teacher education at its state colleges, which were then called "Normal Schools," from the French *école normale*. Robert Frost briefly taught at the Normal School in Plymouth, New Hampshire, now called Plymouth State University.

Many other states and Great Britain also revised their school systems in the wake of World War I. Britain extended the age for compulsory attendance, its "leaving age," from twelve to fourteen and added a non-compulsory option for upper grades. Britain also shifted most funding to national sources, although this was hampered by the country's economic downturn in the late 1920s.[88]

In passing the 1919 legislation, the New Hampshire House of Representatives committee that first considered the proposal focused on state-wide equality of opportunity:

> The committee takes the position that the assuring of equality of educational opportunity is a function of the state and a measure of self-protection as well and that the cost of providing a fair chance to a child who happens to live in a town financially incapable of maintaining standard schools throughout a full school year is a legitimate and essential charge upon the state.[89]

The state of New Hampshire's share of funding in 1919 rose from about 7 percent to 12 percent, with the bulk of the state funding being in the form of a foundation aid program. Foundation aid programs are designed to establish a minimal funding base for the poorest districts. Local monies supplement the foundational funding. Wealthy districts fund themselves based on local taxes with little or no foundational support.

After a year or two, the minimum foundation aid level provided to the poorer districts dropped, perhaps as a result of New Hampshire's declining economy or a reluctance to spend tax revenues to educate an increasingly foreign-born population.[90] By the 1930s, the likely entities to tax in order to raise state revenues were in financial trouble. New Hampshire's dominant textile and paper mills were in bankruptcy. New Hampshire's Boston and Maine Railroad was also in receivership. Except for a one-year blip in 1949, the state's funding for public education never rose higher than 7 or 8 percent of its overall cost. Local communities bore the vast brunt of the obligation to fund public schools.[91]

New Hampshire has always relied more heavily on local taxes to fund schools than other states, and it's not clear why. It's almost as if the leaders of New Hampshire lack commitment to the common good.

This reliance on local property taxes makes the widely varying value of local property more of a problem than elsewhere because the ability of local communities to raise local monies for schools is tied to the value of the property in those communities. The more valuable local properties are, the easier it is to raise money for schools.

A Failure of Economic Development

Having chosen an approach to school funding dependent on local property wealth, New Hampshire had a moral obligation to even out property values where it could through state economic development efforts. It hasn't.

In many ways, New Hampshire's school funding problems are as much about its failure to do economic development as its overreliance on property taxes. New Hampshire has not regularly helped communities with new capital, cut-rate loans, or retraining when dominant businesses fail.

When major businesses, or entire industries, in a community fail, property values plummet. This is true in New Hampshire and in states across the country. Higher taxes amidst the death of a dominant business lead to municipal death spirals, as was recognized by the Texas Supreme Court in the Kirby case. The fact that fewer jobs are available also may encourage more students to stay in school, increasing the financial stress on schools and making the problem even more acute.

New Hampshire was an agrarian and mill economy from colonial times through the 1930s. The Manchester Millyard, where I once had my law office, was a dominant textile manufacturing center in the 1800s.

Lincoln visited Manchester soon after his Cooper Union speech in 1860, on his way to the presidency. Nineteenth-century textile mills flourished through the 1930s. The Amoskeag Mills' bankruptcy litigation occurred in 1936.

To the north, paper mills and shoe factories provided good jobs in and around Berlin, New Hampshire. Converse All Stars were once manufactured in Berlin, as were paper towels, pipes made from paper and tar, and polyethylene Saran Wrap, an invention of the Brown paper company. Strong businesses supported property values.

The mill owners in Berlin also invested in their unionized workforce, including by providing kindergarten for workers' children long before the rest of the state did. New Hampshire was the last state in the nation to require all districts to provide at least a half day of public kindergarten. This requirement was not instituted until 2009, even though the state's board of education had endorsed the concept of public kindergarten as early as 1984.[92] In 1990, only eighty-three of New Hampshire's 154 school districts offered public kindergarten.[93] Local decisions not to fund kindergarten were largely driven by the absence of state funding. Local kindergartens had to be funded by local taxes, and this meant local leaders had to support tax increases.

Berlin High School was among the leading schools in the state when businesses in Berlin were sound. Unfortunately, the mills failed and no one came to help. The federal government did not focus on current-day concepts like economic patriotism and rural re-development.[94] There was no Infrastructure Investment and Jobs Act to help the failing businesses or to replace them.

Berlin's once vaunted position as the papermaking capital of the nation faded and was replaced by a prison economy. In 2000, a 750-bed state prison opened, joined in 2012 by a 1200-bed, medium-security federal prison. Berlin's non-prison population fell from 17,821 in 1950 to about 9,500 today, with a median household income of $39,479. Over the same period, New Hampshire's population grew from 529,880 in 1950 to 1.4 million today, with a current statewide median household income of $83,449, almost $10,000 higher than the national average.

New Hampshire's population became wealthier and more than doubled, while Berlin's decreased by almost as much and its income level plummeted.

In the last few decades, Berlin has had among the highest school property tax rates in the state, often in excess of $20 per $1000 in property value—approximately twice the state average. While running for governor in 2020, I met a teacher who had recently moved to Berlin so her spouse could take a job at the federal prison. The family bought a modest three-bedroom home. The annual property taxes on the house were higher than their mortgage payments.

Berlin is failing to thrive. Its last elementary school, Brown School, closed in 2019, forcing its youngest students to be moved to the middle school, which required emergency renovations when it became clear the youngest children could not easily climb the adult-sized stairs.[95] Berlin's mayor, Robert Cone, elected in 2023, notes that half the downtown's storefronts are empty.[96]

Claremont has experienced a similar downward trajectory. Textile mills shuttered and machining businesses faltered. The Sullivan Machinery Company, a machine manufacturing business, was New Hampshire's largest employer in the 1920s. In 1946, Sullivan merged with Joy Mining Machinery Company to become the Joy Manufacturing Company, Claremont's largest and most dominant employer. Joy Manufacturing moved out of Claremont in the 1980s due to the recession and lagging sales. Even an almost unanimous vote by its unionized workers to accept a 30 percent pay cut did not save the company.[97]

Claremont's median household income today is half the state's median. By the early 1990s, Claremont had the highest local property tax rates in the state and a failing school system. Its high school lost accreditation in 1991. In the early 2000s, during our litigation, the city of Claremont offered to give property it seized for failure to pay taxes to businesses willing to relocate to the city. There were no takers.[98] Today, although one of the downtown mill buildings has been developed into apartments and another into office space, one quarter of the downtown buildings remain empty.

The Influence of Racism and of Privilege Protecting Privilege

It is interesting to contrast what happened in Berlin and Claremont with Salem, New Hampshire. Salem is in New Hampshire's southern tier, thirty-nine miles from Boston. The comparison both exemplifies the importance of property values and introduces the self-serving influence of privilege and racism in New Hampshire.

In 1950, the population of Salem was 4,750. Today's population in Salem tops 30,000 and its median household income exceeds that of the state by almost 10 percent.

Salem is among the reddest towns in the most conservative county in the state. In a state where there are four hundred state representatives elected every two years, Salem has elected only one Democratic state rep in twenty-five years—and Salem elects ten representatives to the New Hampshire House in every election.

Salem is also the stronghold of the conservative Republican Sununu political family. John H. Sununu was a three-term New Hampshire governor from 1983 to 1989. He then became, for a very short time, the chief of staff to President George H. W. Bush. His son, John E. Sununu, was New Hampshire's US Senator from 2003 to 2009. Before that he was a two-term member of Congress.

Another son, Chris Sununu, was elected New Hampshire's governor in 2016 and will complete his fourth term as governor in 2024. I was elected to and served on New Hampshire's Executive Council, which acts as a state board of directors, during Chris Sununu's first two terms, from 2017 to 2020.

The I-93 route between Salem and Boston opened in the summer of 1961. Salem's growth and general success are not fully explained by its easy work commute to Boston.

Through the 1960s and 1970s, Massachusetts state leaders began to desegregate Boston schools, which, at the time, were among the most segregated schools in the nation. The Massachusetts legislature passed the Racial Imbalance Act in 1965, which required desegregation. Judge Arthur Garrity, enforcing federal law, ordered busing to respond to public school segregation in 1974.

The reaction to Garrity's order was immediate and violent. An iconic photo of a White man using an American flag to attack a Black lawyer headed to court cemented Boston's image as a racist city. Famed Celtics coach and center Bill Russell described Boston in the 1970s as "a flea market of racism."[99] Boston-area families fled the city to avoid busing, the related violence, and integration. Many moved to southern New Hampshire, where Salem was one of the primary beneficiaries of this White flight.

Before New Hampshire readers protest the above characterization, they should consider the statewide newspaper, the *Union Leader*, and its publisher, William Loeb, whose heyday was also in the mid-1970s. After a horrible murder in Roxbury, Massachusetts, Loeb wrote and published a front-page editorial that claimed the murder was:

> typical of the savagery of some of the blacks in this country. They hate whites. . . . They have no more feeling . . . than jungle savages from the darkest parts of Africa. It is because this newspaper wants to avoid this kind of thing happening in New Hampshire that we are hopeful that the Black population will never increase from its present minimal level.

The next census, completed in 1980, revealed that New Hampshire had 920,610 inhabitants, of which, 3,990 identified as Black. At the time of the 1970 census, New Hampshire had 737,681 inhabitants, of which 3,505 identified as Black.

When questioned about the Roxbury editorial during an interview by Bill Moyers, Loeb dug deeper: "I wouldn't back off one inch. . . . Many of them are just like children. . . . This is not an environmental problem. This is really genetic. They're years back in evolution."[100]

On September 11, 1975, Loeb wrote a front-page editorial "to newcomers only." He noted:

> In the last few years, New Hampshire has been blessed by having a great many people from other states in the Union, especially Massachusetts, come to live in the Granite State. Many of these

people have crossed the border into New Hampshire for the purpose of escaping from excessive burdens of taxation, political cor-
ruption and unpleasant conditions which surrounded them in the
states from which they came.

The reference to "unpleasant conditions" is not much of a code given
this editorial was written the year after Judge Garrity's busing order. A
few days earlier, the *Union Leader* editorialists had written: "If Shake-
speare were alive today, he would have been able to write a tragedy based
on the busing situation to equal any tragedy ever written." Loeb also
characterized the television series *Roots* as "a Russian plot."

Peter Powell is a leading businessman from Lancaster, New Hampshire, and the son of the late Governor Wesley Powell. When interviewed
for a documentary about Loeb, Peter said that although people were critical of Loeb, they needed to come to terms with the fact that Loeb flourished in New Hampshire after failing in Vermont and Massachusetts.

That's something New Hampshire needs to understand about
itself because you have to admit to it in order to deal with it. . . .
There's something about the history and culture of politics in
New Hampshire that were not so much a result of [Loeb's] being
who he was as a result of our being who we were.[101]

Loeb's third wife, Nackey Scripps Loeb, took over as publisher after
her husband passed away in 1981. Nackey Loeb was from the powerful
Scripps newspaper publishing family. Former *Concord Monitor* reporter
and now Northeastern University journalism professor Meg Heckman
uncovered the Loebs' connection to the White Citizens' Council, an
organization created to fight desegregation through economic reprisals
and boycotts.[102]

Historian Clive Webb referred to the Citizens' Council as "the Ku
Klux Klan without the hoods and the masks," and noted their involvement
in the Reverse Freedom Rides that tricked Southern Blacks into traveling
to northern states to take jobs that weren't there. New Hampshire was

one of these destinations and, according to Peter Powell, Loeb's *Union Leader* was behind inviting the Reverse Freedom Ride buses to Concord, New Hampshire, during Wesley Powell's term as governor. President Kennedy's Cape Cod home was another destination for the Reverse Freedom Rides.[103] Current Texas Governor Greg Abbott and Florida Governor Ron DeSantis are channeling the White Citizens' Council of the 1950s and 60s when they mimic this tactic by busing unsuspecting immigrants who have crossed the southern border with Mexico to northern cities and to Cape Cod with false promises of good jobs and stable living conditions.

Heckman also documented that the Citizens' Council published a political cartoon drawn by Nackey Loeb denouncing the federal troops who protected the Little Rock Nine, the students who challenged desegregation in Arkansas in the wake of the *Brown* decision. The Citizens' Council republished the cartoon in 1972 when William Loeb spoke at their leadership retreat, and again in 1981 when Loeb died. Heckman wrote, "William Loeb saw supporting segregationists as a strategic move that might benefit conservatives" by driving away African Americans and turning the GOP into "the white man's party."[104]

Perhaps the saddest chapter of the Loebs' racist influence on New Hampshire involves their newspaper's effort to prevent the adoption of a state holiday to honor Dr. Martin Luther King Jr. The effort to have Dr. King recognized with a federal holiday began just after his assassination in April of 1968. A federal holiday was adopted in November 1983. It took seventeen more years for all fifty states to adopt state holidays commemorating Dr. King, and New Hampshire was the very last.[105]

Vanessa L. Washington Johnson was the first person of color elected to the Manchester school board, in 1988. (Manchester is New Hampshire's largest city at about one hundred thousand people.) Shortly after her election, Johnson convinced the school board to honor Dr. King with a local holiday.

The *Union Leader*, under publisher Nackey Loeb and editor James Finnegan, missed the original vote and so organized a reconsideration motion a few weeks later. According to the then head of the New

Hampshire chapter of the American Friends Service Committee, Arnie Alpert, "The *Union Leader* used its editorial page much as advocacy groups now use their web sites and social media, informing readers about the time and place of the hearing, providing talking points, and listing the names and phone numbers of school board members."[106]

Fortunately, the reconsideration vote failed. But according to Alpert, the *Union Leader* published one hundred editorials or editorial cartoons vilifying Dr. King or opposing a holiday in his name between 1988 and 1991. Ms. Johnson's father, Lionel Washington Johnson, was the first Black person elected to the New Hampshire House of Representatives, in 1996. Eventually, the New Hampshire legislature agreed to recognize Dr. King with a state holiday in 1999.[107]

Loeb's *Union Leader* flourished and was a dominant political force in the 1970s, 1980s, and 1990s, despite the fact that Loeb featured overtly racist front-page editorials—or maybe because of his editorials. Loeb's approach to racism found a home in New Hampshire. The paper still publishes today, but has been beset by financial struggles since the early 2000s.

New Hampshire's Tax Pledge

William Loeb and his statewide paper were also instrumental in shaping state tax policy. His preference for those of privilege went hand in hand with his efforts to starve the state of resources, and with his racism.

New Hampshire has a political slogan called "the Pledge." It's not the Pledge of Allegiance or some other kind of pledge to God, country, or high ideals. It's a promise by most politicians running for state office never to institute a broad-based sales or income tax.

The Pledge protects the wealthiest in New Hampshire from paying their fair share of taxes because it focuses the state's revenue raising options on local property taxes. Wealthy residents maintain less of their wealth in their homes than middle- and working-class families. Without an income tax, their wealth escapes state taxation while middle- and working-class folks bear the brunt of taxation, which is focused on the value of their homes.

The Pledge originated in the early 1970s in a gubernatorial primary between the incumbent Walter Peterson and the nasty, pre-Libertarian tax hater, Mel Thomson.

Thomson was 0 and 2 against Peterson, having lost in the 1968 and 1970 Republican primaries. In 1972, William Loeb took up Thomson's cause and pummeled Peterson and his family with front-page editorials and unflattering news coverage in his statewide paper. He also boosted Thomson whenever he could. Loeb went so far as to attack Peterson's teenaged children as libertines. Thomson won and New Hampshire leaders promoted the political importance of Loeb's Pledge without fully understanding the singular role of malicious sustained publicity.

Why was Loeb so upset with Peterson, who was a well-liked and responsible governor?

Peterson understood the state's financial needs and the fairness of the various ways those needs could be met. He proposed a broad, flat-rate state income tax in 1972. Peterson's proposal wasn't that unusual. New Hampshire was one of only seven states without an income tax. Pennsylvania and Rhode Island had enacted state income taxes the year before, in 1971.[108]

The ire of William Loeb, however, was raised and the Pledge was born. Fifty years later, the Pledge remains a cornerstone of New Hampshire politics, particularly among Republicans and the most entrenched members of the Democratic Party. In the 2024 run to replace Governor Chris Sununu, who is retiring, four of the five candidates have taken the Pledge. Two of the candidates promising not to touch New Hampshire's regressive system of taxes are mainstream Democrats, one of whom is the former mayor of Manchester.

When I ran for governor in 2020, the advice that leading politicians gave me was to just lie. Promise not to enact a broad-based tax while campaigning and then do what I wanted after the election. I refused this advice.

The Pledge fails the test of economic history. It's a great injustice to the state's taxpayers because modern-day property taxes do not reflect a taxpayer's ability to pay, as an income tax does. The modern property tax is also not the same as the original general tax on property.

Like many states, New Hampshire in the nineteenth century funded government at the state and local level with a general property tax. That property tax, however, wasn't the same as what we think of as the modern-day tax on real estate. The property tax was based on the income property produced. A farmer's wealth was tied to the productivity of the land that was farmed. A gristmill owner's wealth was tied to the value of mill equipment, which was taxed as property. The shopkeeper was taxed on the value of inventory, or "stock in trade." The approach was a fair one.

Perhaps the tax philosophy was influenced by the New Testament, Matthew 25:15 ("from each according to his ability and to each according to his need"). Of course, this is also Marxist theory, but don't tell anyone.

Today, forty-two states have a state income tax, as do some municipalities and counties.[109]

The first state to adopt an income tax as we now understand the term was Wisconsin in 1912, after a statewide referendum showed support for the concept as a way to make taxes fairer. At the time, farmers paid a higher percentage of taxes than wealthy businessmen because the tax was on land, not income.[110]

The states that border New Hampshire all tax wages as income; some have done so for a very long time: Vermont (1931), Maine (1969), and Massachusetts (1916). All the other New England and Mid-Atlantic states have income taxes.[111]

The first federal income tax was imposed in 1861 and repealed in 1872. Congress adopted the nation's first income tax with progressive marginal rates in 1913, after the passage of the Sixteenth Amendment.[112]

At its outset, the general property tax in New Hampshire was a reasonable measure of local wealth. However, over time, beginning in the 1930s, wealth diversified away from the ownership of tangible property to the ownership of stocks and bonds.[113] Businesses also played games when it came time to assess the value of their property for tax purposes.

A well-known auto dealer in the Concord area, for example, moved his inventory of vehicles from sales lots in Concord to his location in the adjacent low-tax town of Bow on assessment day. He'd then quickly move the cars back to his Concord lot.

In the 1970s, starved for funds, New Hampshire introduced both a tax on the business profits of large corporations and a tax on interest and dividends. The Business Profits Tax (BPT) was an income tax on businesses, but politicians did not acknowledge this. The tax rate has fluctuated between 7.9 percent and 9.56 percent (in 1983).

The Interest and Dividends (I&D) Tax is considered a narrow income tax because it isn't imposed on regular wages and excludes capital gains, the profit made on selling a business or other assets. The I&D Tax was set at a flat 5 percent. In 2022, the I&D Tax was producing in excess of one hundred million dollars a year. Governor Sununu and the Republican-led legislature are phasing out this tax over the next two years, without a replacement for the lost revenues.

Small and medium-sized businesses generally escaped the BPT because they converted their business profits to wages paid to the working owners. By 1990 or so, the state's largest employer, a tech company called Cabletron, paid 10 percent of all the BPT tax revenues collected by New Hampshire. Its founders, Robert Levine and Craig Benson, didn't like it.

In 1992, Cabletron filed suit against the state, arguing the BPT was unconstitutional. Cabletron claimed the tax was unfair because it was imposed on too narrow a group of businesses, and that too many businesses easily avoided payment by paying out profit as compensation at the end of the tax year.[114] When Cabletron was starting out, it too paid out profit in the form of compensation to the founding shareholders, but as it grew to be a large, sophisticated company that was publicly traded, it stopped this practice.

When Steve Merrill was elected governor in 1992, the BPT lawsuit became his problem. Benson and Merrill were not on particularly good terms because the Cabletron founders supported one of Merrill's opponents in the Republican primary. Nonetheless, Merrill was in a difficult position, and he approached Benson to settle the case when it was clear the state would lose the suit.

According to Benson, their negotiations included discussion and consideration of the concerns for tax fairness that motivated Cabletron to file suit and the dangers of too narrow a tax base. Eventually, the two settled on the Business Enterprise Tax (BET), which is a tax on the compensation paid by small and medium-sized businesses before the compensation is paid out as wages. This closed the previous loophole in the BPT.

Benson specifically recalls that he and Merrill realized that taxing wages in the hands of small businesses was very close to an income tax, but Benson said it didn't matter. Merrill was stuck, and Cabletron was not backing off.[115]

The legislature enacted the BET at Merrill's insistence in 1993. A former Republican state rep and tax lawyer, Bill Ardinger, was the primary draftsman of the bill. The initial rate was .02 percent of all compensation paid by the business, whether or not the business was profitable. The rate trended up to .05 percent, and has since moved down slightly to .047 percent.

The greatest irony here is that Merrill settled the Cabletron BPT suit by enacting an income tax on small businesses. He did this after he castigated his opponent in the 1992 election, Arnie Arnesen, for openly supporting an income tax. Merrill, by the way, wasn't alone in chastising Arnesen. She and her campaign received a good deal of grief from members of the New Hampshire Democratic Party, particularly those associated with the party's leadership. The Democrats who snubbed Arnesen did so even though failing to support her ensured Merrill's election.

Merrill took the Pledge when he ran for governor in 1992. He did the same in 1994, when he ran again. Benson later became governor, in 2003, on a Pledge-infused platform.

Now, with limited state resources stemming from the absence of a state tax effort, the only game in town is for the state to shift as many expenses of state government as possible to the local property tax, one of the most regressive and inelastic revenue sources available. Local taxpayers must pay their property taxes regardless of whether they have the income to do so. Property taxes do not rise with a new job that increases income or fall when a taxpayer has a medical problem that puts a homeowner out of work.

The consequences of state tax avoidance fall not only on schools but on individuals. The stories of Jill Shaefer Hammond from Peterborough and

Donna Lee McCabe are recounted in a circa-2000 Granite State Fair Tax Coalition video. The Granite State Fair Tax Coalition was funded by the New Hampshire Council of Churches to respond to the Claremont rulings.

After living in her own home for decades, Jill could no longer afford the taxes and had to move to a modest apartment. "I don't believe that it's right that the home I've lived in for twenty years—I get taxed out of."

Donna Lee paid 25 percent of her very modest income to property taxes and still said, "I don't resent paying taxes . . . it's what makes us part of civilization . . . we support each other."

The stories of Ms. Hammond and Ms. McCabe repeat themselves over and over. More than twenty years after the Granite State Fair Tax Coalition video, the *Concord Monitor* reported the front-page story of April Stoddard, who is being taxed out of her small, manufactured home. Stoddard is seventy-five and lives on a fixed income. When Stoddard purchased her home in 2021, it was assessed at $51,000. Two years later, the assessment was $79,200, resulting in a 55-percent increase to her property tax bill.[116]

Particularly at budget time, New Hampshire politicians do a very good job of selling how overburdening taxes are in our state in order to justify inaction—even if the claims are not true. Governor Walter Peterson had it right when he once said we should teach people how to objectively understand taxes.

The bottom line is New Hampshire residents do not pay high state taxes. According to the Tax Foundation, a nonprofit think tank, in 2024, New Hampshire ranked fiftieth in the nation in *state* tax collections per capita, at $2,497 per person. The national average was $4,374.[117] New Hampshire's *combined state and local tax burden* places it in the bottom twenty states. Maine and Vermont, by comparison, are top ten in combined burden.[118]

While low in overall tax burden, New Hampshire ranks at or near the top in property tax reliance. New Hampshire residents don't pay much overall in taxes, but what is paid is overwhelmingly from the property tax.

In fiscal year 2020, when the national average of state and local revenue from property taxes was 32 percent, New Hampshire derived 64 percent of its state and local revenues from property taxes. New Hampshire's neighbors were much more modest in their reliance on the property tax, with 44.6 percent for Maine and 44.3 percent for Vermont coming from property taxes.[119]

Property taxes have a different look and feel than sales or business taxes, which generally add only a small additional cost to the purchase of goods or services. Both the incremental cost of a sales tax and that of a business tax are often considered just a part of the price of the goods or services being purchased. People don't stop to think, *This is the cost of my government services.* They don't connect school costs directly to general state sales taxes paid. No one thinks, *If only schools weren't so expensive, my dinner out would cost five dollars less.*

Property taxes are different. They are paid in significant amounts a couple times a year. A tax of twenty-five dollars per thousand on a house that's worth $300,000 is $7,500 per year. People notice when they pay their property taxes in a way that doesn't apply to other kinds of taxes. The payments become a point of resentment against schools.

I do an experiment when I speak about schools and taxes in New Hampshire. I ask audience members to guess which state has the highest state and local combined tax burden out of New Hampshire, Vermont, Maine, and Massachusetts. The audience members always choose New Hampshire, which has the lowest burden among the four states. It's because they feel the burden of property taxes so much.

One last point worth mentioning is that New Hampshire spends a lot on its public schools, on average. This sometimes confuses people, including our current governor Chris Sununu and elected Democratic leaders, who use the high spending to claim there isn't much of an equity problem. Each year, the Education Law Center rates states on their support for public education. While New Hampshire rates high on its overall spending in support of schools (an A grade), it receives an F in terms of the equity in how the money is raised and a C for effort, a measure that compares the personal wealth in a state versus its spending on schools.

New Hampshire is among the least equitable states in the nation in terms of how it funds its schools.[120] And this inequity is what leads to litigation.

Chapter 5

Building the Claremont Case

T he Claremont case wasn't the first effort to challenge New Hampshire's method of school funding. A couple of cases tried to force change, and failed, and the legislature capitalized on the failure to ignore the problem. Although the prior efforts were unsuccessful, they shaped what we did in *Claremont*.

In 1971, at the time of the first *Serrano* decision, a lawyer from Laconia, New Hampshire, tried to use the arguments made in the California case while representing the Laconia School Board against the Laconia city government. The two municipal entities were fighting over which controlled local appropriations for schools. That lawyer was Arthur Nighswander.

Nighswander was a distinguished lawyer and bar president. He was also a community activist who served as school board president, president of Lakes Region General Hospital, and chair of the board for a school for disabled children. As a bar president, he was committed to protecting civil liberties and encouraging lawyers to engage in pro bono efforts. Nighswander lived until he was 100 and practiced law almost until the day he died. The New Hampshire Civil Liberties Union awarded Nighswander its highest award, the Bill of Rights Award. I am honored to say that I received the same award years after Nighswander did and served on the Civil Liberties Union board with Arthur's son, Warren.

The New Hampshire Supreme Court declined to consider the issue of funding equity raised by Nighswander because it was raised too late in the litigation, but mentioned the equity issue in its opinion that found against Nighswander's client.[121] Courts don't generally write without some purpose and the court's mention of *Serrano* in its reported decision was likely intended to send notice to New Hampshire's elected officials that there was a problem with how New Hampshire funds its schools that required legislative attention.

Although the legislature ignored the suggestion, the State Board of Education, in its statutory report to the legislature for the biennium, 1970–72, recommended that the state "completely revamp the total program [of school funding] and to fund [schools] at a level which largely eliminates the need to raise local funds through the property tax." This call to action was also ignored.

Two years after the Laconia case, Nighswander and a lawyer named Jack Middleton argued in a federal court case that education is a fundamental right and that the New Hampshire funding system was unconstitutional. Nighswander represented school boards and Middleton represented the National Education Association (NEA) teachers' union. Both lawyers were New Hampshire heavyweights.

Today, at the age of ninety-six, Jack Middleton continues to practice law at the firm that bears his name. Like Arthur, he was a president of the New Hampshire Bar and active in his community as an advisor and board member for many nonprofits, banks, and businesses.

Judge Hugh Bownes presided over the case that Nighswander and Middleton filed. He was probably the best judge they could draw for the matter. Bownes was supportive of civil liberties and was likely to rule that education is a fundamental right.

US Supreme Court Justice David Souter said of Bownes, "He was an old-fashioned liberal, yet it seems to me, some of the liberalisms Hugh was such a staunch proponent of shouldn't only be assigned to liberals."[122]

Unfortunately, the *San Antonio* decision, written by Justice Powell, was released early in the litigation before Bownes, forcing him to dismiss the case. As a lower federal court judge, Bownes was obliged to follow the *San Antonio* precedent from the country's highest court. Litigation over fair school funding in New Hampshire then lay dormant for almost a decade, as matters grew worse.

Middleton returned to litigate school funding again in 1980 in a case called *Jesseman v. State*. He again represented the NEA and was assisted by Bill Glahn, a former assistant attorney general under New Hampshire Attorney General David Souter, before he became a justice of the US Supreme Court. Dick Goodman, a University of New Hampshire education professor, helped organize the effort. Arthur Nighswander served as co-counsel.

Wendell Jesseman, for whom the suit was named, was and is a wonderfully committed supporter of public schools. For most of his career he has been the CEO of the New England Wire and Cable Company, now called New England Wire Technologies, in Lisbon, New Hampshire, an isolated mountain community of about 1,500 people. New England Wire employs over 400 people in this rural area of northern New Hampshire. The New Hampshire Business and Industry Association awarded Wendell its lifetime achievement award in 2013. The co-recipient that year was former Speaker of the New Hampshire House, Donna Sytek.

At the time the Jesseman suit was organized, a part of Lisbon High School was a converted chicken coop. There were huge safety issues at the school that included exposed wiring, absence of fire doors, exit doors that swung the wrong way, and improper storage of flammable materials. Years after the suit, Lisbon passed a bond and built a new high school. Cost overruns caused the funding to be short, and the high school gym was going to be significantly reduced in size. New England Wire and Cable, Wendell's company, donated the extra funds needed to build the full-sized gym. His company also wired the high school for Internet access.

The Jesseman suit asserted that education is a fundamental right under the New Hampshire Constitution and challenged New Hampshire's overreliance on local property taxes to fund its schools. The state's top litigators were assigned to defend the suit. Really, what they were defending was the New Hampshire way of life, which eschewed broad-based income or sales taxes and relied heavily on local property taxes.

Assistant Attorney General Leslie Ludtke was one of the state's lead litigators in the Jesseman suit. The key expert supporting her efforts, Paul Snow, was an engineer who worked at the state attorney general's office as a data analyst. From the outset, the state's strategy was to exhaust the resources of the poor school districts who were plaintiffs. Even though the school districts were in a state system that required extensive financial and academic reporting to facilitate oversight by the state board, demands for the plaintiff school districts to produce data were continual and exhausting. Everyone who was part of the plaintiff school districts' efforts, it seemed, was subjected to intense hours of questioning in formal depositions. All of these efforts were unnecessary to address the merits of the case. They were instead designed to keep the case from being decided on its merits. This is generally the approach taken by attorneys general who defend corrupt state funding systems. Since they can't win on the merits by proving their systems are fair and unbiased, they try to kill cases before they reach final decisions.

State expert Snow, perhaps echoing *Edgewood* and the absence of typewriters at its schools, claimed computers were unnecessary to learn computer science, and asserted: "The State of New Hampshire supplements local financing of public schools [through foundation aid] to ensure that every pupil can receive a well-funded education."[123] Interestingly, Snow wasn't a tax expert, economist, or experienced in examining school finance systems. He was just the attorney general's data management guy.

By 1985, the plaintiffs were still some distance from a trial in their case and their resources were exhausted. John H. Sununu was the governor and Stephen Merrill was now his attorney general.

At the time, the state's contribution to public education was about 6 percent of the overall cost.[124] Sununu and Merrill convinced the legislature to create a foundation aid pool—a small pool—and the plaintiffs voluntarily dismissed their case. Sununu was adamant that the new funding remain untethered to any principle of educational finance, such as funding sufficient for a basic education or an equal education. The amount of funding that Sununu allowed to be put into law had to be completely at the discretion of the legislature. Sununu vetoed a first version of the law because it contained language that said the state's policy would be "that all children in New Hampshire [are to] be provided with equal education opportunities."[125]

Eventually, Sununu agreed to have the state contribute an additional 8 percent in state funding targeted towards New Hampshire's poorest districts. An education funding expert from Colorado named John Augenblick was hired to craft the formula to distribute the funds. The result was called the "Augenblick formula."

No one in the education community seriously believed that an additional 8 percent in funding was enough to materially improve the lot of the poorest districts. As it turns out, Augenblick didn't think it would make a difference either, although he didn't say so for more than five years. In an interview with Jeff Feingold, then a young reporter with the *New Hampshire Spectator*, Augenblick admitted the new foundation aid plan was doomed to fail because Sununu did not allow the legislature to significantly increase overall education aid. "Typically, when there's such a change as in New Hampshire, more money is also pumped in. In New Hampshire's case, they took money from one pot and put it in another."[126] Just as bad, Governor Sununu continued to divert about half the state's school funding to programs that were not weighted towards the poorest districts. Sununu insisted that $18 million of the state's $39 million of school funding be distributed on a per-pupil basis that did not consider the wealth of the district that received the money.[127]

Regardless of whether an 8 percent foundation aid program distributed according to the Augenblick formula would have made a difference, the state never fully funded it during Sununu's years in office (1983–1989) or through the administration of his successor, Judd Gregg (1989–1993). Because the plaintiffs had not dismissed their case as part of a formal settlement, there was no mechanism by which the poorer school districts could enforce the promise to target an additional 8 percent of funding. The promise was ethereal, as is much of politics.

Governor Gregg, who followed Sununu, was also part of a political family. His father, Hugh Gregg, was governor from 1953 to 1955. Judd Gregg served four terms as a member of Congress before becoming governor, and two terms as a US senator after leaving the governor's office.

The interesting thing about Judd Gregg's neglect of the 8 percent promise is that one of the initiatives he undertook while in office was to convene a commission that studied New Hampshire's future, entitled the Governor's Commission on New Hampshire in the 21st Century. The commission, composed of many state dignitaries, issued a report in January 1991. The 21st Century Report could have been an important effort to improve the quality of New Hampshire's schools or to suggest ways to make taxes more fair and more stable into the future.

It wasn't.

The commission members muzzled themselves and the 21st Century Report did not comment on New Hampshire's tax system or public schools. This passage from the report explains why: "A good idea that can be accomplished is worth a dozen that can't."[128] Of course, nothing happens without leadership, and Gregg and his commission members squandered this opportunity to provide leadership.

When people complain that lawyers and advocates for school funding equity, or any other kind of social change, resort too quickly to litigation, or that it's only about the lawyers and their litigation, remember the 21st Century report, which failed to talk about the inequity of education funding as an example of why litigation becomes necessary.

The 1980s ended with a failed school funding suit and an empty promise of more aid. Things just continued to worsen for New Hampshire's public schools and taxpayers.

After years of issuing warnings for Claremont's Stevens High School to upgrade its failing buildings, the accrediting agency for high schools in New England finally pulled the plug and revoked the school's accreditation in early 1991.

Interestingly, New Hampshire never revoked its approval of Stevens High School, even though Stevens did not meet state standards and only 19 percent of its graduates went to college. The state average was 54 percent. The state did not even place Stevens on probation. It just let Stevens soldier on and slowly dwindle away—while Claremont's taxpayers paid higher school taxes than taxpayers elsewhere in the state.

The loss of accreditation hurt the community's psyche. *After paying taxes that were higher than anyone else's,* they thought, *we have still failed and we are marked by our failure.* This failure particularly affected Tom Connair, who was a relatively new member of the Claremont School Board when Stevens was placed on probation and then lost its accreditation. Tom was an Ohio transplant, a former Navy commander, and an idealistic lawyer. Tom graduated from New Hampshire's only law school,

Franklin Pierce School of Law, in 1980, served a prestigious clerkship with the New Hampshire Supreme Court, and moved to Claremont with his young family to take a job with the best-known general practice law firm in this small city. The firm was known as Leahy and Denault. Albert "Albie" Leahy Jr., the senior partner, was also the part-time judge in Claremont, as was his father before him.

After getting established in the community, Tom was soon elected to the school board and, later, joined the board of the Claremont Savings Bank. The local chamber of commerce was one of his pro bono clients. There were many others. George Bailey, the lead character in *It's a Wonderful Life*, who sacrificed personally to protect his community, would have been proud of Tom Connair. Decades later, Tom was named Claremont's Citizen of the Year.

Tom organized the Claremont School Board to seek help from the state when Stevens lost its accreditation. Tom understood that the school board was doing all it could. The loss of accreditation required additional investment in the high school, while the middle school and elementary schools had needs, too. Taxpayers were at their breaking point. By 1989, the Claremont School District had already cut sports and kindergarten to save money. Tom understood the unfairness of it all and, when the state refused to help, he began researching legal remedies. Tom found the Serrano and Rodriguez cases and learned about the Jesseman case, which was litigated before he joined the school board.

Tom sent letters asking for help to half a dozen lawyers, including the leaders of New Hampshire's largest law firms and some people who were on Judd Gregg's 21st Century Commission. He invited them to Claremont to view the schools and discuss a potential lawsuit. None responded to Tom's letter except his former constitutional law professor at Franklin Pierce, Arpiar "Arpy" Saunders.

Tom also sought help from the New Hampshire School Boards Association. The association's executive committee turned him down for fear of alienating wealthy communities.

Tom and Arpy began collaborating. Arpy visited Claremont and learned the schools were failing despite the heroic efforts of Claremont's taxpayers. He concluded that a lawsuit was legally viable, but a very long shot.

Arpy Saunders was a former ACLU lawyer in Washington, DC, and had been a legal aid lawyer in New Hampshire before joining the law school's faculty. At the time, New Hampshire legal aid lawyers and New Hampshire public defenders hung out together.

I was a former public defender and Arpy and I became friends. Our young children were the same age. After defending against the death penalty in the South and then serving as a New Hampshire public defender in Manchester, I joined a Concord law firm in 1987. Arpy and I were part of a group of lawyers who ran most days from the Concord YMCA.

One day, as I was changing in the locker room after a good run, Arpy told me about Tom Connair and Claremont, and asked me to be the trial lawyer on the team. We later asked John Garvey, another lawyer who also ran at lunch time, to join us. By New Hampshire standards, we had a pretty good team. Arpy was a law professor with access to students who could do research and John Garvey was an insurance defense lawyer at a large firm with resources. I was a trial lawyer with extensive experience trying cases for appeal, which meant I planned to lose at trial and focused on establishing the record for the later appeals. We thought we had spread the risk well and had the necessary resources even if our client, the Claremont School District, was near destitute.

Were we ever naïve! We expected to donate a lot of our time. As it turned out, our clients didn't have the money to pay us at all. Our fundraising efforts were necessary just to raise enough money to hire experts and pay for out-of-pocket litigation expenses like deposition and hearing transcripts. Still, our clients, having expanded to five school districts, raised $50,000 to get us started.

After the School Boards Association executive committee voted not to support a suit, Tom snuck up on them and put forward a resolution supporting a lawsuit at the next annual school boards meeting. It passed by a wide margin. Tom also pitched the lawsuit at the school district meeting in March of 1990 before a packed gym of about 200 voters at Stevens High School. Every voter at the meeting voted to support filing a lawsuit. Eventually, the School Boards Association agreed to send a letter to its members soliciting support for a lawsuit. Four other districts agreed to be plaintiffs and another twenty-three agreed to be affiliate members of what became known as the Claremont Coalition. The twenty-three affiliates included some wealthy districts that believed in a high-quality public education for all students, no matter where they lived. The Gilford School District stands out in this regard.

Arpy, John and I began meeting with Tom to plan a lawsuit. We researched the San Antonio and Serrano cases and caught up with legal developments in Kentucky and West Virginia. We were introduced to Dick Goodman at the University of New Hampshire, who had been involved in organizing the Jesseman suit. We met David Long, a long-time school-funding litigator who helped us craft the suit.

There were two legal issues and one big practical issue for which we needed to plan from the start. The legal issues were standing and justicia-bility. "Justiciability" asks if courts have any proper role in deciding how to address a problem. Some societal problems are solely committed to the other branches of government. How to spend revenues is a good example of an issue generally committed to legislatures, not courts. Another aspect of justiciability is the question of what standards a court should apply to determine if a constitutional right is violated. We would soon find out the court's position on both aspects of justiciability.

"Standing" is a separate question that asks if the plaintiffs suffered legal harm. Not every bystander or concerned citizen is legally empowered to sue the government over decisions the citizen doesn't like. The decision being challenged must cause the person who brings the suit some direct legal harm. With David Long's advice, we decided to address the issue of standing with belts and suspenders. We had five school districts as our clients: Claremont, Allenstown, Pittsfield, Lisbon, and Franklin. School districts are legal entities, and they are entitled to sue and be sued.

We added students as plaintiffs in case the school districts could not show they suffered the legal harm sufficient to prove standing. Students went to the substandard schools and suffered through educational experi-ences that often left them unprepared to compete with their counterparts in wealthy districts. Students, as minors, however, do not generally file suits. They are required to file suit through their parents or other adults. As we needed to involve the parents anyway, we decided to make the parents plaintiffs, as they owned their homes and thus paid property taxes. This left us with five school districts, five students, and five taxpayers as plaintiffs. Surely one of these groups would be legally recognized as suffering harm. Now we had to find the students and taxpayers who would join our suit.

For ethical reasons, we were hesitant to directly solicit students and parents, so we asked Tom, as a school board member in Claremont, to work with school board members in the other five districts to recommend clients. The school boards each suggested citizens prominent in their communities to become our clients.

Peter Viar, for example, was a selectman in Allenstown and his wife Ann was the head of the Parent Teacher Association. Ann had recently organized a successful fundraising drive to build a much-needed playground at one of the two Allenstown elementary schools. Unfortunately, the roof began to leak badly at the elementary school that needed the playground, and the money for the playground was diverted to fix the roof. The Viars' son, Michael, who was then in first grade, became our student plaintiff.

John Fitzgerald is another example. He represented Lisbon. John was on the Lisbon School Board. He was also the COO of New England Wire and Cable. Wendell Jesseman arranged for his participation. Wendell also arranged for John's later replacement, Lana Superchi, another New England Wire and Cable employee. John's fourth-grade daughter, Meredith, was our student representative from Lisbon.

Richard Elliot Sr. and Annette Elliott from Claremont with their son Richard Jr., in eleventh grade, became the Claremont plaintiffs. Joan Osborne and her daughter Naida, then in kindergarten, represented Franklin.

Franklin was the first community in New Hampshire to enact a tax cap, which required a supermajority vote to raise local property taxes above the rate of inflation. The cap was enacted under Mayor Brenda

Elias. The result was that, not only did Franklin suffer from the structural problem of low property values, it also taxed itself at a lower rate due to the cap. At times, Franklin experienced million-dollar shortfalls in its school budgets, requiring layoffs of nearly half the school staff. Mayors would claim that the tax cap stabilized tax rates and thus attracted business to Franklin, a claim belied by Franklin's ever-dwindling population and dying downtown. Later, Manchester voted to impose a similar tax cap that led to some of the same desperate results as in Franklin.

Patrick Duffy and his daughter Rebecca, in eleventh grade, rounded out our group of plaintiffs. They lived in small, rural Pittsfield.

In addition to describing the state's system for funding public K–12 education in our complaint, we decided the best way to clearly show the shortcomings of our five client districts was to pair them with five nearby, relatively well-off school districts of similar size and grade configuration. This allowed us to describe what our kids were missing in very concrete terms.

We pointed out in our complaint that the Franklin School District did not offer any advanced placement courses to its high school students, had cut all English and social studies electives, and had some students attend three study halls a day, all due to its difficulty staffing its schools. Franklin also experienced almost a 50 percent annual turnover in its professional staff. Gilford, Franklin's comparison district, by contrast, offered seven advanced placement courses, offered English electives in writing, journalism, drama, and public speaking, and offered social studies electives.

We also included a table of tax rates and property values, expressed in equalized values on a per-pupil basis, for each district. Equalizing property values means the values are all presented at 100 percent of their fair market value. Dividing the equalized value by the number of pupils in a district allows you to control for the different sizes of school district.

An equalized value per pupil is a good measure of the financial strength of a district in a system that depends heavily on property taxes to fund schools, because the value of the property being taxed is one of the two primary determinants of how much money can be raised. The other determinant is the rate of taxation.

Our comparisons ranged from Allenstown, with an equalized valuation of $201,407 of property per student, to Moultonborough at $2,237,553 per student. Tax rates varied from Allenstown's at $17.24 to Moultonborough's at $3.34. The state average school tax rate at the time was $9.54.

The complaint showed that Pittsfield, which spent $3,665 per student, had a tax rate almost five times that of Moultonborough, yet Moultonborough's per-pupil spending was more than twice that of Pittsfield.

We made our complaint as factually rich and compelling as possible in preparation for an expected motion to dismiss our case. But before we filed suit, we asked Governor Gregg for a meeting. We waited for a response, but none came. As we were deciding what to do in the spring of 1991, we ran into Governor Gregg's lawyer on the streets of Concord. His name was Art Brennan. Judd Gregg later appointed him to the trial bench and he became a pretty good judge, but at this point, he had to do his client's bidding. Art candidly told us not to expect a response.

So much for avoiding litigation.

We filed suit on June 12, 1991. Named as defendants in our case were Judd Gregg, Governor; Ed Dupont, Senate President; Harold Burns, Speaker of the House; Judith Thayer, Chair of the New Hampshire Board of Education; Charles Marston, Commissioner of Education; Stanley Arnold, Commissioner of the Department of Revenue Administration; and Georgie Thomas, State Treasurer. I remember our press conference announcing the filing. My wife, Amy, had our two small daughters with her. Bekah was in a backpack and she held Mollie by the hand. Our son, Josh, was in fourth grade.

Leslie Ludtke, who had defended the state in the Jesseman case, led the defense team. Assistant Attorney General Doug Jones assisted her. Later, an assistant attorney general fresh from a big law firm in Boston was assigned to the case. His name was Patrick Donovan. He's from Salem and Governor Chris Sununu appointed him to be a justice of the New Hampshire Supreme Court in 2019.

We knew the state would try to exhaust our limited resources with nonsense discovery requests—as the state had done in *Jesseman*. As proof of this intent, the state, with Ms. Ludtke as its counsel, claimed it was without sufficient information to admit to the accuracy of the financial data we cited in our complaint, even though the data came from reports that were published by the state.

We were determined to confront the state's strategy and thought the best way to counter it was to encourage the state to file a motion to dismiss our case. A motion of this kind requires the courts to treat the factual allegations made in the complaint as true and then to rule whether there is a potential case or not. The motion is filed generally at the start of the case, before much time and money is spent on formal discovery efforts. The discovery stage is where the state wore out the *Jesseman* plaintiffs.

We decided the best way to encourage the state to file a motion to dismiss was to ask Leslie Ludtke not to file one; so, I baited her. We also quickly filed Requests for Admissions that asked the state to admit the truth of our factual allegation based on the state's reports. We did this to put some pressure on the state to put up or shut up. In a curious twist that we hadn't planned, presiding judge George Manias told us not to conduct discovery until after the state had filed its motion to dismiss. This meant the state could not make discovery demands either. A deadline was set for the state to file its motion to dismiss. Our strategy was working.

The state claimed, as we expected, we lacked legal standing, the issues raised weren't justiciable because school funding was committed solely to the legislature's discretion, and there were no legal standards on which the court could decide the case.

We opposed the motion to dismiss, citing our belt-and-suspenders approach to standing and all the cases around the country where claims were found justiciable. Soon, however, Judge Manias ruled there was not a legal basis for our suit and dismissed our case. Judge Manias concluded that the language in our state constitution's education clause was merely "hortatory," or aspirational, and provided no standards for a court to enforce.

The New Hampshire education clause, Part II, Article 83 of the New Hampshire Constitution, was a copy of the Massachusetts clause, which was written by John Adams. It was written in eighteenth-century language, and directed the state to "cherish the interest of literature and the sciences, and all seminaries and public schools" because "[k]nowledge and learning, generally diffused through a community, [are] essential to the preservation of a free government."

Our whole case hung on the meaning of "to cherish." What did this all mean when it was adopted on June 2, 1784, and how should it be applied over 200 years later?

We were off to appeal our case to the New Hampshire Supreme Court. Either our case would soon be over and we would have accomplished nothing or the state's supreme court would find the education clause was real and not merely aspirational. No education funding case in New Hampshire had gotten this far. Now, the question was, could we win this appeal?

The first step in pursuing the appeal was the filing of the notice of appeal. At the same time as we filed our notice of appeal, we moved to recuse Justice Stephen Thayer from participating in the case. We intentionally made Judith Thayer, the chair of the State Board of Education, a defendant. It made sense legally because the state board has full powers over school districts. Judith Thayer was also on the state commission that approved the Augenblick formula. Suing Judith Thayer also made practical sense because Judith was married to the most conservative justice on the New Hampshire Supreme Court, W. Stephen Thayer.

We thought the recusal was a slam dunk because a Supreme Court rule expressly provided for the excusal of a judge (called a "recusal") when a spouse is a litigant.[129] The state, by the way, thought that Thayer didn't have an ethical problem and would be just fine. Recusal motions are generally addressed when raised. The justice who is the subject of recusal has a lot to say about the ruling. Justice Thayer refused to recuse himself. Instead, he put off ruling on the motion until just before the oral argument, when, without explanation, recusal was granted on September 7, 1993, nine months after we made the request. Retired superior court judge William Grimes was appointed to take Thayer's place for the purposes of our case.

Grimes was a major improvement in terms of judges who might be receptive to our argument. We still, however, had much to overcome, and we worked hard to put in place the building blocks for a successful public policy decision.

The 1992 state elections happened while our appeal was pending. One of our defendants, Senate President Ed Dupont, retired from the senate to run for governor and lost. A group of Democrats and moderate Republicans conspired to elect moderate Republican Ralph Hough from Lebanon, New Hampshire, as the new senate president. With the switch in senate presidents, Ralph Hough became a defendant in our suit.

After attending one of the national conferences for school-funding litigators, I came up with the idea of approaching a named defendant to switch sides. Hough became our target. A change like this made no difference legally but would be a public relations victory and garner significant media coverage. Legal substance and public engagement are both always at issue in this kind of case.

As a defendant, however, Hough was now theoretically represented by the attorney general and we could not ethically approach him. The representation was merely theoretical because the attorney general was not consulting Hough as a client. He took his orders from the governor, who, after the 1992 election, was Stephen Merrill, Governor John Sununu's former attorney general when Augenblick was enacted.

We let it be known to some friends in the state senate that Hough could ask court permission to change sides for the appeal. Senator Wayne King from Rumney was particularly helpful in organizing his colleagues to support Hough's switch. Senator Susan McLane from the Republican side was also a big help. Senator Jeanne Shaheen was in the state senate at the time and was instrumental in getting Hough elected to the senate president's position, but, according to King, Shaheen disappeared whenever the idea of a switch was broached. She wanted no part of it.

Ralph Hough agreed to switch sides and we asked Bill Glahn to represent him and write an appellate brief. Bill was the former senior assistant attorney general who worked on the Jesseman case with Jack Middleton.

Hough announced his decision on April 20, 1993, saying, "[I am] deeply troubled to find myself held responsible for a funding mechanism

I have questioned and challenged throughout my career in the House and Senate. Furthermore, I find any suggestion that, as a defendant, I might be expected to defend the state against this action especially offensive."

Hough switching was a major coup, but we thought we still needed more help. Arpy, John and I were good lawyers who had accomplished a lot in our young careers, but we weren't leaders in the New Hampshire Bar and we weren't the contemporaries of the justices. We were also pursuing a case that most political wags and some national commentators picked us to lose.[130]

We noticed at national conferences that many of the legal teams were associated with major institutions in their states. The New Jersey team had connections to Rutgers, the New York team was led by a Yale law professor, lead counsel for the Alabama team was Bo Torbert, the retired chief justice of the Alabama Supreme Court. We didn't have these connections to a university or to a local luminary like Torbert. This led me to develop the "more juice" strategy.

If you think of state supreme courts as policy-making bodies that don't just interpret the law, you realize they consider public opinion and the opinions of influential leaders in the legal community. This isn't formally done, of course, but the justices are not completely cut off from society and pay attention to what society thinks about what they do.

Remember the US Supreme Court's *Plessy* decision, where eight of the nine justices supported the consensus of the day in upholding Jim Crow segregation? The same was true in the Korematsu case, where the court shamefully bowed to public pressure to uphold property seizures and internments of Japanese American citizens during the frenzy of World War II. To borrow a term from the economists, supreme courts are "trailing indicators," in that courts generally act after others have cleared the way. They are more likely to be followers than courageous leaders for change.

In the "more juice" strategy, we deliberately set out to recruit the most senior lawyers in our state to our legal team for purposes of the appeal. We focused on the big names who we thought the individual justices trusted. In effect, by signing on to our case, we wanted these big-name lawyers to give the court permission to rule for us. They gave us legitimacy. The leaders of most of the state's major firms were very kind to us and agreed to join our efforts. We added more than a dozen new appellate counsel as part of this strategy. We also added two experienced and skilled appellate lawyers to help us write the briefs, Ed Damon and Diane Perin.

The more juice strategy led to a comical courthouse scene at the oral argument. After the parties and friends of the court (called "amici") file their briefs, which are complex written legal arguments, the parties appear before the justices for oral argument. A good oral argument involves each team of lawyers presenting carefully planned speeches to the justices for about twenty minutes. The justices ignore what the lawyers planned and, instead, ask so many questions that the lawyers find it hard to stay on track.

The oral argument in our case took place on September 14, 1993. Spectators arrived early and the small courtroom was packed. There weren't enough seats for our new appellate counsel and they were asked to wait outside. When we saw this, we explained to court staff that these dozen very senior lawyers were co-counsel, and convinced the staff to squeeze in more chairs up front, around our counsel table.

Chief Justice David Brock entered the courtroom when our case was called, looked over at the state's table, and nodded to Ms. Ludtke. He then looked over at us and visibly did a double take. We could see he had to suppress a smile. There was so little space that the dozen new senior co-counsel, plus John Tobin and Bill Glahn, appeared to embrace the three of us who were litigating the case.

The arguments of the parties were well rehearsed and the questions from the bench were many. Leslie Ludtke argued for the state. Attorney General Jeff Howard sat beside her as her co-counsel. We chose Arpy to argue for us because the legal argument focused on the meaning of the constitutional language and he was our constitutional law professor. Arpy looked and acted the part.

One other thing that we did that was unusual was to split off five minutes of our argument time for John Tobin of New Hampshire Legal Assistance (NHLA). John argued the tax clause part of the case, which centered on the claim that the taxes to pay for the state's responsibility to fund education were state taxes and, as such, the school taxes should be uniform across the state, which they weren't. John and his team of NHLA lawyers were the strongest advocates for this claim and it was their clients, people living in poverty and elderly residents living on fixed incomes, who most suffered from the tax inequities. Some observers thought we gave John time to separately argue the tax claim because the idea of tax fairness in New Hampshire was even more outlandish than a claim for equal educational opportunities, and that the contrast made Arpy appear more reasonable. This idea wasn't true.

The case was fully submitted to the New Hampshire Supreme Court on a beautiful fall day in New Hampshire and we waited for the Court's decision. The state and our team had submitted lengthy briefs, as had Bill Glahn for Senator Hough and five amici (NHLA, the NEA, and the School Boards Association on our side and the Granite State Taxpayers Association and an individual against us). We waited through the rest of September, through all of October and November, through most of December until, on December 30, 1993, the Court issued its decision.

We won.

The Supreme Court rejected Manias's conclusion that Article 83 was merely aspirational ruling: "We hold that part II, article 83 imposes a duty on the State to provide a constitutionally adequate education to every educable child in the public schools in New Hampshire and to guarantee adequate funding."[131] Because Judge Manias's conclusion that Article 83 was unenforceable so permeated the decision to dismiss the case, the Court reinstated our entire case, including the tax count that was argued by John Tobin.

It helped that the highest Massachusetts court interpreted their education clause, on which the New Hampshire clause was based, six months earlier in the *McDuffy* case. The Massachusetts interpretation fully supported our position. As an interesting side note to *McDuffy*, Jonathan Kozol, the author of *Savage Inequalities*, was an amicus supporting the school districts in the Massachusetts case.

We could also see in the Court's opinion references to the history of Article 83 that were submitted in the Hough brief that reflected the input of a local wordsmith, Richard Lederer. We had approached Lederer, an English teacher at a well-known private boarding school in Concord, Saint Paul's School. Lederer wrote about his retention as an expert in one of his many books about the English language, *A Man of My Words: Reflections on the English Language*. In particular, the Court defined the word "cherish" using a dictionary from 1780, as Lederer suggested. The meaning of "cherish" was "to support, to shelter, to nurse up."

The justices did not go quite so far as to determine the right to a public education was a fundamental right. Instead, the opinion identified education as at least a middle-tier right under the New Hampshire Constitution and left the question of fundamentality for another day.

The Court also did not define the parameters of a constitutionally adequate education. Instead, noting that it was more than reading, writing and arithmetic, it placed its "confiden[ce in] . . . the legislature and the Governor [to] fulfill their responsibility with respect to defining the specifics of, and the appropriate means to provide through public education, the knowledge and learning essential to the preservation of a free government."

The case was sent back to Judge Manias for further proceedings leading to a full trial. Governor Merrill and the legislature could have obviated the need for a trial by crafting a new school funding plan. They didn't.

Years after the decision was issued, Chief Justice Brock ran into Arnie Arnesen, who ran for governor against Merrill, and thanked her for making the Court's decision possible. How did she make the Court's decision in the Claremont case possible?

In the 1992 Democratic primary for governor, Arnesen ran against Ned Helms, the state's former commissioner of Health and Human Services and chair of the Democratic Party; and Norm D'Amours, the sitting congressman from the district that included the state's largest city, Manchester. Arnesen beat them both by advocating for an income tax, and faced off against Merrill in the general election. The fact that Arnesen did so well gave the court confidence that the public wanted the problem of uneven school funding fixed.

My relationship with Arnie started one day after our case had been dismissed by Judge Manias. I was sitting in the statehouse cafeteria, trying to eat lunch between meetings and reading a court opinion. A thin woman with big glasses plunked herself down in front of me and said she could not continue her run for governor if I didn't support her. Other than being famous for nursing her child in Representatives Hall while waiting to vote, I didn't know much about her, and she was keeping me from reading an opinion that I thought important. Arnie quickly told me that she believed in everything I was doing in the Claremont case and that we were right. She said if I didn't support her, she was not credible and couldn't go forward. She asked me to hear her speak the next night. I promised to go, mostly to get rid of her.

The next night, I was completely bowled over. She was smart and articulate, and she believed in tax fairness and a good education for every child in the state. I agreed to support her campaign, and soon became the campaign's general counsel.

The fact that Arnie did so well in the gubernatorial race while talking about fair taxes and fair school funding, despite long odds and nonstop snubs from the Democratic Party (Bill Clinton's handlers even made sure she wasn't photographed next to him), gave the members of the Court confidence that their efforts would not be ignored. Arnesen didn't make the legal argument. She made a moral argument and showed it could fly. That was among Arnie's major contributions to the cause.

The Court's decision was greeted by the press and political officials as one would expect. The *Union Leader* headline of December 31, 1993, read "State Must Aid Schools." Next to the headline was a front-page photo of Governor Merrill above a caption that read "Still no income tax." The article that went with the photo repeated Merrill's refrain that the decision would not result in an income tax, but started with this lede: "A stunning landmark decision by the state's highest court has strengthened advocates of radical change."

In a separate summary piece, Merrill went after Arnesen, who, for her part, fired back, "It's in your lap [Governor Merrill]. . . . It is your responsibility. You don't have to worry about your political campaign pledges . . . you have an obligation to fix it for our kids, including your son, Ian."

Former Governor Meldrim "Ax the Tax" Thomson said the "Court is absolutely wrong. . . . The first thing I'd do as governor is cover the back door, make sure it's locked tight [against those endeavoring] to give us a broad-based tax." The paper itself told the court to "Read our lips!" pontificating that the court's decision was at odds with "300 years" of history. As New Hampshire had only been a state for 205 years at the time of the ruling, one could see the *Union Leader*'s editorial penchant for exaggeration. Former Governor John Sununu called the decision "dumb."

The progressive *Concord Monitor*, my hometown paper, celebrated the decision under the headline "Court Sides with Schools." Tom Connair was quoted on the front page, saying, "I'm elated. The winners here are the thousands of schoolchildren across the state." True to form, Merrill said, "I totally reject the concept that this decision means we have to have an income tax." Leslie Ludtke stated her confidence in winning the upcoming trial.

And now, we were off to trial. If we could prove our factual claims, the New Hampshire school funding system would be no more.

Chapter 6

We'd Come So Far

I did not think we'd make it to a trial.

We convinced the New Hampshire Supreme Court to recognize the constitutional right to a public education. The court's ruling in December 1993 was the first recognition in over two hundred years that Article 83 was an enforceable right. Now we had to survive two years of abusive discovery. What's worse, our team faced personal and political calamities that appeared insurmountable.

Judge Manias scheduled us for trial in April 1996.

During 1994 and 1995, the state issued nine rounds of interrogatories that required formal written answers, and endless requests for us to produce documents. The interrogatories and requests for documents created a ton of work for us that produced the same information about our districts that the state already possessed.

What's more, the New Hampshire Supreme Court had ruled that a constitutionally adequate education was not so much a personal right of an individual but a right held by society as a whole. This conclusion is, in part, drawn from the fact that Article 83 is not a part of the individual rights portion of the New Hampshire Constitution. It is in the section of the Constitution that describes New Hampshire's form of government, making clear that John Adams, who wrote the provision, thought of it as foundational to the success of democracy, not necessarily the success of any individual.

Adams's approach diminished the importance of any individual student's performance in school. Despite this, the state required every plaintiff to be deposed. Plaintiff Naida Osborne was in second grade when she was deposed. Michael Viar was in third grade.

It appeared to us that Leslie Ludtke was employing the same tactics that the attorney general's office used to scuttle the Jesseman case, which was to make the plaintiffs spend so much time and resources to comply with discovery demands that the plaintiffs run out of money and give up. In *Jesseman*, it worked.

Thank goodness for Arpy, who methodically coordinated our discovery responses. Even with Arpy devoting most of his time to gathering discovery materials, the state wasn't satisfied and moved for us to be held in contempt.

In late 1995, Judge Manias had had enough, ruling "the Court finds no impropriety on the part of counsel for the petitioners [or plaintiffs] regarding any of these matters. The basis upon which the State seeks sanctions is questionable at best, and the Court finds that the State is not entitled to them. Furthermore, the Court will not entertain such requests at every turn in this proceeding. It is up to counsel, as professionals and officers of the Court, to find some way of cooperating throughout the discovery and trial process."[132]

Having seen Manias refuse to help us obtain basic data from the state, and now realizing he wasn't going to hold us in contempt, I backed us off from devoting our resources to providing data that the state already had. I thought, *Rather than waste our resources, let the attorneys general complain; Manias won't do anything about it.*

For most of 1994 and early 1995, John Garvey and I shared responsibility for defending against more efforts to dismiss our case—sanction motions and creative motions designed to make our lives miserable. At one point, the state moved to dismiss our actual clients and substitute a nonprofit entity that helped fund our efforts, the Claremont Coalition, under the theory that the coalition and its chair, Tom Connair, were diabolically controlling our actions. Manias found the motion "lacked merit" and backhanded the claim by the state that filing the motion was just seeking a final binding conclusion to the trial.

Attached to the state's motion was the coalition's check register that the state had subpoenaed. I think the state included the check register to embarrass us. It showed we were subsisting on small donations, sales of bumper stickers, and the proceeds of a bake sale.

In 1995, John took a paid sabbatical to travel with his wife and daughters. When he returned at the end of the year, the Sulloway and

Hollis firm conditioned his return to the partnership on his withdrawing from our case. We were never told the exact reason for the law firm's insistence that John leave. John only said there was a "conflict," but we assumed that we had become too contentious a matter for the Sulloway firm to stomach.

Other larger firms that had previously supported us also felt concerns about the contentious nature of the litigation. On one occasion, Jack Middleton, now the leader of the McLane Middleton firm, and John Crozier, the head of the Business and Industry Association, were thrown out of a meeting with Governor Steve Merrill, who told them they would not do business with the state if they continued to support us.

As we approached trial in April 1996, we faced more calamities. Arpy's wife, Linda, suffered serious injuries in a sledding accident in the winter of 1995–96. Her injuries required surgery and months of convalescence. Their children, Arpy Jr. and Alice, were in middle school at the time. Arpy had to split his time between answering discovery and caring for his family.

In the fall of 1995, my law firm imploded. There were several reasons for the breakup, but it likely came down to too many alphas in the same room. The thing is, we had survived hiccups before.

Generally, there was tension between two partners, Bob Stein and Steve Gordon, but Bill Shaheen and I had quelled the problems in the past. In the fall of 1995, Bill disappeared when it came time to help me convince Bob and Steve to get along with each other. To this day, I am convinced that Bill took advantage of this opportunity to separate the *Claremont* litigation from the law firm that bore his name, as Bill's wife, State Senator Jeanne Shaheen, was about to announce her run for governor.

The law firm of Shaheen, Cappiello, Stein, and Gordon was formed in 1982 after Bill Shaheen left his position as US Attorney and took his first assistant, Steve Gordon, with him. They were joined by Merrimack County Public Defender Bob Stein, and by Dan Cappiello, a general practitioner from Dover. I joined the firm in 1987. By 1995, we were about a dozen lawyers. We owned real estate in common. We had clients in common and litigated many cases together. Negotiating the breakup was painful. I led the effort for Bob Stein, Peter Callaghan, and me. Two aspects of the negotiation are relevant here.

First, even though Arpy Saunders went with the Shaheen half of the firm, he and I negotiated permission for him to return to the Claremont case for the trial. Second, I negotiated a provision of the breakup agreement that provided for my side to take the entire attorney fee award if ever we were successful in winning our case and collecting fees. I remember the other side laughed at this request because we were a long way from winning a trial, and the New Hampshire Supreme Court had never recognized a right to attorney fees for successfully litigating constitutional violations against the state.

The new firms, Shaheen and Gordon and Stein, Volinsky and Callaghan, became effective January 1, 1996, four months before our trial. With the firm breakup, Arpy's hiatus, and John's departure, all the lingering discovery disputes and pretrial preparation fell to me. Efforts to recruit pro bono help from the larger firms went nowhere.

As this was happening, the state pressed for depositions of our experts. We scheduled the depositions of Kern Alexander and Dick Salmon in Blacksburg, Virginia, for January 6, 1996. Both were professors at Virginia Tech. The Kentucky litigators had highly recommended this team.

I went to Blacksburg a few days before the depositions to do a final prep with the witnesses. Rather than cooperating, Alexander was furious with me because the state had interfered with their team's access to data, and we were behind in paying them because our clients, the school districts, had trouble raising funds for the suit. Alexander refused to meet me absent an immediate payment, and I wound up giving him my personal check for five thousand dollars, which I hoped would be reimbursed.

We proceeded with Dick Salmon's deposition the next day but did not finish. With Alexander in attendance, he and Salmon agreed to return and complete their depositions. Neither expert was meeting with me to properly prepare.

We all showed up at the appointed time, but Alexander refused to go forward and put a long statement on the record complaining that

I hadn't paid them. Salmon fell in line and the depositions didn't go forward.

To this day, it is my opinion that finances weren't the issue. Alexander was afraid to be deposed by Ludtke. Whatever the reason, I flew back to New Hampshire with a huge hole in our case.

We moved to continue the trial from April to October because of the loss of these experts. We needed to regroup. Rather than six months, Manias granted us six weeks. Trial would start in late May 1996.

Arpy and John asked to meet with me.

We met in our first-floor conference room. They suggested we "sue for peace." We should, they said, take pride in the fact that we had gone further than any legal team before us. We had established a constitutional right that did not previously exist. We didn't have the resources to go on. Rather than losing at trial, we should dismiss our suit and end the litigation now.

At some level, I knew their points were valid. I resisted and asked for time to think about it. I don't think I ever felt so lonely in all my life. We had worked so hard and sacrificed so much to get to this point. I just hated the idea of giving up.

After a few long runs through Concord in the snow, I decided to go forward without them. I thought that if I could just remain standing through the trial, we would win Count Six, the tax count—our claim that taxes were unequal because the state didn't pay its fair share. If we convinced a court to equalize taxes, the privileged communities would pay more and the struggling communities would receive extra resources. I trusted the school boards in the poorer communities to make good use of the extra funds.

A trial limited to Count Six meant I would drop the claims challenging the adequacy of the educational services provided in the poor districts. I also knew that I could count on John Tobin and my friends at NHLA, as they championed keeping the Count Six claim alive during the *Claremont* I appeal.

Our other two experts, Van Mueller and Terry Schultz, were from the University of Minnesota, and both were the kind of committed educators who were willing to hang with us even when money was short. They were deposed by Ludtke without incident.

Some things changed for the better. First, Scott Johnson grew into the role of trial assistant. Scott was a third-year law student referred to me by Professor Dick Hesse. Dick thought highly of Scott, and he was not wrong. Scott helped research and write pleadings, helped our paralegal, Mary Ellen McMahon, organize voluminous data, and eventually became my second chair at the six-week trial.

Second, because I was shut out from seeking pro bono help from the state's largest firms, I started recruiting from my contacts among solo and small firms. These folks didn't depend on maintaining a cordial relationship with Governor Merrill. Eventually, I landed help from Pat Quigley, who was a family lawyer focused on adoptions; Jed Callen, who was a semi-retired environmental lawyer from the EPA; Tom Hersey, who was a pony-tailed ex-Marine and former newspaper reporter who went to law school as a second career; and Dick Hesse, the other constitutional law professor at Franklin Pierce Law School. The New Hampshire School Boards Association also gave us the services of their legal counsel, Ted Comstock. Finally, John Tobin and his team at NHLA really pitched in to sustain the tax claim.

Third, Charlie Marston retired. Charlie was the education commissioner for the state of New Hampshire. He served in the New Hampshire Department of Education for more than thirty years and visited every school in the state. We heard that Charlie was friendly to our cause, but I couldn't speak with him while he was employed by the state, as he was represented by Ludtke. We chose not to depose him so as not to expose him as an ally. After his retirement, I approached Charlie to become our lead-off witness at trial. Eventually, Charlie agreed.

The state moved to prevent us from working with and calling Charlie as a witness. But Manias allowed us to work with Commissioner Marston if we did not ask him to reveal his prior communications with the state's litigation team, which was the correct compromise.

By late February or early March 1996, we had a new, somewhat ragtag trial team, the services of the former commissioner, and a trial management system that was superior to the state's. Thanks to Mary Ellen and Scott, we could find any document in our thirty boxes of materials at a moment's notice. This proved invaluable during trial, allowing me to provide the court with relevant documentation on any issue just as the issue arose. We started calling Mary Ellen our "Della Street," after Perry Mason's assistant.

Lawyers reading this are now chuckling because, today, documents used in litigation aren't stored in boxes. They're stamped or stickered with QR codes and scanned or loaded as one long PDF into a court's trial evidence management system. Finding a document requires little more than sweeping a pen-like code reader over the document, or knowing a page number, to have it projected on screens at everyone's desks.

I tried to learn everything I could about the schools for which we were responsible, because I knew the new lawyers would only have time to learn their small parts of the puzzle of school funding. One of my efforts had me taking my neighbor, Don DeAngelis, who was a fire chief with code enforcement experience, to the elementary schools in Allenstown. We had talked of the condition of the schools as we were making maple syrup in the sugar house we share.

DeAngelis was horrified at what he saw. In one classroom there was a window too high for children to reach in case of a fire. The school had hung an old pool ladder from the window for egress in an emergency. There was also a special education classroom built from flammable plywood.[133]

As we were moving towards trial, we continued to seek press coverage and had to always think about fundraising. I remembered a poster an old friend had of a child's play structure that said "It will be a great day when our schools get all the money they need and the Air Force has to hold a bake sale to buy a bomber." I suggested we hold a bake sale for the lawsuit.

Tom Connair had the idea to invite Governor Merrill to contribute brownies. The invitation to Merrill made the Associated Press's coverage of the event, which was held at a local middle school. Merrill's spokesman said he didn't think the invitation was funny. "The funding of education is a serious matter and it's not something to be made fun of."[134]

A local political cartoonist, Mike Marland, also contributed a limited-edition print, *The Last Bake Sale for Education*, that we auctioned off. I still have a copy of the print on the wall of my office. The name of this book is drawn from Mike's cartoon. Stonyfield Yogurt, a New Hampshire company cofounded by Gary Hirshberg, contributed tons of frozen yogurt for everyone. Although we didn't raise much money, the event was a big success.

top: Ticket to March 18, 1994 lawsuit fundraiser.
bottom: The Last Bake Sale for Education print by Mike Marland, March 18, 1994.

We proceeded to trial with this plan: I would present our core description of the state's educational system, with the help of Scott Johnson, through the testimony of Charlie Marston, his deputy Doug Brown, and Marston's predecessor, Jack MacDonald. I would also cross-examine most of the state's experts. John Tobin would cross-examine the state's tax commissioner.

Our newly recruited lawyers and Arpy would present comparison testimony, describing conditions in each of our school districts alongside a well-funded comparison district of similar size and configuration. Our remaining experts, Van Mueller and Terry Schultz, would come last to explain the implications of the resource differences in the paired communities. They had collected more than two hundred photographs and presented them side by side on two slide projectors set up in the center of the courtroom. Finally, learning from my political experience on the Arnesen campaign, we arranged for Tom Hersey, the former reporter, to be our press contact.

Each day, we would set a "message of the day," just like in a political campaign. Rather than sitting with us, Tom Hersey sat with the press in the audience and explained how each thing we did during the trial contributed to the concept we were featuring that day. We supplemented Tom's play-by-play analysis with formal press conferences a half hour after the trial finished each day.

Judge Manias was scrupulous about ending on time. He wanted to avoid overtime for court staff and he was meticulous about attending a cardiac rehab program at the local hospital. Manias had suffered a heart attack between the time the supreme court remanded the case to him and the start of the trial. One can only guess if our quarrelsome relationship with the state contributed to his stress.

We were ready for trial.

Lawyers try cases on multiple levels. They try cases to the factfinder before them and they keep in mind that their cases will be reviewed by appellate judges based on the trial transcripts and exhibits. Plus, in a public policy case, the lawyers must also pay attention to public messaging and news coverage.

Assistant Attorney General Pat Donovan, who is now on the New Hampshire Supreme Court, realized we were taking a multi-level approach and told the press much later what he saw I was trying to accomplish: "Andy had to do lots of things here. He was not just trying a case; he was out to form policy. He had the big picture in mind when he tried the case the way he did."[135]

Our transcript of trial testimony ran to twenty-six volumes, some sixty-five thousand words. There were also tons of exhibits documenting conditions in the petitioner schools and their comparison schools. Most of the major news outlets had reporters in the courtroom every day. A couple of those young, local reporters went on to report for the *New York Times*, *Washington Post*, *Wall Street Journal*, and the *Boston Globe*.

In a trial without a jury, the trial judge is the factfinder, and this changes the nature of the trial lawyer's first focus. A jury of laypeople must be protected from evidence they shouldn't hear because they can be swayed by irrelevant facts. With a judge as the factfinder, particularly an experienced judge like George Manias, the judge can hear more of the proffered evidence and later sift out that which the judge considers unimportant. This means objections to evidence are less important.

Despite knowing this, the state's lawyers moved to exclude our evidence early and often, resulting in long debates about who did or did not conduct themselves properly during discovery or who was violating the technical rules of evidence.

One of the reporters covering the trial wrote, "[I]t seemed that more time was spent on the lawyers' objections than on actually hearing evidence."[136] Former Justice Chuck Douglas characterized the evidentiary objections as "piddling" and predicted the New Hampshire Supreme Court would go straight to the constitutional questions at the heart of the case.[137]

The best example of the absurdity of the state's objections is the story of the red dots.

Before our trial began, the state asked for a view of all the schools in the five plaintiff school districts. Generally, people think of a view as loading jurors onto a bus to look at a murder scene. Here, the state wanted Judge Manias to visit each of the schools in each of the five plaintiff school districts. However, the state didn't want Manias to visit the comparison districts' schools. We worried that Manias wouldn't fully understand the implications of what he was seeing. We suggested that the state either choose a couple of representative plaintiff schools and a couple of the comparison schools and we'd all go visit them, or we should visit all plaintiff and comparison schools. Manias finally decided to visit all the schools.

Our legal team visited the schools a few days ahead of the view and grew worried because many of the classrooms were heavily resourced with books and supplies that were paid for by teachers, not the school districts. This is often the case. Good teachers don't let their students go without.

It would have been unethical and disruptive for us to ask teachers to remove their personal possessions. I decided instead to have every teacher place a red sticker dot on every book or item that the teacher owned in every classroom. At trial, we planned to have the teachers explain the red dots. We bought boxes of red dots and distributed them.

When Manias arrived for his tour, he was greeted by a sea of red, and Ludtke was furious. In a truly absurd exercise, she asked Manias to exclude the view from evidence, essentially for Manias to unsee what he had seen. Manias said he'd take it all "under advisement," which was his way of saying he would take no action on the state's motion to exclude the view.

Maybe we shouldn't have worried so much. A *Concord Monitor* reporter who accompanied us on the views aptly captured the differences between the high school in Franklin and the one in Gilford:

> At Franklin High . . . they saw a gym that is unusable for sports; cracks in windows covered with duck [sic] tape; many computers that are more than 10 years old; crowded classes and chipped paint . . . [At] Gilford High and Middle School, they found a high-tech, modern building with huge windows and carpeted hallways; a gym with two full courts; a 3-part modern auditorium, complete with lecture hall, performing arts center and a "Little

Theatre" for music; keyboard labs for music students and three computer labs, all with new computers and access to the Internet.[138]

One interaction during the view gave me some small hope about Manias, even though he'd ruled against us on every significant decision to this point. We were visiting one of the old elementary schools in Claremont, a brick affair with windows that didn't work and a cracked pavement walk leading to the school's rusted metal front door. We had both teams of lawyers and an older sheriff assigned to "guard" the judge.

As we approached the school, we walked by an older, poorly dressed, unshaven man who smelled of cigarettes. He turned and was quickly coming at us up the walk and I momentarily stepped in front of him until I could signal the sheriff. As I did so, the man said he was a newspaper photographer and he wanted to see the judge. His name was Carter.

George Manias was tall and thin and as prim and proper as Carter was disheveled. The two men didn't look like they'd ever belonged together. Judge Manias grew up in Concord, New Hampshire, and went to Tufts University and Suffolk Law School. He then worked as an assistant attorney general before joining one of the more conservative law firms in the state. He'd been on the bench for more than a decade at the time of our trial. He was appointed by Governor John Sununu.

When Manias looked at the photographer, he paused for a moment and then said, "You're Carter?" and to the rest of us, "We used to box together." He then put his arm around Carter's shoulder and walked off to talk with him for a few moments. It was obvious that the years had been tough on Carter, while Manias prospered. Nonetheless, Judge Manias was as kind to Carter as he could be. Maybe Manias was human after all?

Chapter 7

The Trial

The trial was held in Merrimack County Superior Court Room One. The courtroom was one of two in a nondescript building from the fifties. We could climb a wide, winding staircase to the courtroom, or load boxes, no more than six at a time, on a small elevator that ran from the lockup in the basement to the two courtrooms. The courtroom itself had a jury box to the left with a wood-paneled railing. The judge's bench was elevated to the front, with the witness stand between the two.

In front of the judge's bench was the well of the court where we did battle. Behind us, the audience and press sat in pews. There was a painting of a retired judge, William Cann, that adorned one wall. Later, a painting of Judge Manias would be added, a few years before the building was torn down. Ironically, William Cann was the judge who presided over the aborted Jesseman case.

Prior to trial, Tom Hersey provided the press with an outline of the likely testimony and a schedule of witnesses. Each week he wrote a "Week in Review" memo and we faxed it to the press. We kept a stack of "Fax Cover Sheets," one for each media outlet, that we used again and again. It was a different world in the 1990s, when fax machines were used and the media was not yet consolidated.

The media outlets had a variety of views of our case. Our goal was to make friends of all of the reporters, or at least to make the most opinionated reporters stand out for their bias.

The Commissioners

The trial began with retired commissioner Charles Marston. Marston was New Hampshire born and bred. He spoke with a flat New England accent and was a commissioner dedicated to the mission of supporting public schools. He knew about Lisbon's use of a chicken coop for classroom space, the loss of Stevens's accreditation, and Allenstown's dilapidated "temporary" classrooms that were in their second decade of use.

Marston was well-respected and a very credible witness. He would lay the foundation for the rest of the trial. This is what you want from a first witness. Marston explained that graduation rates and the number of students going to college were measures of the quality of the education a school provided. Graduation rates were considered "at least one measure of a school's effectiveness."[139] He noted that many fewer Stevens grads went to college than Lebanon High School grads. Franklin sent fewer than a quarter of its grads to college, which was bad regardless of any comparison, but its comparator, Gilford, sent more than 75 percent to college.

Marston explained that the widely varying property values in the districts represented "[t]he relative fiscal ability of each of [the] districts [which] varies considerably."[140] We listed on a piece of newsprint the equalized property values for each of the client and comparison districts. Rye, for example, had five times the property value as Allenstown for each child in the district and, as a consequence, its school tax was $6.87 while Allenstown's was $24.99. Marston testified that the ability of school districts to fund their operations based on their property values varied widely across the state, and the state's small funding contribution was not enough to make a difference. This was the key issue in our case and we credibly addressed it with our very first witness. Ludtke objected and the judge wouldn't let Marston say that state funding was "inadequate," but everyone knew Charlie's opinion on the matter.

The state's underfunding of schools was bad enough, but the state also did not fund its own department of education. Lack of resources prevented the department from doing its job or providing real leadership to the state's schools. More than 10 percent of the positions at the New Hampshire Department of Education were vacant due to a lack of funding, and 80 percent of the remaining positions were federally funded. The New Hampshire Department of Education was little more than a federal outpost.

Marston testified that the Augenblick formula that Governor Sununu put in place was never fully funded. It should have provided just over $80 million to poor school districts, but was funded at $47 million—and this was out of the $1 billion spent overall. Even if fully funded, Augenblick funding would not have been enough to make a difference, according to Marston.

We briefly had Marston explain the "Move Package," which contained the reports routinely sent to people who inquired about the quality of schools in a particular location. We introduced these reports about graduation rates, equalized property values, tax rates, and spending per pupil over the state's objection that the data was not reliable.

The state did not enforce the minimum standards for school approval because the only enforcement mechanism Marston had was to punish noncompliant districts by withholding funds. As Marston knew the reason school districts failed to meet minimum standards was mostly lack of funds, he explained that cutting funding made no sense. He refused to do it.

Marston also explained that when he ran the minimum standards bureau, there were three employees assigned to visit schools. When he retired, the process was assigned to one person, half-time, and the visits were discontinued. The process took place completely on paper and was based on self-reporting. It was New Hampshire's way of approving substandard schools with a wink and a nod.

Marston testified that the chair of the State Board of Education, Judith Thayer, prohibited the Department of Education and the Board of Education from crafting a definition of adequacy as required by the 1993 *Claremont* decision.

We followed Marston with his predecessor, Jack MacDonald, and then with their deputy, Doug Brown. MacDonald became an assistant secretary of education at the US Department of Education after leaving his post as New Hampshire education commissioner. MacDonald had been New Hampshire's education commissioner from 1986 to 1990. Brown's focus as Marston's deputy commissioner was on school buildings.

MacDonald testified about the need for a seamless system of education with articulated standards from grade to grade. He said that kindergarten should be a part of this system but "the issue here is financial and there is not political support for publicly supported kindergartens . . . It's a serious problem with disadvantaged children in particular."[141] He noted Governor Sununu, a former professor of engineering, initiated a "computers in schools" program in the 1980s when MacDonald was commissioner. No one expected those same Apple IIe computers to be in use more than a dozen years later, as they were in our plaintiffs' districts. "I thought with the beginning of an initiative so innovative as what John Sununu put in place, that . . . New Hampshire would be able to stay ahead of the curve on it."[142]

Arpy Saunders questioned Doug Brown. When Pat Donovan objected immediately after Arpy's first question, Arpy's response was, "[You object] to his name?"[143]

Brown was the only staff person in the state's building aid program from 1976 to 1990. When he was promoted to deputy commissioner in 1990, no one staffed the school building aid program. Brown kept that responsibility as the deputy commissioner. When he retired in 1992, no one was hired to replace him as deputy commissioner.

Brown helped plan the school renovations in our client districts of Lisbon, Franklin, and Pittsfield. Over many years, he visited schools after they were renovated or replaced, and testified to the impact of fixing broken school buildings:

> Well, I think it was the attitude; working in a cheery building, bright, comfortable, modern services in terms of what was available in the building. Just an attitudinal change basically occurred among faculty. Behavior was different. Care for the building was different.[144]

When Arpy asked about the importance of school buildings, Brown testified, "For many school districts, particularly smaller school districts, high schools in particular are a real focal point of the community and are really a major source of pride."[145]

John Tobin was up next to examine the state's revenue commissioner, Stanley Arnold, who we called as an adverse witness because he supported keeping the current system in place. Arnold carefully stuck to the technical side of explaining New Hampshire's tax system and didn't offer much more.

The Plaintiffs' Definition of Constitutional Adequacy

Arpy then introduced our definition of constitutional adequacy through the testimony of a Concord-based education professor and former local school board member, Rob Fried, EdD.

Fried earned his master's degree from the University of New Hampshire, where he taught English and administered basic education programs for the university. After earning his doctorate at the Harvard Graduate School of Education, Fried worked as a consultant with small school districts throughout New Hampshire. He also worked at the New Hampshire Department of Education before becoming certified as a New Hampshire school principal and serving at a school in Gilmanton.

After his time as principal, Rob Fried worked closely with Ted Sizer, who created and led the Essential Schools movement. Sizer's schools eschewed traditional lectures, saw teaching as "coaching," and worked to reduce school size and school bureaucracy. Sizer started with about a dozen "essential schools" and grew the coalition to more than six hundred schools nationwide. Fried's experience with Sizer's essential schools directly influenced Rob's work in crafting our definition of adequacy.

Of course, the state objected to Fried's testimony. Ludtke argued it was improper for us to offer a definition of educational adequacy because that was a legislative and executive branch function. Given the state's failure to devise a definition since the *Claremont* I decision two and a half years earlier, and its refusal to negotiate with us for six years, the objection was a remarkable display of chutzpah. The judge allowed Rob to testify.

Rob is built like a stick figure. He's tall and thin with a bushy head of hair. He has the mien of a college professor. You could almost picture him in the flowing robes of a Cambridge don. His definitional work was intended to provide children with a fair and reasonable opportunity to obtain a constitutionally adequate education. Rob broke the definition of an adequate education into four cornerstones, the first of which focused on the building blocks of "the materials, the facilities, the staff, the equipment, the books, the computers, the stuff of schooling, the things that we normally associate with a good learning environment."[146]

Fried's Cornerstone Two focused on providing the services necessary to meet children where they are. Fried gave the example of a child from a foreign country floating across the Atlantic and up the Merrimack River to Concord. All the materials in Cornerstone One would be of no use to that child if she did not speak English and was not prepared to learn. The same, according to Fried, was true for children with social or emotional problems that impeded their ability to learn. They couldn't benefit from the building blocks outlined in Cornerstone One.

Cornerstone Three focused on management, in that a school must be an efficient and effective learning organization. It must be capable of learning and growing, utilizing resources and managing conflict.

Finally, Fried's fourth cornerstone dealt with outcomes: that these learning organizations must actually produce a high percentage of children who have learned the core skills and knowledge, attitudes, and values that allow them to be good, productive citizens who can learn on their own.

We blew up a poster of Fried's "Four Cornerstones of Adequacy" definition and Arpy placed it on an easel in Manias's line of sight. Every time Donovan or Ludtke moved the easel, I moved it right back. It was sad and comical to watch how hard the attorneys general worked to keep the blow-up out of Manias's view.

Claremont/Lebanon Comparison

After Fried, we began the testimony that compared the plaintiffs' schools with the comparison schools. The Claremont and Lebanon pairing was first.

The full complement of Claremont's school leadership testified about conditions in their schools. Barbara Krysiak, EdD, the school district's former superintendent, led the team of witnesses. Krysiak's testimony was summed up by reporter John DiStaso of the *Union Leader*: "In Claremont the will is there to succeed . . . but the money is not."[147]

Ludtke again bombarded us with objections in an effort to obstruct a smooth and compelling presentation of testimony. She complained bitterly that we hadn't been forthright in our responses to interrogatories and had failed to disclose key information. I met her objections each and every time, but Manias, rather than being drawn into the minutiae, ended her complaints with this: "Is it a surprise to the State that someone from Claremont would be coming in here and talking about funds that they didn't get that they thought they needed? I mean, really."[148]

Also, as we began the Claremont testimony, the state's lawyers realized they had a problem.

The two sides pre-marked exhibits in advance of trial, and each side advised the other which exhibits would be admitted into evidence without objection and which were contested. The exhibits admitted without objection were denoted as "full exhibits," and were given a number if introduced by us and a letter if introduced by the state. The state objected to many of our exhibits. I decided that we wouldn't object to any exhibit the state wanted, because some of the reports we wanted in evidence were in the state's pile of exhibits and it appeared they didn't realize this. Because we didn't object, the state's exhibits were now all full exhibits that could be used for any purpose by either side.

The state's lawyers realized what we had done on the third or fourth day of trial, when they objected to our use of their exhibits. They tried to withdraw 110 of their 550 exhibits. One reporter called this a "curious maneuver."[149] Manias expressed his displeasure with this new skirmish by putting his hand completely over his face, a posture that he adopted whenever he wished he was somewhere else. He did not allow the state to withdraw their exhibits because both sides had prepared for trial relying on them to be available.

The Claremont-Lebanon pair of districts that we presented underscored the difference property wealth makes in a school district's ability to provide services that prepare children for the rest of their lives.

The first pair also made clear the shortcomings of representing schools—that is, educators are too nurturing. No matter how difficult the circumstances, teachers and administrators always send home hopeful beginning-of-the-year letters. They'll also work well beyond what they are paid to do to compensate for a lack of resources. The state cross-examined some of our Claremont witnesses, rubbing their noses in the cheery notes sent home to encourage children at the start of the school year.

The principal of Stevens High School, Margaret Sullivan, testified that she regularly worked seventy-hour weeks because the school lacked curriculum coordinators, department heads, and a building maintenance coordinator. Sullivan did all these jobs plus provided staff leadership, supervised scheduling and discipline, and engaged in day-to-day operations.

Dr. Krysiak recounted the factors that made her concerned about the children of Claremont: "[T]he number of children on free and reduced lunch . . . [t]he education of parents . . . teenage pregnancy rate . . . school attendance rate . . . [d]ropout rates . . . [t]he number of child abuse reports . . . [and] the transiency of students."[150]

Probably the most compelling testimony we presented concerned the treatment of younger children with identified learning needs in Claremont. Dr. Krysiak testified that in this high-poverty district with low parental education levels, she and her staff identified sixty children each year who required specialized assistance with reading—but there was only money to provide the required services to fifteen children.[151]

Think about it.

The research was clear by the time we went to trial in 1996 that if a child was not reading at grade level by about the third grade, the child would likely never catch up. Kindergarten through grade three is when kids learn to read. Thereafter, kids read to learn. If the skill of reading is not mastered in time, children do not learn the substantive material provided to them later in school.

Here, in Claremont, Krysiak identified sixty children as needing specific help in reading, but could not help three-quarters of them for lack of resources. These children would likely never catch up.

Superintendent Krysiak knew Claremont's struggles. She grew up in a tenement in Lowell, Massachusetts. Her parents were millworkers who did not complete high school. She could relate to Claremont. Yet she found she lacked the resources to make a difference. Worse, when she asked for help from the state, there was no response. The cavalry never arrived.

Krysiak also testified that Claremont had a kindergarten program but could not afford to pay for transportation for the kids. She recounted how high school seniors donated their college scholarship money to help pay for kindergarten transport.

Finally, Krysiak related her concerns about Claremont's lack of health education at the middle-school level, as the community had among the highest level of teenage pregnancies in the state.

DiStaso, the *Union Leader* reporter, focused on the textbooks from Claremont we introduced at trial. They were twelve to sixteen years old and still in use. On a form stuck to the inside cover of a geometry book, where the condition of the book was to be described, a student had written "Beyond Hope."[152] The state's response was to point out that all the pages were there. A middle school science book—in use in 1996—taught students that we hoped to someday put a man on the moon, an achievement that occurred in 1969.

Later in the trial, during the state's case, the new state board chair, Ovide Lamontagne, testified that books were unnecessary in a successful school. When questioned about the poor condition of schoolbooks, he claimed that a good teacher could use books in any condition, and disagreed with Superintendent Krysiak's testimony that the condition of books and materials undermined efforts to motivate less-skilled students. Lamontagne didn't think falling-apart books were an impediment, and noted what he called a trend away from using textbooks at all.[153]

I remember meeting with Barbara Krysiak and her staff and just feeling so angry at the opposition we faced from the state leading up to the trial. My work with Krysiak helped me to better understand the motivation of those who oppose change.

Fear is their primary motivation. They fear that their privileges will be compromised, that their child's school will sink to the level of a Claremont. The other fear I came to understand, particularly as I later ran for state office, was that politicians are fearful of the risk inherent in making change.

If things are bad, politicians blame forces beyond their control, or blame their predecessor. If politicians advocate for change, then they own it. This is a calculus that is ingrained in every officeholder, and only the best can overcome it. New Hampshire doesn't generally elect the best.

Years later, I was asked to give Krysiak's eulogy and expressed my deep admiration for her work in Claremont and at trial.

We also skirmished over John Sununu's 1985-era computers. Claremont was one of the communities still using the Apple IIe computers in 1996. The *Concord Monitor* described the computers as being from the "technology ice age."[154] Apple stopped producing the IIe in 1993. But during questioning, the state ignored the quality of the computers and focused on the ratio between students and Apple IIe computers.

Even the ratio wasn't great. For example, there were only thirty computers for the 250 high school students who wanted to take a computer applications course in Claremont. The Lebanon School District's technology coordinator—the fact that Lebanon had a coordinator and Claremont did not was beside the point—had to explain to the state that even if the Apple IIe computers weren't beyond repair, he still wouldn't use them. They provided drill and practice work—like electronic flash cards—and couldn't really go beyond that stage. He also testified about Lebanon's exposure of its kindergarten students to technology and the district's use of modern-day networking equipment through all grades.

Tom Hersey's press release on May 13, 1996 featured this exchange between Ludtke and Krysiak:

> **Krysiak:** The school district is still using the same Apple IIe computers that were bought when John Sununu was the governor over ten years ago.
>
> **Ludtke:** Certainly, you would agree that the Apple IIe is not unsuitable for an elementary school classroom?
>
> **Krysiak:** It certainly is unsuitable if you can't get parts for them, so they just sit there.

Many of the Lebanon school kids also had access to computers at home. Claremont kids did not.

Claremont is in Sullivan County, New Hampshire's poorest county, with low parental educational achievement. Lebanon is in Grafton County, adjacent to Hanover, where Dartmouth College and Medical

School and the Dartmouth-Hitchcock Medical Center are located, and where significant numbers of physicians, faculty, and staff live.

Claremont also had a high number of children who qualified for special education services. Claremont's budget for these services was in the range of $1.2 to $1.5 million each year. Depending on the year, the state provided between $50,000 and $100,000 to defray this expense. The federal government contributed about $250,000 a year, leaving a million

top: Claremont's Stevens High School circa 1996.
bottom: Alternative Education program located in basement of Stevens High School.

dollars or more each year of special education costs to be paid from the local property tax. It was no wonder that Claremont taxpayers experienced a 20-percent increase in their taxes during the three years Superintendent Krysiak was there.

WPA era mural in Claremont's Way Elementary School.

Finally, the testimony showed that eventually the community passed a bond to address Stevens High's accreditation failures, but the community couldn't raise enough funds to obtain a new site for the high school that met state standards. The state instead issued a waiver to renovate the school on its substandard lot. To this day, Stevens sits on that same substandard lot across from Tom Connair's law office where it was located at the time of trial in 1996.

Pittsfield/Moultonborough Comparison

The Pittsfield-Moultonborough pair was presented by Patricia Quigley. Pat and I knew each other through our children. Pat is now a probate judge.

The Pittsfield and Moultonborough school districts are both small. The full-time residents are very similar. Both communities had a significant number of children whose poverty allowed them to qualify for the free or reduced-price school lunch program. The communities had below-average household incomes. Household incomes are based on the earnings of full-time residents, not on the plentiful second homeowners with property on the lake in Moultonborough. Moultonborough's lakefront real estate is very valuable, providing Moultonborough with a huge financial advantage over Pittsfield.

Ken Greenbaum, the superintendent of the Moultonborough district, testified that his practice was to have his staff design an individualized education program for each student in the district. He took the concept from special education, where students are entitled to individualized plans called "IEPs." His goal was to have 90 percent of his students enrolled in some meaningful educational opportunity after their high school graduation.

To reach this goal, curriculum and extensive resources were deployed to meet students' needs, and to encourage them. There were numerous advanced placement courses as well as work apprenticeships. Every classroom was networked and had at least one modern computer. Apple IIe computers were not used because they couldn't deliver quality educational programming.

Moultonborough residents had passed a budget about six weeks before trial that included spending $125,000 to implement the first two of five steps in a multiyear technology plan. In addition to new hardware and software, the plan included in-depth training for teachers, and would result in every classroom containing networked computers that could perform desktop publishing, aid with music and graphic arts programs, and connect to the Internet.

Teachers with appropriate subject matter certifications taught music and art in Moultonborough. Foreign language instruction began in kindergarten. The district ignored minimum standards because they were set too low. It didn't have to change anything to address newly adopted higher-level curricular frameworks that described what should be taught, because Moultonborough's faculty helped write the state's new frameworks based on what the district was already providing.

The average teacher in Moultonborough earned $34,000 per year as compared to the average teacher in Pittsfield, who earned $24,000. The two communities are less than forty miles apart. Greenbaum testified that teachers were the single most important component of his school system, and he could pay them almost 50 percent more than his counterpart in Pittsfield.

Pittsfield was a very different situation. The district had two schools: one elementary school and one combined middle and high school. The middle-high school did not meet accessibility requirements. A student who used a wheelchair had to go outside to access the cafeteria. The main part of the building was built in 1940. Water came through the brick walls in the middle-high school when it rained, and puddled on the floor. Voters, who already paid very high education taxes, continually rejected funding to fix dangerous wiring problems or improve lighting as that would have increased their taxes even further.

The district did not offer any advanced placement courses and could not upgrade their curriculum to meet the new state curricular frameworks. A single foreign language was offered, beginning in ninth grade. Only one classroom computer in the entire school district was connected to the Internet, even with technology funding from a local charitable trust. Teacher turnover was a constant problem because of low pay. Many of the books and other equipment used in Pittsfield had been previously discarded by other schools. Science books were thirteen years out of date. The vast majority of Pittsfield programming was designed to meet minimum standards, and it was failing even at that.

The industrial arts are important in Pittsfield, yet the program was in a homemade building separate from the middle-high school. There were no emergency lights, and the heating system was inadequate for New Hampshire winters. Children with asthma couldn't take industrial arts courses because of dust problems.

Hugh Sanborn, who taught most of the shop courses, testified that his budget for classroom materials was a quarter of what it should have been. He also testified that he was recognized with a grant from the RAND Corporation for designing an applied technology program. He taught the

Makeshift Industrial Arts building (brown building) circa 1996.

program for one year before being assigned to lunch supervision duty, and the course was not taught again.

There was something else about Hugh Sanborn. His daughter was graduating from Pittsfield Middle High School and had been accepted to a very good college, Smith College in Northampton, Massachusetts. Only a quarter of Pittsfield's students went to college, and this young

The Pittsfield Industrial Arts teacher scavenged wood from downed trees for his program.

woman was going to a very good school. We knew that Ludtke would try to make hay with this information and so prepared Sanborn in advance. When cross-examined, Sanborn was able to testify that he and his wife paid more than $28,000 for his daughter to attend supplemental private art and music classes during high school. She also took college courses at the community college in Concord, at her parents' expense, to compensate for the absence of honors or advanced placement courses at her high school.

The assistant middle-high school principal, Mark Jarvis, was questioned about why the district had spent so much on a new elementary school half a dozen years earlier. Why, for example, did they need a gym in the elementary school? Jarvis explained that the gym was a community asset used for town meetings and civic functions that could not be held at the run-down middle-high school.

Effie Topouzoglou, a Pittsfield School Board member and former chair, testified that the elementary school was already overcrowded and should have been built for a larger capacity. She also testified that small budget surpluses were returned to the taxpayers, who already paid well above average taxes, to keep faith with them when the board promised to fund only certain services.

Pat Donovan cross-examined the Pittsfield biology teacher. When pressed, she said working in Pittsfield was like putting a Band-Aid on a cut jugular.

In an article entitled "Plaintiffs Show How Rich Live," John DiStaso recounted the financial evidence. In 1996, Moultonborough spent $5,400 per elementary school pupil and $8,900 per high school student. For Pittsfield, the corresponding numbers were $4,000 per elementary pupil and $5,800 per high school student. Despite this discrepancy, Pittsfield taxpayers paid much higher education taxes.

The reason? Moultonborough, with its second homes on the lake, had $1.3 million in taxable property for each child in the school system. Pittsfield had $121,000 per pupil.[155] Donovan was described in the next day's paper as having tried to "use Greenbaum's testimony to show the state's funding system works well for his district."[156]

The state, and its lawyers, just didn't get it. Of course the system worked well for communities with high property wealth. These communities generally had second homes on a lake or ski condos. These second homes increased property values without adding children to the schools. The system failed the children who didn't live in these communities. That's what the trial was about.

Allenstown/Rye Comparison

Jed Callen, our retired EPA lawyer, presented the Allenstown and Rye pair.

Allenstown and Rye are both kindergarten-through-eighth-grade districts, with children attending high school in another district. Rye high school students attend one of the best high schools in the state, Portsmouth High School. Allenstown students attend a five-district collaborative called Pembroke Academy.

Rye is located on the New Hampshire seacoast. The 2024 average home price in Rye is $1.3 million. At the time of trial in 1996, it was similarly property-rich, with an equalized value per pupil of $1,092,289.

Allenstown is not located near any major highway. Allenstown once hosted active and productive textile mills powered by the Merrimack and Suncook Rivers. The pattern of failed economic development efforts holds true for Allenstown. Allenstown has a lot of manufactured housing developments and transience. More than 25 percent of the children in the elementary schools move into and out of the district each year. Allenstown's equalized valuation of property per child was $128,279, about 10 percent of what Rye had.

Allenstown has two elementary schools, the Armand R. Dupont School for grades five through eight and the Allenstown Elementary School for kindergarten through fourth grade. The Dupont School was previously a bowling alley and community center, originally constructed in 1954. The bowling alley and community center were sold to the school district by the Catholic Diocese of Manchester in 1987 for a nominal fee. The bowling alley school wasn't replaced until 2022.

According to superintendent George Cushing, Rye students came to school ready to learn. Four students—not four percent, but just four—students participated in the free and reduced-price lunch program. Starting with kindergarten, all teachers integrated technology and focused on employing best practices. The district had active music and art programs. There was a technology lab with networked, modern computers that had been donated by Craig Benson and Cabletron. Teachers with one or two planning periods each day coordinated their efforts and applied for external grants that leveraged their already abundant resources. Grants funded an elementary school project to coordinate with NASA, and another to track roadkill across the country.

Allenstown, by contrast, did music and computer education "on a cart," taught by homeroom teachers not certified in music or art or trained in technology. In this approach, rudimentary musical instruments were rolled on a cart from classroom to classroom. A single Apple IIe computer was strapped to a different cart so the younger elementary students

Allenstown music on a cart.

Allenstown computer education on a cart.

at the Allenstown Elementary School could see what a computer looked like. There was no computer curriculum.

Discipline was a problem at the Armand Dupont School and, to deal with it, the district tied red and blue gym pads to the wall of a three-sided alcove in which to hold students until parents or police could retrieve them. These children were roughly ten to thirteen years old.

According to superintendent Tom Haley, Allenstown didn't meet state minimum standards for school approval and had been "conditionally approved" for three years. Allenstown schools lacked a required media generalist, full-time music teacher, full-time art teacher, and a reading specialist. Haley hoped part-time personnel would be enough to satisfy the state. Haley, by the way, was the superintendent for five districts in a consolidated supervisory unit. Allenstown had dismissed one of its two building principals the year before trial to save money. The remaining principal covered both schools.

Reporter Jo Becker with the *Concord Monitor* wrote, "Haley offered a bleak view of education in the poor mill town. . . . The buildings needed work but there's only $5,000 in a capital improvement plan. There are no computer classes available to younger students. Though Allenstown kids represent only 20 percent of the students at Pembroke Academy, they represent 35 percent of the dropouts."[157]

Ludtke gave Haley an especially hard time. She cross-examined him about central office employees receiving raises as the salaries of school-based employees stagnated. Tom had to explain that the employees who got the wages were teachers, not administrators like him. They were employed by the central office rather than one of the five school districts because their teaching occurred across multiple districts. The teachers traveled from district to district to save money. She also went after Tom because the superintendent's office spent $76,000 on computers while students went without. Again, Tom had to explain the need for central office computers, and that the person overseeing the installation of the computers was a teacher and half of his pay was to teach in one of the districts.

Franklin/Gilford Comparison

The Franklin and Gilford school district pairing provided more of the same, only more so because Franklin has a tax cap. Ted Comstock, our lawyer on loan from the School Boards Association, was ready to present the testimony. But at this point, we offered to proceed by way of an offer of proof for the rest of the paired school districts because this would expedite the process. In proceeding by way of an offer of proof, the lawyers simply talk the judge through what the evidence would be in summary fashion rather than proceeding witness by witness. The state, of course, objected as we expected they would, but the offer got us off the hook for "taking so long."

In addition to having low property wealth and high needs, and consistently spending less than the state average, Franklin has self-inflicted problems stemming from its tax cap. The *Concord Monitor* published a multipage spread about Franklin as our trial started.[158] The article pointed out that a vote after a change in city council membership caused extensive teacher layoffs. A prior city council had approved a bond for a new middle school outside of the regular school budget, which was subject to the tax cap that limited tax increases. With the change, the school budget

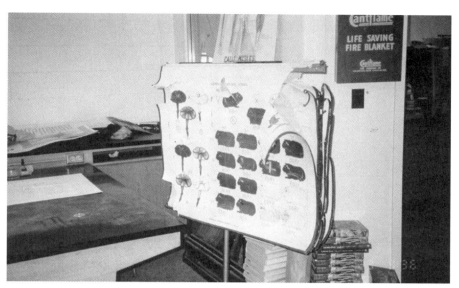

Franklin High School science class circa 1996.

subject to the tax cap was required to absorb the bond payments, causing a huge shortfall.

Franklin was the only client where a community leader testified against us and against the interests of his community. Franklin's mayor, Ken Merrifield, came to trial and testified for the state. The *Concord Monitor* article referenced above disclosed that all the extracurricular activities in Franklin were student funded through ticket sales, bake sales, and students volunteering to clean at the local racetrack in exchange for the raceway's contribution to the school. The article pointed out that two high school students raised $600 for drama productions, which was almost twice what Mayor Merrifield paid that year in school taxes.

According to the *Monitor* article, students in Franklin could choose among only eight high school electives over their four years because that was all the high school offered. In the prior year, "[f]ifty kids were shut out of the school's only art class. Seventy-five others couldn't take a basic computer class, and thirty more were denied access to a health class. All three classes are requirements for graduation."[159]

Franklin's superintendent, Edgar Melanson, testified that he shamed the city council into funding an alternative education program to reduce

Franklin High School classroom with broken windows and shades.

the high number of dropouts, but in doing so, the council required him to lay off teachers in other areas. Franklin has a one-quarter turnover of teachers each year because of low pay and poor conditions and, in some of the city's schools, the teacher turnover rate approached 75 percent. Melanson testified that computers were so outdated they'd be good for boat anchors. The district obtained a lot of them from military bases where they were being replaced.

I met students while preparing for trial. They didn't testify, but I remember the Franklin student athletes. The athletes were among the first students to notice their school's problems because they competed at other schools and saw the facilities. They often took to heart that they weren't from a place as good as their competitors.

Franklin had a dirt running track. Its high school basketball gym floor was so uneven and had so many dead spots that visiting teams complained it gave Franklin players an unfair advantage because they knew which spots on the floor to avoid. As well, the band room was located under the gym and asbestos from the gym floor rained down on the band students when someone bounced a ball on the floor. Consequently, the basketball teams had to practice and have their home games at the middle school.

The high school principal, Bob Retchless, testified that Franklin kids were among the neediest he had ever worked with. On cross, Ludtke questioned him about the slogan he had posted in his office: "Quality is not about money alone but the result of hard work." Bob explained that he uses the slogan to keep his kids from feeling second rate.

Gilford High School, Franklin's comparison district, offered twelve advanced placement courses to the one at Franklin, which wasn't offered every year. The Gilford witnesses testified about the difference that resources make. Perhaps the most compelling witness was Rhetta Colon, the chair of the Gilford English Department.

Rhetta had previously taught at Franklin High School. Franklin didn't have department chairs, but Rhetta was the most senior English teacher in the high school before she transferred to Gilford. She remembers standing at the counter in the main office and throwing away every job application from teachers who had more than three years' experience, because she knew the Franklin School District could not afford to hire experienced teachers. As Gilford's English chair, she only considered teaching applicants who already had three years' experience.

While all the teachers who testified at trial were good witnesses, the most impressive were the ones who had experience teaching in both the property-poor and the property-wealthy districts. They could really explain and describe the difference that having resources made. Rhetta Colon was the best of this group.

Lisbon/Lincoln-Woodstock Comparison

The Lisbon and Lincoln-Woodstock pairing came last, presented by Arpy Saunders. Lisbon is an isolated mountain community. Lincoln-Woodstock is a combination of two school districts located on the extension of I-93 called the Franconia Notch Parkway. The Parkway is a two-lane scenic highway through New Hampshire's ski country.

Lincoln is the home of the Loon Mountain ski resort. It has lots of second homes, which increase property values without contributing additional children to the school system. Woodstock is a very similar neighboring community.

My image of those who lived in Lisbon is driven by a conversation I had with the Lisbon high school principal, Steve Sexton. I was in Sexton's office and he noticed me looking at the shooting trophies on his wall. He correctly guessed that I wasn't someone who favors gun ownership, and sat me down to set me straight. He said that many of the families in Lisbon wouldn't eat meat for the winter unless Dad "got a deer or a moose." He said hunting is not only part of the lifestyle, but also how people survive in Lisbon, where winter work is hard to find.

Lisbon's school tax rate, despite its poverty, or more likely, because of its poverty, was 60 percent above the state's average, according to John Fitzgerald, the chair of the Lisbon School Board. Only 5 percent of the school budget was discretionary, and a large portion of that small percentage related to the cost of kindergarten, which still wasn't required in New Hampshire at the time of our trial in 1996.

The state's lawyers impeached most of our school witnesses with their prior writings. An impeachment, when done crisply with clearly contrasting statements, is a very effective way of undermining a witness's credibility. A witness who, prior to trial, for example, tells the police that a traffic light was red is not credible when he later testifies at trial that the light was green.

I remember wincing at the first couple of impeachments. I thought, how could you have written that letter home or that report, knowing what you know? Over time, the impeachments were so frequent and expected that we began to ignore them. After all, we weren't in a criminal trial with drug dealers ratting out their competitors for a lighter sentence. The witnesses in our trial were educators and community leaders whose motivation for cooperating with us was both clear and commendable.

Looking back, I wish I'd prompted a witness to explain why he'd told a white lie in a letter home or in a report. He hadn't had the heart to tell his students that no matter how hard the students worked, the school just didn't have the personnel or resources to prepare them to compete against the sons and daughters of doctors and lawyers who attended the school across the river or up the street.

The Education Professors

The financial disputes with the team of experts led by Kern Alexander at Virginia Tech left us without financial experts. We relied instead on Commissioners Marston, MacDonald, and Brown, and some state reports. We relied on homegrown expert Rob Fried for a definition of educational adequacy.

The only outside experts we presented at trial were Van Mueller and Terry Schultz, two University of Minnesota education professors who provided a qualitative analysis of New Hampshire's two-tiered school system, one for the haves and the other for the have-nots. We first needed to overcome significant problems with their report, which had factual and data errors in it. Manias took the errors, mostly found by the state's hired gun, Paul Snow, under advisement and we proceeded.

At the time, we thought we were innovative in how we presented the Mueller and Schultz testimony. Looking back, I realize how rudimentary our courtroom technology really was. We borrowed two slide projectors and two screens from friends in the wealthy districts and set them up side-by-side in the well of the courtroom. We advanced the slide carousels by hand. On the left, for example, the judge would see the Apple IIe strapped to a cart in Allenstown, and on the right, he would see the bank of networked modern computers in the elementary school in Rye.

We started Van's testimony by tying it to Fried's adequacy definition. Van considered Fried's Four Pillars of Adequacy to be comprehensive, and used it to frame his qualitative study. He noted that New Hampshire state statutes require provision of a quality education to all children, and that New Hampshire did not live up to the laws on its books. Van testified that he saw science equipment in one of the high schools he visited that was fifty years old. Van had used the equipment when he took high school physics.

Van's testimony is best summed up by his belief that the New Hampshire statutes and the *Claremont* court decision required the state to have a single school system that local input could vary based on local needs and preferences. He testified that the comparisons showed this wasn't the case. New Hampshire had two systems of education: one failed to meet the needs of its students, while the other excelled.

Terry Schultz didn't pull any punches in her testimony. She considered Pittsfield Middle High School "a seriously substandard, inadequate facility [that] provides an inadequate program."[160] The fact that it was accredited meant that accreditation was "meaningless. . . . The science classrooms . . . [are] very poorly equipped and maintained, concerns about safety in them . . . [there are] pieces of equipment . . . designed for a tech prep curriculum, but there's no funding to support staff development or curriculum integration. So, they have the equipment, but they don't have curriculum integration to support the appropriate use."[161]

Schultz also criticized Allenstown's retention of only one principal for two separate schools. She said this wasn't local control. It was a choice forced upon Allenstown due to financial limitations.

She talked at length about Allenstown's need for a room for students who acted out.

> This is a padded room—an open room in a hallway, so students walk past this classroom every day as they're moving back and forth from classes. Student discipline is a very serious problem. . . . The principal showed us pages and pages of disciplinary logs he's maintained . . . that may perhaps be a result of students having no access to hands-on learning. . . . Students . . . have access . . . only to learning activities that involve sitting passively, listening to teachers talk and writing. . . . [T]he disciplinary problems . . . are so severe that the principal must occasionally restrain students, bring them to an area where they can be out of control safely and guard them until their parents or the police can come and pick them up. . . . [F]or children to have that kind of problem is extremely unusual and I think the consequence of circumstances that we have a responsibility to prevent. . . . I've never seen anything like this in a school. . . . I've never seen a facility like this. . . . This is not local control.[162]

With the conclusion of the Mueller and Schultz expert testimony, we rested. Our presentation wasn't perfect, but I thought our team did an impressive job with what we had. We awaited the onslaught of testimony from the state that would start tomorrow—after yet another motion that claimed our case should be dismissed.

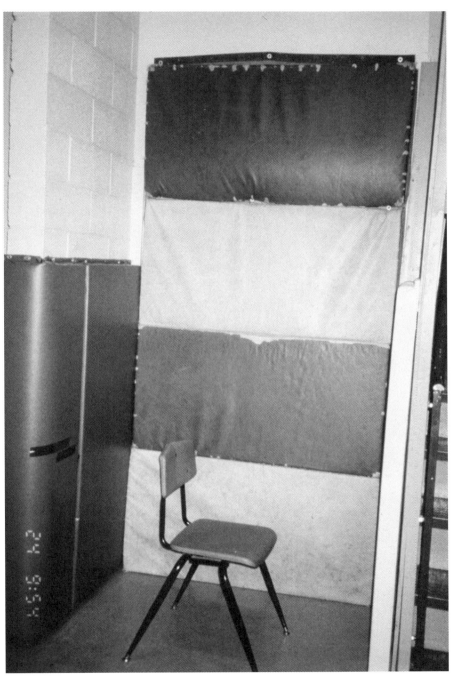

Allenstown padded time-out disciplinary space at the Armand Dupont Middle School.

The State's Economists

The state's testimony was built on the expert opinions of four economists and the factual conclusions of lower-level state education department employees, who testified that everything was peachy keen. The state did not call then-Education Commissioner Betty Twomey to defend the system she oversaw. As mentioned, they did call the politically appointed board of education chair, Ovide Lamontagne, who had taken Judith Thayer's place. More about him later.

Three of the state's economists presented an economics theory of capitalization to justify a system with low taxes in wealthy districts and oppressively high taxes in poor districts. These three economists weren't lightweights—two taught at Dartmouth and one at Harvard. Their application of capitalization theory to public school finance, however, would have flunked Econ 101.

Under capitalization theory, the more an investor commits to a particular investment, the bigger his return should be. The true value of capital is its earning capacity. The more valuable capital is when first invested, the larger its rate of return should be.

A simple example of capitalization theory might be two investors buying $100,000 bonds. The first investor puts down $10,000 and the second commits $30,000 towards the purchase. Under capitalization theory, the second investor shouldn't invest unless he has a better rate of return because more of his capital is at risk. There is nothing about this theory that discriminates against the first investor based on class or race, as is often the case with public school finance. The second investor simply committed more cash at the outset to buy the bonds. The bonds bought with the $30,000 should have a greater return than the bonds that cost $10,000.

The problem with this economics analysis is that the houses in wealthy and poor districts, unlike the bonds in our example, aren't the same. It's not that the homeowner in the wealthy district paid more for the same house and therefore deserves a better payoff in the form of a lower tax rate. The homeowner in the wealthy district paid more because the expensive house is likely larger, in a more desirable location, and has better services, including schools. The house was more expensive to buy because the buyer got more house.

Dartmouth Professor William Fischel tried to make his presentation folksier by sharing that he had bicycled through all the plaintiff districts and all the comparison districts. He claimed he knew them well because of his bike rides.

This testimony gave me the opportunity to ask Fischel the question that put his take on capitalization theory to shame. I asked if, during his bike tour, he noticed that Rye had an ocean and Allenstown didn't. I also asked him if he knew how many of the residents in Allenstown's plentiful manufactured home parks had the money to buy mansions on Ocean Boulevard in Rye.

Caroline Hoxby, the Harvard professor, who was paid more than $10,000 by the state for her testimony, had two contributions that should go down in the annals of things Harvard consultants should not say while on the stand. (Hoxby is now at Stanford.)

First, when questioned about the fact that she had only recently earned her PhD, Hoxby testified that she was actually at the most productive age for economists. This left us all to wonder about the state's older economists, whom Hoxby must have considered well past their "sell by" date.

Second, Hoxby also testified that people in poor school districts have a "lower demand" for education, and therefore deserve what they get. It was hard to believe she said this out loud. This sentiment is the basis for every shortchanging of "those people" that could be imagined. Poor people live in tenements because they don't want to live in nice homes. Poor people shop at convenience stores in food deserts because that's what they like best. It's just a short walk from here to the *Wall Street Journal* article that proclaimed "slum kids can't learn."[163]

Hoxby's testimony oozed racial and class-based discrimination, whether this was her intent or not. Her opinion was also based on the incorrect assumption that poor people paid less for their schools and therefore deserved less.

Hoxby's claim that poor people had a "lower demand for education" didn't account for the fact that our clients paid higher education taxes than homeowners in wealthy districts. It also missed the fact that, with lower incomes, taxpayers in the poorer communities paid a higher percentage of their incomes in taxes.

A homeowner in Pittsfield in 1994–1995, for example, paid a $25.26 school tax rate on a $60,000 home, or $1,515.60 a year, as compared to the owner of a $240,000 mansion on the lake in Moultonborough, who paid a $5.56 school tax, or $1,334.40 a year. The residents of the poorer districts paid more in taxes, whether considering the rate of taxation or the amount of the annual payment. In terms of Hoxby's economic theory, this should have meant they had a right to demand more because they paid more.

The other problem with the economists' theories was that their economics opinions ignored who went to school and what the purpose of public education is. Children don't generally choose where they are born or where they live. The quality of their education in a single state (or, I would argue, in America) should not be determined by geography.

A strong democracy is inclusive. It doesn't depend upon a child getting a good education only if her parent can afford the "price of admission" by buying a fancy house on a lake. The children of Claremont have the same right to vote as the children of Lebanon. They shouldn't be poorly equipped to participate in New Hampshire's democracy.

Colin Campbell, an older Dartmouth economics professor emeritus, led off the state's case. His testimony was so muddled, and it was clear he had such a hard time following Ludtke's questions, that Arpy and I decided not to question him at all. We also knew that Fischel would present the same economics testimony, which we could challenge later without being cruel to an elderly, clearly confused witness.

This left Erik Hanushek. Hanushek was an economics professor at the University of Rochester. He was the darling of state attorneys general because, for a small fee, he would come to your state and offer the opinion that, in education, money didn't matter. That, unlike any other activity that requires resources, schools did not do better—all other things being the same—when provided with more resources. He and a couple others were the progenitors of the "slum kids can't learn" school of economics. Hanushek was the state's last witness.

We knew what he would say, so we spent much of the trial asking witnesses, "If poor school districts had more resources, would it help them provide a better education to their children?" We also asked the witnesses from the wealthy districts what they did with their more plentiful resources to help the children in their districts. By the time we got to Hanushek, the writing was on the wall. He changed his opinion from "money doesn't matter" to "money spent well matters." We could live with that proposition. No one supported wasting money.

As previously noted, Hanushek's claim that money doesn't matter was thoroughly debunked by a team of economists at Northwestern University led by a labor economist named C. Kirabo Jackson.[164] In 2016, Dr. Hoxby also dumped Hanushek's theory and agreed that better funding makes a difference.[165]

Summing Up

The highlight of the "educators" presented by the state in its case had to be Ovide Lamontagne, the politically appointed chair of the state board of education. To deflect testimony about the old and tattered textbooks, he testified that textbooks were unnecessary.[166] He also testified that he and Ludtke had drafted a state definition of a constitutionally adequate education and submitted it to the state board, which approved it with four votes, three members being absent.[167] Lamontagne's definition was created for trial. Lamontagne and Ludtke had not consulted any teacher, administrator, local school board member, parent of schoolchildren, or taxpayer, except for the members of the state board who happened to be present for the vote.[168]

At the end of the evidence, we all agreed to submit our closing arguments on paper. Arpy and I split about half a dozen radio interviews that Tom Hersey arranged, and spoke to the press that had diligently covered the trial. Our theme was that the state had the constitutional duty to educate New Hampshire's children and was failing. Despite heroic efforts by taxpayers and educators, children were not receiving the quality of education they deserved and needed in order to succeed in a competitive society.

I had some buttons made that said I Survived the Claremont Trial and gave them to the reporters and court staff. The other side's lawyers declined them. I also bought a fake set of eyeglasses with a nose and moustache attached and gave it to *Union Leader* reporter John DiStaso, so that we could see each other for coffee in the future without him getting into trouble with his editors, who were opposed to the equity we sought. When I ran for governor in 2020, DiStaso told me he still had the glasses with the fake nose.

Judge Manias's Ruling

Judge Manias issued his ruling at the beginning of November 1996.

It ran to 190 pages and we got hammered. Manias ruled against us in every way imaginable, while asserting that the problems we did prove were not the state's fault.

Manias construed the New Hampshire Supreme Court's *Claremont* I ruling as not requiring any consideration of equity or equality, even though the Supreme Court described the Education Clause in terms of a competitive model of adequacy. The court had written, "The State's constitutional duty extends beyond mere reading, writing and arithmetic. It also includes broad educational opportunities needed in today's society to prepare citizens for their role as participants and as *potential competitors* in today's marketplace of ideas."[169]

Manias rejected the paired district comparisons, even though this approach had been used in every school funding trial since *Serrano* I in the early 1970s. It's why, quite frankly, Hanushek and his ilk developed their side hustle testifying that money didn't matter. None of this mattered to Judge Manias. Equity was not his concern.

Manias found that we failed to establish a standard for a minimally constitutional education and, therefore, did not carry our burden of proving the poor districts fell below any recognizable standard. The idea that a Pittsfield Middle High School graduate would compete against a Moultonborough grad for a place at college or in the job market simply did not register with Judge Manias.

Manias rejected Rob Fried's definition of adequacy because he hadn't done enough research to satisfy the judge, even though Fried was a professor of education and a former school board member. Instead, he adopted the definition written by Ovide Lamontagne, the political appointee.

Manias relied on Professor Emeritus Campbell's testimony. He characterized it as "unrefuted" and adopted Campbell's conclusion that "local property taxation provides a stable, dependable, and expandable source of revenue for the provision of public education."[170] Ironically, Campbell was the only economist mentioned in Manias's order. Manias also expressly concluded that "tax rate" does not equal "tax burden," which was an unspoken nod toward capitalization theory.

Minimum standards, according to Judge Manias, were not minimal. Charlie Marston's testimony on this point was rejected and the testimony of his subordinates was adopted.

Judge Manias accepted virtually every impeachment offered by the state, accepting as true every "letter home" or sympathetic report that painted a rosy picture of a school or district, even though his own eyes saw a different story when he visited the schools or saw photographs in court.

It is hard to imagine that we could have done much worse. Once again, we were headed to the New Hampshire Supreme Court with an albatross around our necks. Only now, we couldn't deploy the tactics of a senate president switching sides or a group of senior lawyers adopting us. It was November when Manias ruled and the days were growing darker, as was our mood.

The Politics

State Senator Jeanne Shaheen announced her run for governor while we were in trial. Steve Merrill decided not to run for reelection, and took a job with the public relations arm of a national law firm soliciting work from other former attorneys general and big businesses. Ovide Lamontagne ran against Congressman Bill Zeliff for the Republican gubernatorial nomination and, to Shaheen's surprise, beat Zeliff. The November election featured Lamontagne versus Shaheen.

Because Shaheen assumed Zeliff would be her opponent, her team had not carefully researched Lamontagne; now they only had a few months to pull together their opposition research. Shaheen's research team was led by Robin Read, who had worked as my criminal investigator when I was a public defender. Robin and I remained friends, and I gave him my trial prep materials on Lamontagne to get him started.

Shaheen handily beat Lamontagne in the general election soon after Manias issued his order finding against us on all counts.

Although I still believed that if we could remain standing through an appeal we would succeed, the forcefulness of the order raised doubts even in me. Should I have taken the advice to declare victory after the first *Claremont* decision and passed off the problem to the next set of lawyers? This question buzzed through my head as we awaited the transcripts and began writing our appellate brief.

The state's lawyers had it easier. They did what any good lawyers would do with a ruling as strongly in their favor as Manias's was: they relied heavily on it in their briefing. Of course, they needed to respond to the legal claims that we set out, but they did so with Manias and his order at their side.

Chapter 8

Is Education a Fundamental Right?

The New Hampshire Supreme Court had gone way out on a limb when it found that education was an important constitutional right, and now, after having lost at trial, we were going further by asking the court to declare the right "fundamental" and to condemn the state for its lack of action during the three intervening years between the two appeals.

The court issued its ruling on December 17, 1997. I was working with a client away from the office when the decision was ready. The court's clerk, Howard Zibel, called my office looking for me and spoke with my law partner, Bob Stein. The decision was being hand delivered to the lawyers in the case and would arrive soon. The court planned to hold the public release of the decision for a few hours to give us time to absorb what was written before the press descended. Scott Johnson, who was finishing his third year of law school, was the first of our team to read the decision.[171]

We won!

The first paragraph read:

> In this appeal we hold that the present system of financing elementary and secondary public education in New Hampshire is unconstitutional. To hold otherwise would be to effectively conclude that it is reasonable, in discharging a state obligation, to tax property owners in one town or city as much as four times the amount taxed to others similarly situated in other towns or cities. This is precisely the kind of taxation and fiscal mischief from which the framers of our State Constitution took strong steps to protect our citizens.

The court adopted our comparison approach starting on the tax side. The court compared the taxable property value per child of Franklin ($183,626) to that of Gilford ($536,761). Manias had characterized the school tax as being "local" because the mechanisms of assessment and collection were exercised by local town officials. The court focused instead on the purpose for the tax, which was to pay for the state's duty to provide a constitutionally adequate education pursuant to Article 83. A state purpose meant the tax was a state tax.

By finding that education taxes were state taxes, the court's ruling required that school tax rates had to be uniform throughout the state for the portion of school costs that were the state's responsibility. This was our Count VI of the complaint.

After ruling for us that taxes must be proportional, which in this instance meant uniform in rate, the court went on to consider the second requirement of the tax clause; that is, taxes must be "just" or "reasonable." The court found, "There is nothing fair or just about taxing a home or other real estate in one town at four times the rate that similar property is taxed in another town to fulfill the same purpose of meeting the State's educational duty."

Now the court linked the education side of the case to their tax findings: "Children who live in poor and rich districts have the same right to a constitutionally adequate public education. . . . [T]he record demonstrates that a number of plaintiff communities are unable to meet existing standards despite assessing disproportionate and unreasonable taxes."

The court, referencing the US Supreme Court's *San Antonio* decision, found that education is a fundamental right under the New Hampshire Constitution because "[f]irst and foremost is the fact that our State Constitution specifically charges the legislature with the duty to provide public education." In other words, that New Hampshire has an education clause in its constitution.

The court also pointed out the importance of education. "[E]ven a minimalist view of educational adequacy recognizes the role of education in preparing citizens to participate in the exercise of voting and first amendment rights. The latter being recognized as fundamental, it is illogical to place the means to exercise those rights on less substantial constitutional footing than the rights themselves." This proposition was rejected by the US Supreme Court's majority but accepted in most of the state court cases that followed. The court relied on the decision in the Kentucky case and the Massachusetts decision in the McDuffy case to outline the broad parameters of a constitutionally adequate education.

The court couldn't help noting, somewhat cheekily, that an equal protection decision written by New Hampshire Chief Justice Doe in the late nineteenth century stated that equal treatment of constitutional rights had been New Hampshire doctrine before the US Constitution's Equal Protection Clause was adopted in 1868.

Rather than detailing how the legislature should proceed, the court expressed its confidence in the legislature and stayed its finding that the current system of funding schools was unconstitutional for fifteen months, until the end of the next tax year on March 31, 1999.

The new crop of legislators and Jeanne Shaheen, beginning her second term as governor, would have fifteen months to craft a constitutionally sound funding system that would be fair to taxpayers and that would provide all children across the state a strong opportunity to "compete in the marketplace of ideas."

Justice Sherman Horton dissented from the court's opinion. Although he agreed with many of the concerns asserted by the court, he did not agree that the court should make "educational policy" for the state. He thought this was particularly a legislative responsibility.

Perhaps it was sensitivity to Horton's concern about separation of powers that led the court to refrain from designing a specific program of education finance for the state to adopt. Perhaps the details of the existing educational shortcomings were not something the court wanted to memorialize in its published opinion. Some of those details were shameful. Regardless, we had won, and nary an economist or misapplied theory of economics was mentioned. Tax rates were considered a perfectly acceptable measure of tax burden, and they were not proportional and reasonable as required by our Constitution.

We were happy that the court did not fashion a specific remedy. We had an education governor in office and friends among the Democratic reps and senators and among the moderate and progressive Republicans. We were ready to work with the governor and legislature to craft a lasting solution.

Concord Monitor reporting described the celebration at my office. "The bubbly flowed freely. So did tears of relief, giddy joy and unabashed pride. . . . Congratulatory messages spit out of the fax machine. Supporters came by with cards and hugs."[172] Claire Ebel, the director of the New Hampshire ACLU, said, "[The decision] totally rips Manias."[173]

The *Monitor*'s editorial of December 19 likened the decision to Dickens's *A Christmas Carol,* where Jeanne Shaheen was now staring at Jacob Marley's ghost. The editorial chided Shaheen and the legislature for being caught flat-footed by the decision because the *Monitor* thought I had a strong oral argument three months earlier. The *Monitor*'s political cartoon by Mike Marland had the caption, "Yes, Virginia, there is a New Hampshire Supreme Court."

Among the supporters who congratulated us were those who fought to keep the suit alive for six and a half years, including those who raised money for us. In a nod to them, I said, "There are a bunch of kids in Franklin who can now hang up their baking dishes, stop selling brownies, and concentrate on their education."[174]

Steve Merrill, the former governor, at first refused to comment on my efforts in the case because he claimed his mother told him, "If [he] couldn't say something nice about somebody not to say anything at all." When pressed, he referred to me as a "movement lawyer straight out of the 60s. He's Abbie Hoffman's brother and he won a huge case and deserves recognition for that."[175]

Years later, Justice William Batchelder was interviewed for the New Hampshire Supreme Court's Oral History Project.[176] Although he recognized the *Claremont* decision may have been "traumatic" for the legislature, he considered the court's finding a "no-brainer" based on 150 years of tax cases that required taxes to be fair. He also considered the act of approving the Augenblick formula and then not funding it to be "political hypocrisy of the worst kind."

Our client from Allenstown, Ann Viar, who organized the playground fundraiser and paid over the proceeds to fix a leaky school roof, was quoted as saying, "It's not over, but it feels like the reinforcements have arrived."[177] Her son, Michael, who was now a thirteen-year-old eighth grader, said, "I think it's great because all those kids in the poor public schools will now have the chance to get a good education. . . . And they won't have to share books anymore."[178]

The *Union Leader*'s ham-handed editorial, under the headline "Statist Decision," read: "Pathetically unable to force a broad-based tax through the Legislature, the barnacles that cling like parasites to the ship of state's hull calculated that they could accomplish their nefarious objective through the courts. They calculated rightly."[179]

You could almost imagine the editorial writer, Richard Lessner, fuming and spraying spittle as he typed. His suggested remedy? Amend the New Hampshire Constitution to preserve "the freedoms and quality of life with which Granite Staters are so greatly blessed." Key the band to play "My Country, 'Tis of Thee."

Like it or not, how we fund our schools and treat our taxpayers was front and center again in the minds of the public. Manchester physician Bill Siroty summed up the response to Lessner and other naysayers with two words: "Franklin and Fairness." Siroty pointed out in his letter to the *Union Leader* that deplorable conditions in Franklin coupled with low pay made it hard to attract teachers. In response to calls for the legislature to take back control, Siroty wrote, "the Supreme Court did what our past and present elected officials lacked the courage and leadership to do. Just as the Boston and Maine Railroad influenced our state's government at the turn of the century, the *Union Leader* has exerted its pernicious influence over the past several decades. It's high time the people take back control of our great state."[180]

What was Shaheen's reaction to the landmark ruling? Was she hopeful? Did she view the *Claremont* II decision as an opportunity to make real changes?

No, Shaheen was described as "somber," "surprised," and "disappointed" by the ruling.[181] Ultimately, she held a short press conference and read a one-page statement that included this quote: "While I disagree with the decision, I am committed to working with the Legislature to address the issues in it."[182] She took no questions and fled the stage.[183]

Chapter 9

The Democratic Governor Responds

Governor Shaheen's State of the State speech in early January 1998 became a big deal because of the *Claremont* II ruling, garnering national coverage, including from the *Washington Post*.[184] Shaheen declined to provide details of her plan to respond to *Claremont* II in the speech, but she did acknowledge the challenges of the *Claremont* ruling. Right after touting the absence of new broad-based taxes, Shaheen characterized the Claremont case as one of many challenges and opportunities facing the state. In rhetoric unmatched by deeds, Shaheen claimed New Hampshire needed a world-class education system, not one that was merely "adequate."

As House Speaker Donna Sytek from Salem noted, "The ramifications are enormous." But Shaheen only said what she was against in the speech. She was against a constitutional amendment to reverse the *Claremont* decisions and she was opposed to any broad-based tax. The *Post* article noted that New Hampshire spent about $1.2 billion on public education at the time and 90 percent of that, about $1 billion, came from property taxes. This was the highest reliance on the single revenue source of the local property tax of any state in the nation. The question for which Shaheen failed to provide an answer was how to raise close to $1 billion for education without upsetting New Hampshire's anti-taxers, and without "dumbing down," in Shaheen's words, education.[185]

Perhaps Vice President Al Gore knew the answer.

Shortly after the State of the State speech, Angus King, who was Maine's governor at the time, and Jeanne Shaheen toured Maine and New Hampshire with Vice President Gore after an extensive ice storm caused massive damage in both states. Many years later, Angus told me that he asked Shaheen how she would solve the *Claremont* problem.

Shaheen insisted she could solve *Claremont* without a new tax. When she left the car, Angus asked Gore how she could possibly do that. Gore responded, "Alchemy. It's how we do everything."

Radical Republicans had other ideas. They wanted to amend the Constitution to get the court out of the business of telling the legislature what to do. There were all manner of approaches suggested. None would have been good for schoolchildren or most state taxpayers.

Ovide Lamontagne teamed with former Governor John Sununu and some rabid anti-tax advocates to form the New Hampshire Advantage Coalition. Their view of the "advantage" was that New Hampshire did not do taxes.

I was invited to discuss the *Claremont* decision with a gathering at the Universalist church in Milford, New Hampshire, one cold weeknight in January. Our daughters, Mollie and Bekah, came with me. Senator Jim Squires and Representative Neal Kurk were also on the panel to respond to my comments. Squires was a reasonable Republican. Kurk was not.

When we got to the question-and-answer period, a state representative from Kingston, Ken Weyler, spoke up. Weyler had been fuming during my entire presentation. He traveled to our church meeting from his home in Rockingham County, an hour away. Weyler, a retired airline pilot, didn't have a question. He wanted to make a statement.

Doing his best to channel 1950s segregationists, Weyler threatened that if we tried to enforce the *Claremont* rulings, he would convert all public education monies to athletic funding and open "rec centers" in all towns to replace public schools. Weyler, an elected rep in a New England state, wanted to replicate the Virginia private academies that were used to educate White children while public schools were closed to Black kids in response to the *Brown v. Board* decision.

Weyler has remained a state rep through my writing of this book in 2024, and his political career has remained extreme. In 2021, he was stripped of his committee chairmanship after circulating a report that claimed COVID vaccines inserted creatures into people's bodies and controlled their thoughts.

It couldn't have been easy for the Shaheen team given the cacophony of amendment advocates on one side and us on the other side. Her *Claremont* response team included her trusted legal and campaign advisor, Judy Reardon, who was a lawyer educated at Dartmouth and Penn; her education policy advisor, Vicki Boyd; the state's tax commissioner, Stan Arnold; Attorney General Phil McLaughlin; and her family friend and future board of education chair, John Lewis. Shaheen made Lewis a judge in 2001.

By mid-January 1998, the Shaheen team had a plan, sort of.

Some wags wondered aloud if Shaheen and her team spent more time naming their plan than working out its details. The name was pretty cool. The plan was called the "ABC" plan, which stood for "Advancing Better Classrooms."

The plan called for increasing state spending by $100 million from existing state taxes and instituting a statewide property tax for the rest. The statewide property tax was just a renaming of a portion of the already existing local property tax, but put that aside for a moment. The smaller problem with the plan was that Shaheen identified only half the state revenue sources. She proposed about $47 million in new state funding from increasing the cigarette tax by twenty-three cents. There wasn't a proposal for the remainder of the $100 million injection of new money. Later, Shaheen claimed instituting video gambling would provide the missing state funds that were needed.

Under Governor Shaheen's vision for New Hampshire, the state would fund perhaps the most important function of government, supporting education, with sales of cigarettes and expanded gambling, and these vices would join New Hampshire's already booming state liquor sales business.

Shaheen's statewide property tax had the same constitutional problem that caused the supreme court to rule for us in the first place. The effective rates of the statewide property tax varied with the wealth of the communities being taxed. The only difference from the existing system was that Shaheen planned to impose a nominally uniform state tax rate. But then residents of property-wealthy communities would receive an automatic tax rebate, so they would never pay the full rate and would not contribute a penny to the statewide funding of adequacy. All of the money raised by the Shaheen ABC plan would be spent locally to pay for each community's adequacy. Communities that couldn't raise enough would receive money from the state's $100 million kitty, funded by the sale of cigarettes and gambling.

On January 28, 1998, I testified before a state senate subcommittee on education to answer questions about the *Claremont* II ruling, and was asked about the ABC plan. I pointed out the problem with not identifying sustainable sources of revenue and the lack of uniformity in state property taxes. I was followed by former Republican governor Walter Peterson. Both Peterson and I testified against a constitutional amendment. "Making a constitutional change a first option would say the current system is fair when the court has told us it is not," Peterson told the panel.[186]

As I was testifying before the Senate, the *Valley News*, the newspaper for New Hampshire's Upper Valley (the region around Hanover and Lebanon), ran the numbers for Shaheen's plan.

> [T]he equalized cost to Claremont property owners of a constitutionally adequate education would be almost four times the cost to taxpayers in New London. Taxpayers in Grantham would pay just a third of what the same minimum spending level would cost taxpayer in Haverhill . . . and Sunapee and Hanover residents would pay less than half of what people in Canaan and Enfield would be expected to pay.[187]

Shaheen's people were counting on the court to back down. Judy Reardon told the *Valley News*: "I think in large part, the court's reasoning will depend on what they really meant by uniformity. . . . I don't think uniformity should be the altar at which people worship."[188] Reardon, joined by the state's tax commissioner, Stan Arnold, claimed the political support for the governor's plan would impress the court. Fred Bramante was given credit in the *Valley News* article for renaming the ABC plan to "Anything But Constitutional."

The editorial that accompanied the *Valley News* article, entitled "School Finance, III," noted that "Gov. Jeanne Shaheen does not aspire to write a new chapter of *Profiles in Courage*" and termed her ABC plan a "massive exercise in political timidity."[189] The same editorial claimed the Shaheen plan only looked good in comparison to the "malice-in-wonderland fantasies of . . . [the] constitutional amenders." While not taking lightly the travails of proposing an income tax, the *Valley News* argued it was a fair, simple, and broad-based solution to the school funding problem.[190]

Judy Reardon also had words for me. "I think every time [Andru Volinsky] opens his mouth, support for a constitutional amendment goes up. . . . He's exhibit A for the constitutional amendment folks. . . . If people think he's going to be marching into court every two months."[191]

The Republicans, as a group, were not trying to help Shaheen. She was the first Democratic governor in sixteen years and she was popular. At their state convention in February 1998, Congressman Charles Bass suggested a campaign tactic that coupled blaming the Dems for the *Claremont* ruling with a swipe at Bill Clinton about Monica Lewinsky. Party chair Steve Duprey denied that Republicans were simply stalling by advocating for a constitutional amendment—which required a public vote nine months hence, in November. Only Speaker Sytek was adamant that the Republicans avoid politics and try to do the best for the state.[192]

Six months later I ran into Duprey in a Concord coffee shop and asked him who he thought had Shaheen's ear. His reply was Judy Reardon and Mandy Grunwald. Grunwald is a top political consultant who worked for Bill and Hillary Clinton.

Duprey, the chair of the Republican party, predicted that Shaheen would win reelection in 1998 by a landslide. If she backed a broad-based tax, she would still win but by a slightly smaller landslide.

In March 1998, I attended the annual education finance conference and litigators meeting sponsored by the American Education Finance Association. Shaheen sent her education policy consultant, Vicki Boyd, to the finance part of the conference. Boyd mostly avoided me, but I arranged for her to sit with us for one breakfast. I told her Shaheen's ABC plan was not constitutional, but if Shaheen wanted to make the plan interim, we might help her buy time. I asked Boyd to carry the message back to Attorney General Phil McLaughlin.

A few days after returning home, I called McLaughlin and described my conversation with Boyd. He said he would get back to me and, about a week later, he called and suggested a meeting the next day at noon. He said he'd bring Judy Reardon, the governor's lawyer, as his "client representative" and that I should bring Kathy Fuller, the Claremont Coalition's advisory board member from Franklin.

Fuller was an interesting choice—as was the idea that McLaughlin should choose which of my clients to attend the meeting. Just a week earlier, Fuller had held a press conference to denounce me for speaking against the ABC plan without authority to do so from my clients. She publicly claimed I was on a mission of my own design.

Fortunately, I didn't operate this way and was tipped to Fuller's close ties to Shaheen and Reardon. Before challenging the ABC plan, I briefed our advisory board about its constitutional shortcomings and received the unanimous blessing of those in attendance to speak against it. Then, worried about Fuller, I sent a confirming letter to every advisory board member and client asking anyone with a different opinion to speak up. Fuller did not voice opposition to the plan or contact me before she publicly claimed I was unethical.

Fuller wasn't invited to the meeting.

Attending the meeting were McLaughlin, Reardon, Scott Johnson, John Tobin, and me. We met in the attorney general's commodious conference room in a former bank building across from the Statehouse. After being lectured by McLaughlin about ground rules, I explained the idea of declaring the ABC plan with a few tweaks as "interim," and jointly approaching the Supreme Court to ask for more time for the state to fashion a proper remedy. I said we were trying to help the state "get out of the box" it was in.

Phil and Judy reacted by claiming the state wasn't in trouble and there was no need for tweaks. Phil said the plan was as good as it would get and we had "better get on the train before it leaves the station." I remember

Phil McLaughlin, who is a big man, doing his best John Wayne impression as he stood over me talking about trains.

I ignored the threat and asked if there was a plan in case the ABC approach was found unconstitutional. Judy said that was not going to happen and snapped shut her notebook. At this point, I got up, said a quick goodbye, and left. We intentionally left Scott and John to linger in case there were any further avenues to explore without me. There were none.

After the "train leaving the station" comment, the next phase of the Shaheen approach kicked in. Reardon called John Tobin and Bill Glahn, who had represented Senate President Ralph Hough when he switched sides. Her message was that ABC was a good plan and that Andy was likely to cause a constitutional amendment to be passed by criticizing ABC. Jeanne Shaheen personally invited John Tobin to lunch at the governor's cottage, called Bridges House, where I was a prominent topic of discussion.

I also heard, repeatedly, that "perfection is the enemy of the good." In other words, I was demanding too much. But ABC wasn't good. ABC was a repeat of the failed Augenblick plan that Sununu instituted, only at a slightly higher level of funding. The additional funding, however, wasn't sustainable, and the plan perpetuated uneven property taxes. My assessment was that ABC, at best, was an unsustainable plan built on a foundation of the-supreme-court-can-go-to-hell. Neither aspect of the plan was attractive and I was committed to shoring up the effort to find a better plan.

By early May 1998, Shaheen realized she couldn't pass the ABC plan without Speaker Sytek's help, and they forged an alliance based on a compromise between their two plans. Sytek's plan was called "SMART." By this point, I lost track of the meaning of the acronyms. Shaheen dropped her funding target by $28 million and Sytek increased her target by $45 million. At Sytek's request, video gambling was taken off the table and the cigarette tax increase was lowered by ten cents a pack, which helped the retailers in Sytek's border community that sold cigarettes to more highly taxed Massachusetts residents. A one-time state surplus filled the gap. The backbone of the plan remained the Shaheen statewide property tax, with its rebates and uneven property tax rates. There was also no definition of adequacy. That work was put off until after the next election.

The big fly in the ointment was that the state senate was excluded from the negotiation between Shaheen and Speaker Sytek. When the compromise ABC plan was sent to the New Hampshire Senate, the Senate voted to refer the plan to the New Hampshire Supreme Court for an advisory opinion, which is allowed under the state's constitution.

In an extraordinary move, the court invited a select group of non-lawyers to join the lawyers and argue for or against ABC. I'm not aware of any appellate court making a similar move, and when I later discussed the invitation with Columbia professor Mike Rebell, he thought it was unique, too. I've never been told this, but I think the court wanted those invested in state government to feel that they were truly heard. Also, I think the court wanted more policy input than the lawyers would provide.

At this point, the members of the court appeared to still believe the elected leaders would, in time, do the right thing. The lawyers from our team and for the state were asked to coach the non-lawyers through the process of a supreme court oral argument. We had Fred Bramante and Jim Rubens assigned to us. Rubens was a Libertarian state senator, another Dartmouth grad, and an unflinching amendment advocate. He ran for governor against Shaheen later in 1998 and lost handily. My advice to Fred Bramante was not to wear boat shoes to court. I ended up buying Fred a pair of shoes.

The groups supporting approval of the ABC plan included Shaheen, represented by her attorney general, the board of education led by John Lewis, Senate Democrats, Speaker Sytek, a handful of House Dems, and Tax Commissioner Stan Arnold. Joining us in claiming the plan was unconstitutional were the right-wing Republicans, Bramante, and Fred Upton, who was the son of a US senator and a prominent moderate Concord lawyer. It's fair to say those arguing against ABC had very different agendas: the right-wingers sought to turn the clocks back, and we hoped to move forward after clearing away the debris of Shaheen's failed plan.

After quickly brushing aside procedural arguments, the court concluded that the ABC plan was unconstitutional as written because it violated the tax proportionality provisions of the New Hampshire Constitution by imposing non-uniform rates. The automatic rebates didn't cut it. The court also refused to use the advisory opinion process as an excuse to backtrack from its *Claremont* decisions.

In response to the Shaheen group's argument that the state doesn't like taxes, the court wrote, "Social unrest cannot be a factor in the court's constitutional review of a bill."[193]

The underlying thesis of the ABC plan, focused on local funding as a prerequisite to local control, was rejected. New Hampshire is not a confederacy of localities. "[I]t is basic to our collective well-being that all citizens of the State share in the common burden of educating our children."

The court ended its advisory opinion by congratulating the governor and legislature for their hard work and by thanking the approximately one hundred organizations and individuals who had submitted comments in advance of the ruling.

It was now June 23, 1998, and the clock was ticking. The legislature would usually go out of session for the summer, but this year, it did not. We all went back to work, with legislators proposing plans and our team responding, mostly through an ad hoc group we called Citizens for Fair Education Taxation, or CFET.

CFET developed a list of nine basic reality checks and graded each proposal on the measures, issuing education-themed scores that ranged from a dried apple core to four apples. The group included friendly legislators like Dave Allison from Claremont and Gordon Allen from Antrim. Gordon had a PhD in economics. Sam Mekrut, who ran an advocacy group called New Hampshire Citizens Alliance, joined us. Educators joined with us who understood schools and school finance, including Dean Michener from the School Boards Association, Mark Joyce from the School Administrators Association, and Barbara Krysiak, who moved from her superintendency in Claremont to teaching at UNH's education school. Dennis Murphy from the NEA helped. A client of mine, Bill Duncan, also became involved.

It took a minute for me to realize that before becoming a software executive, Bill Duncan had been a community organizer in Berea, Kentucky. His wife, Cynthia, also was a sociologist at UNH and became the first director of the university's public policy school, where I now teach. Bill Duncan eventually was appointed to the state board of education in 2014 by Governor Maggie Hassan.

Among the legislators we talked with was Ned Gordon, a lawyer and state senator from Bristol, New Hampshire. Ned was born in Franklin and now represented a senate district with expensive homes on Newfound Lake. He had both rich-town and poor-town experience. Ned had been a senior executive at New England Telephone when he accepted an early retirement package and went to law school. He clerked for progressive Judge Hugh Bownes after graduation.

Ned was a Republican, but in my conversations with him, I found him both reasonable in his approach to solving school funding and honest about what the court had ruled. Ned was open to an income tax and thought he could bring others along with him. The price he wanted for his cooperation was a single statewide teachers' contract, rather than the norm, which was district-by-district collective bargaining agreements.

Liz Hager was a Republican state rep from Concord at the time, and had been Concord's mayor. She lost in the three-way Republican gubernatorial primary in 1992, the year party nominee Steve Merrill beat Arnie Arnesen in the general election. Hager's chief policy person was Doug Hall, with whom I have worked extensively since the 1990s.

Although trained as an electrical engineer at Stanford, Doug Hall is a fantastic data analyst. He served a couple of terms in the New Hampshire House of Representatives as a Republican representing a rural community. Doug also ran a think tank at the University of New Hampshire called the New Hampshire Center for Public Policy Studies. Hager's press secretary was a young *Concord Monitor* reporter named Felice Belman. Belman went back to the *Monitor* after Hager lost, and later became an editor at the *Boston Globe* and then at the *New York Times*.

Hager sponsored an income tax bill to address the funding side of the *Claremont* suit. She teamed with then-fellow representative Clifton

Below from Lebanon. Representative Below then ran for the state senate against constitutional amendment advocate Jim Rubens. He went to every town in his senate district to explain the exact consequences of the income tax bill he co-sponsored with Hager, and the drawbacks of New Hampshire's heavy reliance on local property taxes. Below became the first Democrat elected to the state senate from Lebanon in decades, proving that refusal to take the Pledge is not always fatal.

Democratic senator Mark Fernald and state reps Gordon Allen of Antrim and Martin Feuerstein of Franklin also joined Hager as co-sponsors. Mark had won a race similar to Below's in the Peterborough area. The bill they all co-sponsored was called the Hager-Below Income Tax Bill.

The bill was introduced in March 1998 but didn't get much attention until the supreme court shot down ABC. The Hager-Below bill, in its final iteration, combined a 4 percent personal income tax with a statewide property tax on business properties and vacation homes to raise north of $700 million for education funding. None of the taxes were rebated. Personal exemptions protected taxpayers of low and modest means. The income tax was applied at a flat 4 percent rate because the New Hampshire Constitution, which requires uniformity in rates, barred a progressive income tax with higher rates for higher levels of income.

A two parent/two child family was not taxed at all on the first $28,000 of their income. The $28,000 exemption would equal $54,400 in today's dollars.[194] At the time, the median household income in New Hampshire was about $49,500. Fifteen percent of the households in New Hampshire would not pay any income tax under Hager-Below. About an equal 15 percent of New Hampshire households earned more than $100,000 per year[195] and would pay about $2,880 in taxes on their annual incomes, after the exemption.

Mike Ettlinger, the tax policy director for the Institute on Taxation and Economic Policy (ITEP), worked closely with Clif Below to craft the income tax bill. Eventually, Ettlinger testified before the legislature to explain why an income tax was the fairest solution to the school funding problem. He also had to explain the errors in Stan Arnold's state tax agency's forecast that the income tax bill would be unable to produce the funds that Below and Hager predicted. The short answer to this last question was that Commissioner Arnold's agency didn't understand the tax modeling and made obvious mathematical "mistakes," the combination of which led Arnold to claim the Hager-Below bill would produce a third less revenue than ITEP forecast.

Ettlinger, in his testimony to the legislature, explained that New Hampshire's tax system was "regressive" in that it taxed lower-income and middle-income taxpayers much more harshly than high-income taxpayers. The property tax system was also "inelastic" in that property taxes were levied based on the assessed value of the real estate and not on the ability of the taxpayer to pay them. Ettlinger described income taxes as "progressive," or at least proportional, because the incidence of taxation falls most heavily on higher-income taxpayers. An income tax also adjusts to the loss of income, or the receipt of additional income, and is therefore considered "elastic."

At about this time, Tom Connair sounded off for us in a *Wall Street Journal* article against Representative Neal Kurk. Tom noted that experts hired by the state pegged the cost of state adequacy at between $983 million and $1 billion. The Senate then developed a bill at $960 million, the governor claimed the cost was $946 million, and then the governor negotiated a deal with the House speaker at $825 million. Kurk, for his part, said $825 million is enough and who wants a "first-class or an excellent education, anyway?"[196]

Shaheen's opposition to the income tax was driven by William Loeb's Pledge. An income tax was considered a new broad-based tax forbidden by the Pledge, and Shaheen was up for reelection in November. She would have none of it. She also had her eye on the US Senate.

The Hager-Below income tax bill squeaked through in the House. Despite a threat to veto a slightly different version of the bill in the Senate, it passed there too. The passage of time and the differences in House and Senate versions required a second House vote.

I remember watching the second House vote from the balcony of Representatives Hall. I saw Speaker Sytek stall the vote so that Shaheen and Reardon could call reps off the floor one-by-one into the adjacent cloak room to be bullied by Shaheen to vote against the income tax bill. It was a very long day with us working to shore up the vote during breaks against the advantages held by a speaker and a governor. Ultimately, Shaheen, Sytek, and Reardon narrowly prevailed. The income tax bill lost by a very small margin in the House.

Governor Shaheen easily won reelection on November 3, 1998. On November 9th, she asked the court to delay the deadline set for March 31, 1999, for two years. The court's response was unique in that the motion for delay was scheduled for argument in just two weeks, and the court handled it in a way that mirrored the US Supreme Court's handling of Little Rock's request to delay desegregation in the case of *Cooper v. Aaron*.

Both courts denied the requests for delay on the day after oral argument in an order personally signed by all the sitting justices. The New Hampshire justices cited *Cooper v. Aaron* in their order.

If it hadn't previously been clear, it was now. Our five justices looked upon their duty in the Claremont case as solemnly as the US Supreme Court had in *Brown*.

Years later, my wife Amy and I attended President Obama's inauguration in 2009. We chatted idly with the woman in front of us on that cold, sunny January morning. We were wearing our best ski clothes for this auspicious occasion. A friend of the woman in line in front of us walked up and joined her. Our line-mate turned to us and apologized for having her friend cut the line and said, "but we haven't seen each other since Little Rock." We realized that we were standing in line with two of the Little Rock Nine. Amy said, "Without you, we wouldn't be here. Do you have any more friends to add to the line?"

Just writing this passage makes me choke up at their accomplishment in Arkansas. When we got home, Amy bought an original edition of *Warriors Don't Cry*, a book about the valiant efforts of these women when they were teenagers. The book sits on my shelf as I write.

All right, then. No ABC and no delays. It appeared to be a good time for the state to start working with us.

Instead, since the court would not approve ABC as a permanent funding mechanism, Shaheen sought to pass a plan that assigned an arbitrary cost to adequacy and that used property tax rebates for five years before being phased out.

Back to court we went, to challenge the rebates and other aspects of the legislation, and the court shot down the phase-in. The Supreme Court issued its opinion on October 15, 1999.[197] The court noted it had been sixteen months since the decision in *Claremont* II and stressed that justices were not appointed to manage educational policy for the state. This, for us, raised a key point of tension.

We weren't asking the court to run the New Hampshire Department of Education. We were satisfied with the court's rulings, and had suggested that the court simply declare the system unconstitutional and then give the state time to devise a remedy. Now, however, we were past the deadline and there needed to be consequences—or at least backup procedures put into place. The state's failure to meet the *Claremont* II deadline had already resulted in every teacher in the state being pink-slipped; that is, officially warned they might not have a job in September.[198] New Hampshire's bond rating had also come under scrutiny.

As Shaheen's plans were shot down, we relied on our contacts across the country to understand what was happening in cases in other states at their remedy stages. Scott Johnson also compiled a list of all the possible remedies that we could request by reviewing the written opinions in all the school funding cases decided to date. John Tobin was by now the executive director of NHLA, a position he held for eighteen years. We asked John to compile a similar list of possible remedies from his legal assistance colleagues who tried complex welfare and housing cases.

Finally, we asked true New Hampshire school lawyers how education laws worked in a practical sense, looking for helpful options based on existing practices. Gordon Graham and Barbara Loughman of the Soule, Leslie firm and Jim Allmendinger of NEA-NH were a big help in this regard.

Poor Attorney General Phil McLaughlin didn't know what to do with us. He hired Hale and Dorr, a staid, big firm from Boston, to get some help. Like the assistant attorneys general before them, they were good lawyers, but their experience with school funding cases was limited and they didn't have our national network. The only state lawyer with school funding litigation experience by this point was Leslie Ludtke, and we just weren't seeing much of her after the *Claremont* II loss.

About this time, my law partner, Bob Stein, decided to start serving breakfasts of scrambled eggs and bagels at his home in the South End of Concord. His breakfast guests were Attorney General McLaughlin and me.

We established a weekly back channel and we kept our conversations secret, except that Phil felt compelled to keep Judy Reardon and the governor informed. For his part, Phil just needed some help. He told me hypothetically what the state was planning and I told him hypothetically how we'd respond. Bob mostly stood by with a congenial "master of the house" grin, more coffee, and an occasional dad joke.

In December 1999, the court finally took up the question of attorney fees for us. I was aware of the right to attorney fees in constitutional litigation and knew that some courts awarded fees in school funding cases, too.

New Hampshire, however, did not have a law that granted a right to fees. Our claims that our poor clients shouldn't have to pay our fees and we shouldn't have to work for free were just, but, again, we asked a lot of the court. However, the court came through for us. Although it wouldn't require the state to reimburse our expert expenses and most of our out-of-pocket costs, the court ordered the state to pay our reasonable attorney fees. This right has now been used by other litigants in New Hampshire arguing constitutional matters unrelated to education funding.

I didn't want us to appear greedy or engage in a full-blown evidentiary hearing to determine the amount of attorney fees. Months earlier, I had asked the lawyers in the case to give me a tally of their time. With huge discounts and an intent to compromise, we agreed among our team that we would settle for $750,000.

Phil and I met for breakfast. I convinced him to settle at $775,000 and the state cut a check to me. I shared the money proportionately with all the lawyers who worked on the case, except my old firm, which had traded away the right. At one point, I calculated that my current firm was paid about ten cents on the dollar up to nine years after the work was completed.

The *Concord Monitor* used the quick agreement on the amount of fees as an example of what could be done in the overall case.

> Andy Volinsky and Attorney General Phil McLaughlin have been arguing opposite sides of the Claremont school tax case for years now with Volinsky's team . . . beating McLaughlin's like a drum. But when the Supreme Court ordered the two of them to negotiate the Volinsky team's legal fees, they sat down together . . . and reached a reasonable conclusion that's in the public interest. Hmmm. Could there be a larger lesson in this?[199]

Phil and I continued to have breakfast at Bob Stein's house for a few more months, until Judy Reardon thought it was to her advantage to publicly reveal the meetings. She claimed the meetings showed how cooperative her office was with our team. Phil was embarrassed by the disclosure and I begged off further breakfasts.

Shaheen did not stand in any schoolhouse door blocking integration as the Southern governors did, but she and others were committed to undermining the *Claremont* II orders. One of the tactics she used was to punish the court system, headed by Chief Justice Brock, by cutting its budget by millions of dollars. The next governor, Craig Benson, kept the court system's budget reduced to the levels set by Shaheen. These cuts undermined efforts to modernize the court's computer system, which impacted the public, whose access to justice was compromised.

The Republicans now went after Chief Justice Brock as a complement to Shaheen's budget cutting by impeaching him for failing to report improper conduct by Justice Stephen Thayer. Justice Stephen Thayer, the one who hesitated to recuse himself from our cases, caused an uproar when it became public that he attempted to influence Chief Justice Brock's appointment of replacement judges to hear the appeal in Thayer's divorce case against Judith Thayer, the former chair of the state board of education.

Brock, who may have been distracted because his daughter was struggling with a cancer diagnosis, did not immediately report Thayer for the
clearly improper approach. Brock, however, had already made his decision
as to who was on the appellate panel, and he wouldn't budge.

No one challenged this sequence of events. Brock didn't report Thayer's misconduct and he should have. The clerk of the Supreme Court,
Howard Zibel, learned of Thayer's request and reported him to the committee on judicial conduct. The Judicial Conduct Committee asked the
attorney general to investigate.

Talk about a situation rife with personal and ethical conflicts. Brock
and Thayer worked together as justices, but Brock was the boss. Zibel, a
lawyer, managed the supreme court's clerical function, oversaw the staff,
and, at times, represented the court before the legislature. Brock was his
boss, too. Attorney General McLaughlin represented the state in all manner of appeals that were decided by the Supreme Court, including the
Claremont appeals.

We needed a functioning supreme court to advance our school funding efforts. The investigation of the court meant that Brock and Justices
John Broderick and Sherman Horton, who were also investigated, were
suspended from their work. Thayer was already removed from our case.
It was a mess.

A few months later, in mid-July 2000, the New Hampshire House
of Representatives overwhelmingly voted to impeach Brock for failing
to report Thayer and for other charges dreamed up from a ten-year-old
complaint about the chief justice interfering in a case that involved a
former senate president. The impeachment effort was led by then-chair
of the Judiciary Committee of the House, Henry Mock, a conservative
Republican rep from picturesque Jackson, New Hampshire. Mock had
been the state's chief Fish and Game officer before retiring and running
for rep. He was the state's top moose cop.

Although they wouldn't publicly admit it, we heard that Representative Mock and those who voted for impeachment viewed this as payback
for the court's rulings in the Claremont cases. The impeachment, the first
in the nation of a state's chief justice,[200] was a professional and personal

embarrassment for Chief Justice Brock, and there was nothing we could do about it. We had to stay away because our work on the Claremont case may have caused the House to impeach.

Justices John Broderick and Sherman Horton were ultimately not charged with misconduct by the House. Justice Thayer resigned his position on the court in a deal with the attorney general to avoid criminal prosecution.[201]

Brock went to trial two months later, on September 18, 2000.[202] The trial, per the New Hampshire Constitution, was conducted before the New Hampshire Senate and lasted three weeks. A two-thirds vote for conviction was required, and the impeachment failed to gain even a simple majority. Beverly Hollingworth, as the Senate president, presided over the proceedings. She retained George Mitchell, Maine's former US senator, to advise the New Hampshire Senate.

Brock soon returned to active judicial status, and the judicial conduct rules about recusals were clarified. School funding disputes again proceeded apace.

When left to its own devices, the legislature was sure to screw things up. This time, Senator Fred King, a Republican from Colebrook, proposed a funding bill that relied, in part, on local monies to pay for adequacy. Like the Augenblick formula, the amount of money in the Fred King proposal was determined by how much the state could pay without changing New Hampshire's tax system.

King's bill became the subject of yet another request for an advisory opinion. Again, the court was clear:

> The bill contains legislative findings which acknowledge that its proposed funding mechanism would rely, in part, upon local property taxes to pay for some of the cost of an adequate education. These findings directly contradict the mandate of Part II, Article 83, which imposes upon the State the exclusive obligation to fund a constitutionally adequate education. The State may not shift any of this constitutional responsibility to local communities as the proposed bill would do.[203]

We made one more trip to the supreme court, this time about accountability, in September 2001. We argued that it was fine to adopt the Minimum Standards for School Approval and other goals and standards, but nothing was in place to help school districts that failed to meet these guidelines. The court issued its ruling on this final challenge on April 11, 2002, and found that accountability was both required and missing from the current system.

We'd been at it for more than a decade, with eight different trips to the New Hampshire Supreme Court in the Claremont case and another four trips on requests for advisory opinions. The one advisory opinion not mentioned to this point was when the Shaheen group tried to transfer responsibility for deciding how to pay for adequacy to a public referendum. The court concluded that New Hampshire is not a referendum state and sided with us.[204]

Regarding accountability, the court split three to two. The majority decision was written by Justice James Duggan. Before he was appointed to the bench by Governor Shaheen, Jim Duggan was the head of the appellate defender program that was housed at Franklin Pierce School of Law, where he also taught criminal law and procedure.

Just reading Justice Duggan's history of the litigation makes you tired. We, and the court, had been through so much. Thankfully, the court held firm. Accountability standards were meaningless if they could not be enforced. The majority opinion cited relevant cases from Ohio, Massachusetts, New Jersey, Tennessee, and Kentucky. The review of the state's proffered accountability standards was careful and detailed, and the standards were found lacking. Citing a 1991 case, the court wrote, "If the State cannot be held accountable for fulfilling its duty, the duty creates no obligation and is no longer a duty."[205]

The definition of adequacy was obviously deficient, and the majority of the court said so. Back to the drawing board for the state. But now we had two dissenters. Justice Linda Dalianis, a conservative Republican from Nashua, and Justice Joe Nadeau of Dover. Shaheen had promoted Nadeau from the New Hampshire trial court. We knew to be wary of Nadeau because Bill Shaheen's father and Nadeau's father had a long history of political connection in Dover, where Bill's father was the sheriff and Joe's father was a state liquor commissioner. Eventually, Justice Nadeau was promoted to chief justice in 2005, and the Supreme Court, under his leadership, administratively closed our case in 2006, meaning we lost our direct route to the Supreme Court. Any future complaints would be litigated through a more cumbersome process that started in a trial court.

Justice Nadeau gave me a very hard time throughout the argument of the accountability case, claiming I would never be satisfied and telling me every case must close. It was almost like Judy Reardon was now on the bench. I probably shouldn't have, but I told Nadeau he was jeopardizing the credibility of the court. This was all broadcast live on New Hampshire's public television station, another first for our state.

Phil McLaughlin argued for the state. He got a hard time from everyone and had few answers. At one point, Phil said the definition of adequacy was complete and Chief Justice Brock—whom Phil had previously investigated—pulled out a recent edition of *New Hampshire Business Magazine* and read a quote from the new state senate president that the definition of adequacy was incomplete.

For once, the *Union Leader* agreed with us in an editorial. They wrote that Phil looked like a "law school intern" but, more importantly, wrote, "although we think *Claremont* II was wrongly decided, the plaintiffs are correct that the state has not yet complied with that ruling. . . . [I]t doesn't make any . . . sense to declare the obviously unresolved case resolved."[206] Of course, the *Union Leader* wasn't being kind to us. This was part of their argument for a constitutional amendment.

About this same time, progressive reformer Arnie Arnesen and Republican political strategist and former attorney general Tom Rath publicly opined about Shaheen's performance with respect to school funding. Tom and Arnie were brutal in assessing Jeanne Shaheen's work to solve the school funding crisis. They concluded that she led the state during consideration of the most important issue in fifty years and spent not one whit of her own political capital to solve it, despite being elected with a 70 percent majority in her second election. The bottom line from

Rath and Arnesen was that you shouldn't run for governor just to get the license plate.

In 2002, Jeanne Shaheen ran for the US Senate against former governor John H. Sununu's son, Congressman John E. Sununu. State Senator Mark Fernald, who was part of the income-tax-supporting group in the legislature, ran against Craig Benson, the wealthy businessman who cofounded Cabletron. This set up an election season in which the Dems ran a tax-opposed Shaheen with an income tax proponent, Mark Fernald. Both Shaheen and Fernald lost.

Craig Benson was more accustomed to being the CEO of a publicly traded company than a governor, and made a number of enemies while in office. In the 2004 election, he lost to former Democratic Party chair, lawyer, and businessman John Lynch.

Dennis Murphy, the NEA teachers' union lobbyist, worked closely with Lynch's campaign, and asked me to brief Lynch about the *Claremont* litigation and the constitutional principles the Supreme Court established. John Lynch is a likeable, very smart, and sophisticated lawyer, politician, and businessman who clearly understood what the court decided. Lynch won election and became a popular four-term governor with lots of political capital. Instead of using it, he worked in secret to undermine the *Claremont* principles.

On October 21, 2011, Lynch unveiled yet another constitutional amendment and announced that he'd been working with a team of lawyers for seven years to get it right. Lynch secretly negotiated with Republican House Speaker Bill O'Brien and Republican Senate President Peter Bragdon in his effort to amend *Claremont* out of the Constitution.

The team of lawyers with whom Lynch worked was a virtual murderers' row when it came to *Claremont*. The team included Chuck Douglas, Eugene Van Loan, Bill Ardinger, and Martin Gross.[207] Chuck Douglas was Governor Mel "Ax the Tax" Thomson's legislative director and lawyer. Thomson nominated Douglas to the New Hampshire Supreme Court, where he served for eight years, until 1985, when he resigned at age forty-three. Douglas then ran for Congress. After one term, he was defeated by Dick Swett, the son-in-law of California congressman Tom Lantos.[208]

Some commentators thought Douglas's four marriages undercut his family values platform.[209]

Martin Gross was a Shaheen confidante, apologist for the wealthy towns, and, coincidentally, the lead lobbyist for the state's largest utility, whose property tax fortunes rose or sank in sync with the wealthy towns.

Supported by this team of amendment super-lawyers, Lynch put together one of the most disingenuous approaches to amending the state constitution since *Claremont* II was decided. The amendment looked like it was doing good, even though it wasn't. The amendment gave the legislature "full discretion" to "mitigate" disparities in funding by being "reasonable." Reasonableness, of course, is the equal protection standard that limits court review of state action. The amendment would have removed the New Hampshire Supreme Court from the picture, but didn't explicitly say so.

Fortunately, Lynch was too cute by half. Even though he negotiated the amendment proposal with Speaker O'Brien and President Bragdon, Lynch released the proposed amendment without coordinating with his Republican counterparts. Speaker O'Brien would have none of it. O'Brien scheduled a hearing in the House one month after Lynch's announcement of the amendment, and then a vote eight days later. Lynch's amendment had to achieve a three-fifths vote in the House and Senate to get on the ballot. The amendment lost in the House 264-114, and it never made it onto the ballot.[210]

The property-wealthy towns also worked to undermine the *Claremont* decisions by filing to stop a statewide property tax. Led by Portsmouth mayor Evelyn Sirrell, the property-wealthy towns filed suit, claiming the state lacked a uniform, statewide system of assessing the value of property. The suit also asked the court to reverse *Claremont*. In a turn of phrase that would have made Robin Hood angry, the handful of wealthy communities proudly called themselves "donor towns."

Superior Court Judge Dick Galway found that assessment practices were not standardized, and also that some communities ignored the constitutional requirement to update the value of properties every five years. Galway rejected the claim that it was wrong to have taxpayers contribute to a state system of education.

The case was appealed by the state to the New Hampshire Supreme Court and, in a decision issued in early May 2001, the court reversed Judge Galway.[211] The Court concluded that exact equality in valuations wasn't required, and put the burden on Sirrell to prove there was an intentional scheme of systemwide underassessments. As there wasn't proof of a grand plan to cheat the wealthy towns, Sirrell lost.

It helped that the state had already begun to standardize valuation practices under new Revenue Administration Commissioner Kevin Clougherty and Len Gerzon, who was appointed to oversee a new professional standards board for tax assessors. Lynch sought out Clougherty because he had been the chief financial officer for the city of Manchester and before that the state's deputy treasurer. The work by Gerzon, Clougherty and others remains in place today and is valued by all in the field of property tax assessing. The court also made clear that the Department of Revenue Administration must oversee and enforce the requirement for updates every five years.

By 2005, the sufficiency of education funding was back before the New Hampshire Supreme Court, but not by us.[212] Middle-wealth communities challenged the state's approach to adequacy and sought to increase funding.

Our clients were the poorest communities in the state, where major employers failed and no one at the state bothered to help with economic development to replace them. Middle-wealth communities were largely Republican-leaning suburban bedroom communities with modest, non-retail businesses and middle-income taxpayers. Since *Claremont*, the amount of money the state contributed increased from about 8 percent to 17 percent. But New Hampshire was still last in the nation at 17 percent, and its failure to fully address the problem caused it to expand and affect middle-wealth districts.

Superior Court Judge William Groff found the system unconstitutional and the state appealed. The Supreme Court issued its decision in September 2006, in what is called the Londonderry case.[213]

By a three to two vote, the Supreme Court agreed with Judge Groff that the state had not yet carefully defined the components of a constitutionally adequate education. This was nine years after *Claremont* II.

The decision, which was written by Justice Gary Hicks, ended with a succinct three-sentence statement of what was required of the state. Hicks wrote:

> Any definition of constitutional adequacy crafted by the political branches must be sufficiently clear to permit common understanding and allow for an objective determination of costs. Whatever the State identifies as comprising constitutional adequacy it must pay for. None of that financial obligation can be shifted to local school districts, regardless of their relative wealth or need.[214]

Hicks ominously noted, "Deference, however, has its limits."[215] Justice Duggan dissented, in part because he thought the court should do more. Dick Galway, now a supreme court justice, also dissented because he thought the court should do less.

By 2006 or so, Tom Connair and I had been working on school funding in New Hampshire for sixteen years. All of the lawyers and advocates had lost time with our families to work on school funding issues. We were part-time school funding lawyers and public-school advocates who relied on other parts of our jobs to earn a living. This meant we worked many weekends and nights.

This isn't a note of complaint. But it puts in context my upset when legislators approached me at times to say they had just voted for a school funding plan that was unconstitutional, but that they knew I'd fix it by going to court. These very words were said to me by a senior Democratic senator from the seacoast and an experienced state representative from the southern part of the state. The fact that they both expressed the same reliance on me to fix things made it clear this was a sentiment shared among the Democrats. Their comments remind me of Phil Ochs's lyrics about liberals.[216]

In 2016, I was elected to the New Hampshire Executive Council, a state board of directors meant to keep our governors in check. Pittsfield superintendent John Freeman invited me to a non-public school board meeting to consider filing another school funding suit.

I met with the Pittsfield School Board even though I could no longer sue the state. I suggested that before the board looked for another lawyer to bring suit, it should have a public meeting to explain how school funding works. Community input about a new suit could then be solicited.

I asked John Tobin and Doug Hall to join me for the meeting, and we asked the head of the School Boards Association to spread the word in case other districts wanted to join a possible suit. The auditorium was packed.

Doug created a slide presentation and I painted lines on an eight-foot scrap of wood to show the relative financial strength of school districts across the state based on their equalized property values. Claremont and Berlin had lines at the bottom of my stick. Manchester was just above these cities. Portsmouth was at the tippy top of the stick. Moultonborough was five lengths higher than my stick would reach. I just couldn't figure out how to fit a stick that long in the back of my truck.

We called our seminar "Ed Funding 101" and suggested audience members ask candidates what they would do to improve funding for the state's poorest districts. We eventually presented more than seventy seminars—just three old warriors, a PowerPoint slide deck, and an eight-foot stick of wood. It made a difference. Informed voters asked hard questions of candidates, and some heat was taken off school boards, who did not control how money was raised.

School funding was back on the front burner and being talked about. There was a Republican governor, but the House and Senate were purple/blue.

It was Doug Hall's idea to convince the House to form a committee to study school funding and to allow it to hire a consultant. The 2020 Commission to Study School Funding was born and Bruce Baker and the American Institutes for Research were hired to consult. We thought we were in a good position as the commission was chaired by a Democratic rep, Dave Luneau, from Hopkinton, and his fellow rep from Hopkinton was deputy chair.

The commission did some good work. It established that the average cost of special education was about four times the cost of regular education, and that the state defrayed only a fraction of the cost. The commission also suggested funding parameters for teaching kids who live in poverty or are learning English. It also concluded that Manchester spent $10,000 too little on each of its children. This amounted to more than a $130 million shortfall, and it showed.

Governor Chris Sununu's appointee to the commission was Republican tax lawyer Bill Ardinger. As a result of Ardinger's role and weak leadership by Luneau, the commission did not explore alternative funding sources for education beyond the existing state property tax. An income tax was never mentioned. It was as if the Pledge was a member of the commission.

The commission's report is published at the website for the University of New Hampshire's public policy school.[217] Ultimately, the commission supported a targeted or foundation aid approach, which is not legal under our supreme court's interpretation of the New Hampshire Constitution. It's a throwback to Lynch's constitutional amendment.

The commission's report recounted some of the efforts to respond to the *Claremont* rulings. The Federal Reserve Bank of Boston did a better job in its report, cataloguing 150 pieces of legislation since 1998, including personal income taxes, state property taxes, securities transfer taxes, taxes on capital gains, consumption taxes, and business taxes that were dedicated to funding education; not to mention many efforts at constitutional amendments.[218]

A small group of lawyers, public-school advocates, parents, and educators over a period of fifteen years faced these challenges, relying on the justice of the cause, some creativity, and, at times, a scrap of wood. We married an aggressive litigation strategy to public engagement and political work. At least we'd moved beyond selling brownies to support our suit.

While not achieving all our goals, we had a record of putting education on top of everyone's list of most important issues facing the state. State funding also went from about 8 percent to 23 percent. We won in court, repeatedly, and got more money coming into local education budgets. Regular people also began to understand how limited school boards were in controlling spending that was dictated by state and federal laws while local taxpayers were stuck with the bill. New challenges caused by vouchers and charter schools, however, diverted limited public monies to private ends. The unfairness of our tax system also continually made public education a target for libertarians and other anti-taxers.

Was it time to head back to court?

PART THREE

Present Day and the Future of Education

Chapter 10

Don't Make a Fuss

A friend of mine calls me Sisyphus—always rolling the rock of school funding uphill.

In 2020, I ran for governor. I had been on the Executive Council for four years and thought I'd accomplished what I could. I also wanted to make room for someone else. I knew Chris Sununu, who would run to keep the governor's seat, and saw that he had done some good things but also many very bad things.

Perhaps his worst act as governor was to appoint Frank Edelblut to be education commissioner. Edelblut, who had no academic or professional preparation for the job, opposed public education, much like Trump's Education Secretary Betsy DeVos. Edelblut's only qualification was that he narrowly lost to Sununu in the Republican primary for governor in 2016 and Sununu didn't want him to resurface as a primary challenger.

Although I greatly exceeded expectations while rejecting the Pledge, I lost by a couple points in the primary to a party insider who was the Democratic leader in the Senate. The insider who beat me then lost to Sununu by thirty points and dragged down the whole ticket, giving Sununu a clean sweep of the House, Senate, and Executive Council. So much for the benefits of taking the Pledge.

Two events that occurred during my campaign provide lessons for advocates in other states. They're about how entrenched majorities—this time Democrats—justify inaction.

The Next Day Problem

The first involved Judy Reardon, who sadly passed away in 2022. I invited Judy to lunch as I was preparing to run for governor. I figured, know the opposition.

Judy immediately asked if I would take the Pledge, and when I said I would not, she launched into what she called the "next day problem."

Any major social change, including a change to a tax system, will run into this problem.

The next day problem is what happens on the day after you pass an income tax, or some other socially important program, and before the benefits of the change take hold. The campaign to throw income tax supporters out of office begins immediately. Because the benefits of a tax change take time to be felt, you are left with all grief and no improvement when you arrive at the next election, which in New Hampshire occurs every other year. The income tax supporters, according to Judy, then lose the next election, power changes hands, and the income tax gets repealed before anything changes. The only thing accomplished is to lose the next election. This is what Reardon claimed motivated Jeanne Shaheen as governor.

Let's put aside that Shaheen won her re-election by seventy points and was not in danger of losing anything. Even the Republican Party chair thought she'd win re-election by a landslide no matter what she did on taxes. The answer to the next day problem is to plan for it.

Part of the planning, according to former senator Below, involves showing respect for voters and doing the work to inform them. Below co-sponsored an income tax bill as a rep before running for a state senate seat that had been held by Republicans since the Civil War. Against all advice from party elders, Below embraced the income tax and took the time to explain it, in person and in a long and complex mailing, to all the voters in the senate district, not just to the Democrats. He approached Republicans and Independents because he knew the entrenched Dems did not have his back. Below's willingness to be bold in talking about his values allowed him to win his senate race.[219]

Below was also specific. If the average family in his district at the time earned $90,000 a year and had a $200,000 house, he explained that they would pay $2,480 in income taxes, but their real estate taxes would drop by about $2,000. The increased tax burden was also offset by a federal tax deduction, and the system that resulted would better support education—reducing the costs of crime, delinquency, and unemployment, and be more sustainable and fairer.

Doug Hall also won election as a state rep after publicly supporting an income tax. Even though he lost some votes by supporting an income tax, getting things done was why he ran for office. Like Below, he carefully explained his support for the tax and how it applied to local voters. Taking explanations to the local level is what is necessary to pass reform.

Doug didn't put it this way, but his and Below's efforts to go right to voters and explain tough issues rather than run away from them reflect the political approaches of Senator Paul Wellstone and, later, Bernie Sanders. Wellstone was called a "liberal." Bernie Sanders is a "progressive." Both spoke directly about compassion for one another and both showed respect for voters by detailing problems and suggesting specific solutions.

Their stump speeches were amplified by armies of volunteers who engaged local voters in "deep canvassing." Rather than simply counting votes to determine who is for or against you, deep canvassing focuses on winning hearts and minds through engaging voters in real conversations about the problems they face.

Wellstone beat a very popular, multi-term incumbent to become a senator representing Minnesota. Sanders walloped his competition in the 2016 New Hampshire Presidential Primary, Hillary Clinton, and won the New Hampshire Primary again in 2020. In 2016, I was Sanders's New Hampshire lawyer. In 2020, Senator Sanders endorsed me in my run for governor. So did Ben and Jerry, who also named an ice cream flavor for our campaign. It was called Volinsky's Courageous Crunch. (It was vanilla with little cinnamon hearts and busted up Million Dollar Bars to reflect my strong stance on campaign finance reform.)

Planning to change how revenues are raised also requires good timing. There are better and worse times to effect change, even though the need may be constant.

Time the change from a regressive tax system based on property taxes to a progressive system with an income tax when there is a surplus in your state's budget. The budget surplus can be deployed to reduce property taxes while the systems for implementing an income tax are put in place.

The budget surplus can be naturally occurring or result from ticking up existing state taxes in preparation for a major change. Paying attention to federal tax changes that can cause a state surplus is important, too. The federal tax changes in 2015 that caused businesses to onshore their revenues, for example, also increased state business tax revenues in following years, and would have presented an opportunity for change in 2017. Unfortunately, Chris Sununu was governor, having beaten Democratic nominee Colin Van Ostern in the same year that Trump beat Hillary Clinton in the presidential race.

The income tax can also be phased in while the property tax is phased out. This is different than the unconstitutional phase-in that Governor Shaheen proposed. A legal phase-in involves treating all taxpayers equally. Start an income tax at a very low rate for everyone and increase it over a few years as the state property tax is reduced. The danger of this approach, as Doug Hall has pointed out, is that it leaves more time for complaints.

Another option is to use the state's bonding capacity to reduce state property taxes at the outset and use income tax revenues to pay off the bond debt. Timing is important to take advantage of favorable interest rates for the bonds. The use of a bond also makes it harder to reverse course after the change because the bonds must be paid off.

Meeting the Enforcers

The second event that is worthy of mention involved Kathy Sullivan, the long-time former state Democratic Party chair and continuing Manchester Democratic enforcer. Kathy was law partners with the gadfly amendment advocate Gene Van Loan, and with Mike Tierney, who is introduced later in this chapter.

She also was responsible, during my gubernatorial race, for the opposition research on my prior law cases that was used to try painting me as illiberal. The effort didn't work because she and her team didn't understand the complex cases she chose to challenge. They were not anti-consumer or anti-taxpayer. She had more luck challenging a candidate in the 2024 primary who had once lobbied for drug company Purdue Pharma.

No one supports the Pledge more than Kathy Sullivan and, as a *Union Leader* columnist, she controls the official Democratic Party position in Manchester. When I participated in the Manchester City Dems "Meet the Candidates" Gubernatorial Forum during the spring of 2020, Sullivan didn't miss the chance to ask about my refusing to take the Pledge. She asserted it was "disrespectful" to other candidates for me to refuse to take the Pledge. In the forum and around town, she whispered this sentiment to other candidates, telling them that my opposition to the Pledge made them look bad.

My lesson was to be wary of those within your own party who are more afraid of being shown up than showing up to accomplish needed change. I also learned that I should have expected this challenge and worked to defuse it before it was deployed by arguing that I was willing to take the heat for others and they could follow my lead. I wasn't trying to make them look bad.

The Fair Funding Project

While I was involved with my gubernatorial race, John Tobin and Doug Hall approached the largest charitable foundation in New Hampshire to convince its leaders to fund an ongoing advocacy campaign around school funding. John, Doug, and I had provided an Ed Funding 101 briefing for the leadership of the New Hampshire Charitable Foundation that was well received. The leadership of the foundation had changed since the *Claremont* days when the foundation was too timid to help with litigation. The current executive director, Dick Ober, and his board were now willing to assist in changing public opinion even if the effort involved litigation.

The Charitable Foundation provided multiyear funding for a new 501(c)(3) start-up to focus on changing public attitudes about how New Hampshire funds its schools. They were to be the public engagement leg of the three-legged stool. The New Hampshire Fair Funding Project was created (fairfundingnh.org).

Although the Project has had growing pains, it has continued to educate and has become a reliable partner under its new director, Zack Sheehan. The Ed Funding 101 forums have been updated and continue under the banner of the Fair Funding Project. The Fair Funding Project has a research component that produces actionable research on important subjects. They also coordinate with other education-focused organizations in the state, including Reaching Higher New Hampshire (reachinghighernh.org), an organization that Bill Duncan helped to form that focuses on conducting and disseminating high-level research and careful analyses.

Still missing was a direct political effort. Even though nonprofits can do some of this work, the New Hampshire nonprofits were too gun-shy to take on the politicians most opposed to change by recruiting candidates to run against them.

New Litigation

We thought the litigation issue would be solved by a new lawsuit filed in 2019 by a group that did not include John Tobin, Doug Hall, or me. The lead plaintiff for this group was the Contoocook Valley School District, or ConVal.

In March 2019, ConVal, which includes Peterborough, sued the state, challenging its approach to adequacy and using many of the arguments we perfected in the Claremont cases. Kathy Sullivan's firm was the regular counsel for the school district and her partner, Mike Tierney, was assigned the case.

Although we heard about another suit being organized, we didn't know about the ConVal suit until we read a press release about its filing. John Tobin, Doug Hall, and I had barnstormed the state only two years before this suit was filed with our Ed Funding 101 seminars. We would have been happy to provide insights learned from our long experience, but no one asked.

The suit proceeded in fits and starts. Eventually, ConVal won a ruling from a trial court in Rockingham County and that ruling was appealed to the New Hampshire Supreme Court, which reversed the win and ordered a full trial. This was in 2021.[220]

We approached Tierney about his case after the remand and learned he had no need for our assistance, and that he had dropped claims we thought critically important. Tierney wanted to focus the ConVal case exclusively on the amount the state assigned to cover the cost of basic adequacy. The state set the cost at about $4,000 per student and the

ConVal plaintiffs' sole purpose was to raise that amount to $10,000. The average per-pupil cost at the time, including the cost of buildings and transportation, was about $22,000 per pupil.

The claims that *ConVal* dropped involved a tax claim and a challenge to the additional amounts that the state provided to adequately fund education for children who live in poverty, are learning English, or who qualify for special education. The dropped tax claim involved the state again using a special rebate as part of the statewide property tax for education, even though the rebate was condemned by the New Hampshire Supreme Court in 1999 in the context of Shaheen's ABC plan.

The extra aid for the children who lived in poverty, were learning English, or who qualified for special education was called "differentiated aid." These extra increments were arbitrarily set and were not sufficient to cover the additional costs of educating these children. For example, in 2022, the state provided an extra $2,100 for every child who qualified for special education and related services, but the average cost was more than $25,000 per child and expensive out-of-district placements could run as high as $300,000 per child.

When we learned that *ConVal* would not include these important challenges, we organized our own suit with taxpayers as our only clients. We argued that the state's failure to fully pay the costs of adequacy shifted costs to local taxpayers. Local education taxes were imposed at widely varying rates, in violation of the New Hampshire Constitution's tax clause that required state taxes used to pay the state's duty to be uniform across the state. It was Count VI all over again.

The two suits are proceeding as of fall 2024 and the differences in tactics between Tierney's team and our team are a laboratory for two very divergent approaches to how to change public policy. Tierney, the lead lawyer in *ConVal*, doesn't believe in coordinating litigation with public messaging or engaging in politics. We include these approaches to advocacy in our efforts, often working with the Project that Doug and John helped found. Tierney has also gone to extreme measures to keep the two cases apart. He's formally opposed consolidation of the cases and interfered with our access to school witnesses who are involved in his case.

The appeal that ConVal lost in 2021 would have benefitted from public and political organizing. The failure to focus attention on the court or to adopt approaches like our "more juice" strategy made it easier for the court to reject ConVal's claims. By then, as well, Pat Donovan, who had defended the state in the *Claremont* II trial, was a justice on the supreme court. Tierney did not move for him to step off the case, and Donovan wound up writing the decision reversing Tierney's win. Donovan's opinion for the court also invited the state to seek reversal of the *Claremont* cases when *ConVal* came back on its next appeal.

John Tobin and our new school funding colleague, Natalie Laflamme, submitted a friend-of-the-court, or amicus, brief as part of the *ConVal* appeal. They did so to make legal points that Tierney missed, and to show the court the number of school districts challenging the state's funding effort was not limited to a handful of middle-wealth school districts centered around Peterborough. The effort was important but of less impact, because it was not done in coordination with Tierney; it was done despite him.

John and Natalie's clients included twenty-five additional school districts and the New Hampshire School Boards Association. Among the twenty-five additional districts were a couple of the original *Claremont* plaintiff districts (Claremont and Pittsfield) and the three largest school districts in the state (Manchester, Nashua, and Concord). Finally, the school districts participating as amici included the hometowns of the two reps who commonly chair the Education Committee in the New Hampshire House, depending on which political party is in power: David Luneau, a Democrat from Hopkinton and Rick Ladd, a Republican from Haverhill.

Natalie Laflamme is a story in herself. She is from Berlin and had to overcome the severe limitations of that city's underfunded school system. She epitomizes the child who overcomes adversity and deserves credit for doing so, as Justice Marshall noted in the *San Antonio* decision. She was Berlin High School's valedictorian. She attended Georgetown as an undergrad and Duke for law school. She then clerked at the New Hampshire Supreme Court before entering private practice.

John and Natalie also appended a detailed study to their amicus brief by John Freeman, the superintendent of Pittsfield. The study explained what would happen to Pittsfield's schools if the $10 million actually spent was reduced to the $2.6 million in funding the state provided as adequacy. The bottom line was that the Pittsfield School District would be unrecognizable. The state's reply brief backhandedly complimented the amicus brief for this inclusion because Tierney had not submitted a similar study.

Not being able to coordinate with the ConVal case, we filed our suit in Grafton County in 2022. Our lead plaintiff, Steve Rand, is from Plymouth, New Hampshire, and we sought consolidation with the ConVal case for trial. Other than the exchange of expert reports and expert depositions, we offered to waive all other discovery so that the *ConVal* schedule would remain intact. We also promised to refrain from filing common pretrial motions to keep the ConVal case on track for trial. Tierney joined the state in opposing our entry into "their" case, and the request to consolidate was denied.

We had help in our case from a national law firm's New York office. White and Case offered us pro bono assistance if we would allow their junior lawyers to gain experience as litigators.

Two young White and Case lawyers, Michael Jaoude and Morgan Brock-Smith, traveled from New York for our first court argument, in which we sought an injunction against the use of the statewide property tax with its preferential rebates for taxpayers in wealthy towns. Before our case was called, we watched the presiding judge, Lawrence MacLeod Jr., berate an appointed lawyer and his young client for not understanding the terms of a plea bargain. The judge was not in a good mood. Eyebrows raised all around, Michael and I repaired to a conference room to tighten his planned argument.

Michael Jaoude's presentation was well-rehearsed and rearranging his planned argument was not a problem. His arguments were logical and tight and made our points while answering all the expected objections. It was fun to watch this young lawyer from New York in his trim gray suit making arguments on our behalf in a courtroom that had a faint smell of the manure recently spread on the neighboring field.

Assistant Attorney General Sam Garland presented the state's case. He is a very good young lawyer who knew his arguments well, even though he speaks too fast. Also, Sam had been up all night with his young children, who had conjunctivitis. Sam shared this last tidbit so we wouldn't shake hands as we introduced ourselves.

The first hearing was about our request to enjoin the state's property tax, called the SWEPT (StateWide Education Property Tax) because it included the prohibited rebate provisions. If granted, our injunction would stop the use of the SWEPT unless the provisions were dropped. Ultimately, the decision to grant or deny a preliminary injunction is discretionary. We had answers for all the state's legal arguments, but knew, ultimately, the judge would likely hesitate to enjoin an entire state tax.

Our goal, however, wasn't necessarily to win this motion. We wanted to begin to educate the presiding judge about the unfairness of the system. Any recognition of this unfairness by the judge would be a good start for us. This was also part of our public engagement strategy.

The Fair Funding Project posted our pleadings on their website and echoed our arguments in their presentations. We wanted the general public to understand that taxpayers who lived in a few towns with high property wealth got special treatment in the form of a discount on their education taxes that most taxpayers did not get. We hoped that, armed with this knowledge, voters would complain to their elected officials.

Even though we filed our motion for preliminary injunction more than a month before the hearing, a lawyer for a group calling themselves the Coalition Communities 2.0 contacted us the night before the injunction hearing to ask if he could participate in our case, representing intervenors who were a group of the wealthy school districts. The state readily agreed to the intervention request because it gave their arguments two bites at every turn. We declined and told the Coalition Communities to file a formal motion, which they did, an hour before our hearing began. Judge MacLeod either did not know of the intervention motion or chose to ignore it, and the coalition's lawyer did not participate in the hearing.

Wealthy Portsmouth also sent its deputy city manager all the way from the seacoast to monitor the proceeding, more than a two-hour drive each way. The lead organizers of Coalition Communities 2.0 were the elected and appointed leaders of the city of Portsmouth, a traditionally

Democratic, beautiful city on New Hampshire's small coast. Portsmouth and the coalition were spending substantial sums derived from their local taxes to hire lobbyists and lawyers to protect their advantages. In time, the chair of the coalition switched from Portsmouth to Waterville Valley, New Hampshire, the home of the Waterville Valley Resort and ski area, which is owned by concerns controlled by the Sununu family.

Judge MacLeod did not ask a single question. He basically didn't say anything during the hour-long argument, and had the appearance of a deer in headlights.

Five days later, MacLeod issued an order recusing himself from the case because he had a conflict of interest based on his ownership of real estate in Lebanon, New Hampshire. Most judges own a decent house or two in a well-off community with good schools. Did this mean no judge could sit on our case? Was MacLeod, who verbally abused the young lawyer in the case before ours, just the bully whose bluff had been called?

Rather than consolidation with *ConVal*, an early ruling, or a start on educating the presiding judge, the recusal meant our case went back into the queue for reassignment to another judge. This time, the chief judge of the superior court stepped in and reassigned us to the *ConVal* judge. We had our special assignment to the most knowledgeable judge on the bench, albeit in a separate docket from the ConVal case. The two cases still weren't consolidated. The recusal and reassignment also meant we lost our May 2023 trial date in Grafton County and had to settle for a September date in Rockingham County.

Months later, we repeated our arguments for an injunction against the SWEPT before Judge David Ruoff in Rockingham County Superior Court.

Michael Jaoude and Nick Roberti traveled to New Hampshire from New York. Sam Garland repeated his opposition and, this time, John-Mark Turner from the Sheehan Phinney law firm got a speaking part for the intervenor Coalition Communities 2.0. At times, he undercut the state's candid admissions that things weren't quite right with the SWEPT and, at other times, he joined their positions. Although Judge Ruoff appeared sympathetic, he thought ultimately that our injunction request now being heard in November was too late in the tax setting and budgeting process that ran from April to the next March. We were mid-tax year and halting the process would cause more trouble than it was worth.

We did, however, take comfort that we began the process of educating the judge, who noticed there really weren't any factual disputes about our claims of an unconstitutional advantage for the wealthy communities. The SWEPT challenge also generated good press about tax inequities in our state.

We decided to convert our motion for injunction to a motion for summary judgment on the SWEPT issue, and refiled. We did this because of Judge Ruoff's comment that the facts were not in dispute. If facts are not in dispute, a motion for summary judgment allows the judge to decide the legal issues without the need for a formal trial. While a summary judgment motion wouldn't immediately stop the use of the SWEPT, there would be no need for a trial; the judge could issue a declaration that the SWEPT as implemented with the preferential rebates was unconstitutional. A tax declared unconstitutional does not have a long life because the taxpayers who must pay it will loudly complain and avoid paying the unconstitutional tax.

We also were scheduled for trial before Judge Ruoff in September 2023, and *ConVal* was scheduled for five months earlier. This wasn't as good as being in the same trial. But the trial dates gave us the advantage of first watching the state's case in *ConVal* and gave us the opportunity to fill in gaps that we expected the *ConVal* plaintiffs to leave.

John and Natalie, who attended most days of the ConVal trial, essentially took over press relations for the ConVal team with the help of the Fair Funding Project. They explained what was happening during the trial to Project staff, who issued press releases and posted pleadings on their website. The press was extensive and mostly favorable, and resulted from the Project's media efforts. Tierney and his staff only dealt with the press on an occasional basis.

We met weekly with the White and Case lawyers via Zoom as we prepared our case for trial and monitored *ConVal*. Wendy Lecker from the Education Law Center was now a vital part of our team. I developed a great relationship with the team of lawyers at White and Case, especially with Michael Jaoude and Nick Roberti, both of whom took the "gastronomic tour" of Concord-area diners, Bagel Works and the local ice cream shop. The tour ended at our house.

Though both Michael and Nick are very good lawyers, they didn't know the practice of law in New Hampshire or the personalities and proclivities of the judge and opposing lawyers. This is really the job of local counsel, and I happily fell into this role. Eventually, Michael left White and Case for another firm in his hometown of Buffalo, New York, and continues to participate as pro bono counsel from his new firm. Alice Tsier is now our pro bono lead counsel at White and Case.

We added John Freeman and Corinne Cascadden as experts to our team. John is the retired superintendent of Pittsfield who did the financing study that John Tobin and Natalie Laflamme referenced in their amicus brief. Corinne retired as Berlin's superintendent. "Mrs. Cascadden," as Natalie refers to her, was Natalie's elementary school principal. We also added a longtime special education administrator, Jen Dolloff, and a school counselor, Annette Blake, as fact witnesses so that we could explain the insufficiency of the state's funding for special education and student support services.

Our case was starting to shape up for trial when, without warning, Judge Ruoff issued a stay of our proceedings so that he could focus on deciding the merits of the ConVal trial. There is nothing more deflating for trial lawyers than to gear up for trial and suddenly be told to wait, but that is exactly what happened. We waited, and waited, and waited.

Meanwhile, the Fair Funding Project continued to give its seminars about school finance across the state, and organized a special seminar for the lawyers to explain what was happening in the ConVal and Rand cases. Michael Tierney was invited and participated. More than a hundred people attended.

On November 20, 2023, Judge Ruoff issued an order on our SWEPT challenge along with the final order in the ConVal case. Our SWEPT motion was granted, and the administration of the SWEPT was declared unconstitutional. Judge Ruoff allowed the current tax cycle to finish and deemed the SWEPT unusable—unless the preferences were discontin-ued—beginning with the next tax year on April 1, 2024. In *ConVal*, Judge Ruoff ruled that the amount assigned to defray the cost of base adequacy, now $4,100, was constitutionally deficient and the correct number is at least $7,356.01, a statewide increase of half a billion dollars. The press covered the rulings extensively, putting school funding back front-and-center just before the new legislature convened.[221]

Judge Ruoff's *ConVal* ruling relied extensively on the testimony of Kim Rizzo Saunders, the superintendent of the ConVal School District. Judge Ruoff credited most of Rizzo Saunders's testimony. For example, he accepted the superintendent's testimony that she could not hire first-year teachers to fill every teaching position in her schools and then hire a new bunch of first-year teachers every following year, even though this was part of the basis for the state's lowball adequacy number. The state's salary estimate, on which it built its cost model for base adequacy, used the salary of a first-year teacher, $38,867 in 2021–22. This approach was declared unreasonable by the judge, who said an average salary of more than $60,000 should be used. He discounted the average salary by 5 per-cent to reflect that some districts paid more than was necessary to gain a local competitive advantage.

Judge Ruoff also credited Saunders's testimony that health insurance benefits, predominantly paid by the employer school districts, were nec-essary to attract and retain teachers, but reduced her estimate slightly. Some understandable gaps in Rizzo Saunders's testimony led the judge to reject a few of her suggested costs, for example, for food services. The judge accepted that hungry or malnourished children could not learn, but was unconvinced that schools couldn't break even on food costs. So he rejected including food service costs in the calculation of base adequacy.

Ultimately, the judge rejected the state's argument that setting a cost figure was a job exclusively for the legislature. He wrote, "the Court . . . is cognizant that school funding is a complicated and politically-charged issue, with a history that suggests some level of judicial intervention is now necessary." Treading lightly, however, his ruling was that base ade-quacy was *at least* $7,356.01. The legislature could go higher.

The state and intervenors moved to stay both November 20 rulings, which Judge Ruoff denied. Appeals followed and the New Hampshire Supreme Court stayed both decisions while it considered the appeals. We moved to recuse Justice Donovan and to also recuse Chief Justice Gordon MacDonald.

Donovan denied the recusal, in part because the *ConVal* plaintiffs failed to challenge him. MacDonald also declined to step aside even though he was the attorney general actively representing the state during much of the early *ConVal* litigation, which overlaps with ours. MacDonald and I also have a history. I blocked his appointment to the supreme court because he had no judicial experience, was strongly opposed to reproductive rights, and had a close affiliation with an extreme Koch-network-funded enterprise called the Josiah Bartlett Center. MacDonald got to decide his own recusal, which is the custom, and declined to step aside.

Two other points about the appeals: the state challenged *ConVal* for not addressing differentiated aid in the same trial as base adequacy was considered, and the state now seeks to reverse the underlying *Claremont* rulings, as Justice Donovan had invited.

The cases on appeal will not likely be decided until the spring or summer of 2025, after full briefs are submitted by all parties and an oral argument has taken place. A number of non-parties have also weighed in. A group of right-wing Republicans filed an amicus brief seeking an outright reversal of the *Claremont* and *Londonderry* decisions. The Republicans, however, blew their deadline and the Supreme Court informed the ConVal team that it need not reply. Sadly, senior Democrats who served on the funding commission seek to resurrect the failed Augenblick approach. The ACLU and NEA filed a brief that argues the importance of respecting the thirty-year precedent of *Claremont* as did the League of Women Voters.

Meanwhile, Judge Ruoff has lifted the stay in our case and scheduled us for trial in September 2024. True to form, Tierney remains uncooperative, going so far as to ask Judge Ruoff to quash trial subpoenas we issued to witnesses who testified in the ConVal case. He also claimed it would be unethical for us to talk with the witnesses outside of a formal proceeding.

Chapter 11

Politics, Learning the Wrong Lessons, and Some Successes

Even before the November 20 rulings, the Fair Funding Project began to press for legislative action. Their goal was to find friendly legislators to submit legislation that could start the discussion about how to improve education funding by introducing legislation favorable to us. Doug Hall masterminded the plan. Doug and the Project knew it would take more than one legislative session to overcome resistance by Democrats, and they suspected the Republican majorities would be outright hostile to our cause.

Game-changing legislation requires sustained effort over years to make a difference. In New Hampshire, repealing the death penalty and acknowledging Martin Luther King Jr. took decades of lobbying and public advocacy to gain traction. The 1964 Civil Rights Act, signed by President Lyndon B. Johnson, also took years of planning. It likely had its start sixteen years earlier, when Hubert Humphrey of Minnesota advocated for a desegregation plank in the Democratic national platform during his first term as a US Senator in 1948.

The Project made its first approach to Democratic House leadership in July 2023. The House leaders were chosen because the House had almost an even split between Republicans and Democrats, while the Senate was firmly under Republican control. Also, appropriation bills originate in the House. House leaders in attendance included the Democratic leader and his deputy and the leading reps on the House Education and Finance Committees.

John Tobin and Doug Hall, as Project founders, and Zack Sheehan, as the Project's executive director, told the assembled group to expect rulings in the ConVal case in the fall, and alerted them that the SWEPT was also in trouble and may be found unconstitutional. They asked the leaders to help by sponsoring bills to respond to the likely rulings that would start the conversation in the legislature.

The Democratic leaders were unmoved. They didn't want their members "on the record" with respect to bills that required additional revenues. The best the Democratic leaders would do was agree to a bill to once again study special education costs. I think Zack Sheehan, who previously worked as House staff, was deflated by the refusal of the House Democratic leaders to do anything.

The House Democratic Leader, Matt Wilhelm from Manchester, and his deputy, Alexis Simpson from Exeter, are bright and energetic leaders who will lead the New Hampshire Democratic Party into the future. They've done well to rebuild the House after its disastrous 2020 losses, but they've learned the wrong lessons from those losses.

The 2020 elections occurred during the COVID pandemic. The Democratic Party leaders before Wilhelm and Simpson enforced a ban on house-to-house canvassing. In fact, one young rep, Josh Adjutant, was called on the carpet by the party's chair for ignoring the ban and actually campaigning door-to-door. The Republicans, who didn't believe in taking precautions against COVID, campaigned in every way possible to engage voters.

The results showed that engaging voters made a difference. It also didn't help that the Democratic Party's preferred gubernatorial candidate got hammered by Chris Sununu, losing by more than thirty points.

The lesson party leaders took from 2020 was to be more like the Republicans and Sununu in opposing taxes. The lesson they should have learned was about the need to extensively engage voters about your plans so you can convince them your party will make things better. Wilhelm and Simpson showed they could lead campaigns based on the careful engagement of voters when they took back a number of seats in the 2022 election. Unfortunately, they didn't learn from their own success. Rather than offer a clear alternative agenda to the Republicans, they acted as if being Republican-lite was the key to their success.

Rather than accept the leaders' rejection of Zack, Doug, and John, I suggested that Zack and I contact members of the House Progressive Caucus whom I had helped get elected. The Progressive Caucus is small, but when the split between Dems and Republicans is tiny, their votes count. House leadership needed their cooperation on bills outside the realm of education.

A young rep from Peterborough, Jonah Wheeler, quickly agreed to sponsor a bill to raise base adequacy from $4,100 to the $10,000 amount demanded by the *ConVal* plaintiffs. Jonah graduated from ConVal High School just a few years ago. He should have been approached by Tierney and the *ConVal* crowd, but they refuse to do this kind of advocacy.

The chair of the Progressive Caucus, Cam Kenney, agreed to sponsor two special education funding bills. One bill simply boosted differentiated aid for special education from $2,100 per student to $25,000 per student, representing the approximate average cost paid by local property taxpayers for each student who qualifies for special education, after allowing for federal contributions. Of course, we didn't expect the state to pay $25,000 per student regardless of the cost of required services. We just wanted to put the $25,000 figure of unreimbursed expense into the public's dialogue on school funding.

Cam sponsored a second, more important bill that had the state act as an insurer paying all special education costs not reimbursed by the federal government from a central kitty funded by the state. We were prepared to have this bill amended to have the local districts pay a small portion, say 10 percent, as a "deductible." The bill addressed the problem of children with special needs being transient and local districts being unable to plan for expenses associated with children joining their schools without prior notice.

The best thing about Cam's sponsorship was that he received special education services as a child and had an IEP through elementary school. He is now serving his third term in the House while finishing law school at the University of New Hampshire. He is a great example of the impact of well-funded special education programming.

Finally, a veteran legislator and personal friend, Marjorie Smith, agreed to sponsor a bill to fix the constitutional infirmities that we predicted Judge Ruoff would find with the SWEPT. Given her experience and gravitas, Marjorie, a leading Democrat, was able to line up

Republican co-sponsors from property-poor towns for her bill, giving it the best chance of passage of the handful we encouraged.

In January, we learned that the leaders' refusal to bring forward any funding bills wasn't quite accurate. The Democratic Education Committee leaders, supplemented by a rep on the Finance Committee, had their own bill, HB 1586. This bill focused on providing targeted aid to the neediest districts. It would have protected New Hampshire's tax structure and would have furthered the state's two-tiered approach to funding education. The wealthy towns with high property values were free to spend at will the revenues they easily raised for education. The poor towns had to beg the state for handouts. It was the Augenblick formula all over again.

HB 1586 was co-sponsored by Democrats Dave Luneau, Mel Myler, Mary Heath, and Dick Ames, all of whom attended the July 2023 meeting. All are very senior and influential representatives. None of them have had serious challenges to their reelection in years.

Reps Luneau and Myler represent Hopkinton, a bedroom community for Concord and Manchester. It has good schools and very high property taxes that create a dramatic split between the high-income doctors and lawyers and the regular working people who live there.

Mary Heath is from Manchester, where the schools are handicapped by both a structural low-property-value problem and the self-imposed harm resulting from its tax cap. Heath is a former state education official and Kathy Sullivan's sister.

Finally, co-sponsor Dick Ames was tax counsel to the Massachusetts state revenue department before moving to New Hampshire. He represents Jaffrey, a small rural community in the southwestern part of the state with high property taxes and modest educational outcomes.

HB 1586 is a twenty-seven-page monster of a bill that is driven by the Pledge. It rearranges the state's spending to better target limited monies to poorer districts. This is an admirable goal, but in the thirty-year scheme of efforts to improve school funding, it represents a step backwards. It's a little like rearranging the deck chairs on the *Titanic*.

The targeting of aid, rather than paying the full cost of adequacy, also disregards the requirement established in the *Claremont* and *Londonderry* cases that the state must pay the *entire* cost of an adequate education with state tax monies. Under the bill's approach, the state does not pay for the cost of a constitutionally adequate education in all school districts, and property taxes to pay for the state's portion of adequacy are not imposed uniformly across the state. Both of these approaches violate the New Hampshire Constitution.

The bill also switches the definition of adequacy from an inputs model that considers how many teachers, the cost of materials, and the like to a funding model based on outputs that focuses on the results achieved by a school or a school district. Educational adequacy, in the proposed bill, requires school districts to achieve the average state scores in terms of school attendance, high school graduation rates, and assessment outcomes. In effect, HB 1586 adopts a "successful schools" model that, as the name implies, requires all schools to achieve an average level of success.

In theory, the approach is not bad. The problem with this aspect of the bill, however, is it does not identify the components of successful schools that make them successful. Nor does it determine the cost of and fund the necessary components. The bill just accepts the current level of funding and distributes more of it to the poorer districts without ever stopping to determine if the redistributed funds are enough.

HB 1586's failed effort at redistribution can best be understood with an example. It's as if the state knows a good school costs $25,000 per pupil to operate but distributes $4,000 per pupil to every schoolchild in the state on an equal basis. This is, in fact, the current state funding distribution.

HB 1586 changes the distribution formula so that children in poorer districts get $6,000 each and children in wealthy districts get $2,000. The problem is that $6,000 is still insufficient to pay for a constitutionally adequate education. Leading elected officials settling for this "less failing" approach is why there is so much trouble making improvements in our state and elsewhere. Failing by a smaller margin is still failing. School funding challenges are rife with litigation resulting from legislators failing to appropriate funds to meet the requirements of laws they put on the books.

The legal problems with HB 1586 also require a constitutional amendment for the bill to become law. One need only compare the proposed legislation to the three-sentence summary of what is required of the state that was written by Justice Hicks in the 2006 Londonderry case. Contrary to what Hicks wrote, HB 1586 doesn't allow for a common understanding of what is required for an adequate education because the components of what makes schools successful are not identified. The bill doesn't require the state to pay for all of the cost of adequacy. And it doesn't employ uniform tax rates.

As if the constitutional problems aren't enough, HB 1586 doesn't identify a sustainable state funding source. When targeted aid plans like this one don't identify a clear revenue stream, or are built on a rickety one, any economic downturn causes the legislature to reduce the targeted aid funding. The need for the funds, however, doesn't go away. Children still need to be educated, even in difficult financial times. The pressure relief valve in these instances is to shift more of the state's funding responsibility to the local property taxpayer, and this hurts residents of the poorest districts the most. HB 1586, it turns out, is just a differently dressed Augenblick approach to school funding.

How did these leading Democrats go so wrong?

The answer became clear when the bill was presented to the House Education Committee on January 10, 2024. As prime sponsor of HB 1586, Rep. Luneau came down from his committee seat to present his bill from the witness seat. But instead of presenting, he called Bill Ardinger to sit beside him and present the bill to the committee in his place. The moment was breathtaking.

Bill Ardinger's name has been mentioned a few times. He is the best Republican privilege-protecting tax lawyer in the state. He's drafted constitutional amendments to reverse the *Claremont* decisions and personally worked to stymie virtually every attempt to expand New Hampshire's tax base to better fund state services, including education.

In his testimony before the Education Committee and in a later published editorial, Ardinger claimed that New Hampshire has high average spending on public education and suggests the committee take credit for New Hampshire's good average outcomes. Bill's entreaties are a clear effort to overlook the fact that New Hampshire's well-funded public schools drive assessment scores up. The *average* score is therefore misleading because it hides the results from failing districts. Ardinger's focus on overall spending also obscures how uneven our state's funding really is and doesn't even begin to address the taxpayer inequities.

Of course, that's the point. Preserve the tax system at all costs.

If the New Hampshire Supreme Court ever reverses *Claremont*, they'll do it in a way that approves targeting aid because they can use the cover that Luneau and Ardinger have provided. The court will insist that the state share in funding education at some level and pronounce the importance of education. But they'll find the determination of *what level of funding* is purely a legislative function. The guardrails provided by the *Claremont* and *Londonderry* decisions that require the state to fund all of the cost of adequacy will be removed. In doing so, the court will return our state to the Augenblick era.

We'll have Ardinger, Luneau, and the HB 1586 co-sponsors to thank if this happens.

HB 1586 was voted out of committee with a recommendation to send it for further study, and the full House supported that recommendation. The other bills were either amended beyond recognition or simply voted down. We have much work to do, but the standards set out in the Claremont and Londonderry cases allow us to engage in litigation that keeps these issues in focus. These cases provide guardrails we can use to challenge funding proposals. And we're not going away.

Personal Stories

Some people ask why I have stayed with this issue for so long, because it is very frustrating. John Tobin, Doug Hall, Tom Connair, and others have worked on school funding as long as I have. Our colleagues in other states have endured decades of litigation and political nonfeasance. Each of us has our own stories and our own motivations.

I began the journey because of my own school experience. I went to a grossly under-resourced and poorly managed high school marked by racial tensions. I am the only one of four siblings to go to college. My siblings could have been the subject of Jonathan Kozol's books because they were so poorly served by the schools we attended.

Allenstown Elementary School bathroom used as one-on-one tutoring space for children who required special education services.

I knew that I escaped and have always felt a responsibility to do something about it. Although I didn't know I would fall into school funding work, I went to law school to make a difference, not to get rich. Arpy Saunders's invitation at the local YMCA pointed the direction for this journey.

Once I started, I couldn't turn away.

There's also this photo from our 1996 *Claremont* trial that still haunts me. It's of a bathroom in Allenstown, one of the districts we represented. There's the typical metal stall you see in public restrooms in the center of the photo, but you notice there's a poster on the stall. It's a poster of a wolf. Then you notice at the very bottom of the photo, there's a child's desk.

This isn't a bathroom. It's a classroom in a poor school that couldn't afford a real classroom. Not only that, but the children who learn here require special education services.

In this struggling school, the most stigmatized and most often bullied children are those who receive special education services. And the most challenged of these—the ones who require one-on-one tutoring—are pulled out of class to be taught in the bathroom.

You want to know why I keep going after all these years? It's this photo and the shortchanging of student needs that it represents.

I've learned that getting angry isn't enough. The photo scares people of privilege because it means that something must change. Building power over time is the only way to force that change. This book is one small effort to build power by combining public engagement and political efforts with a careful litigation strategy.

The news about school funding isn't all bleak. The results of litigation aren't all delayed beyond utility. Even in New Hampshire, the state's share of public-school funding has increased from 8 percent when we started the *Claremont* litigation in 1991 to 20 percent in 2024.

Success in Pennsylvania

Pennsylvania shows us that successful litigation remains possible and, at times, legislatures listen to courts. A coalition of six school districts, school organizations, and parents sued the commonwealth of Pennsylvania in

2014 in a case called *William Penn School District v. the Pennsylvania Department of Education*. The plaintiffs finally made it to a four-month trial that began in November 2021. They were represented by the Education Law Center, the Public Interest Law Center in Philadelphia, and a contingent of pro bono lawyers from O'Melveny and Myers, a national law firm.

On February 7, 2023, the trial court issued a more than seven-hundred-page order finding the Pennsylvania school system unconstitutional for insufficient and inequitable funding.

Pennsylvania funds 38 percent of the cost of K–12 public education with state money. Only six states have a smaller state share—New Hampshire is the lowest funding of the six. The limited state funding makes school districts reliant on local property taxes; the litigation showed a $4,800 difference in per-pupil funding between the 20 percent wealthiest slice of school districts and the 20 percent poorest slice. Further, more than half the state's Black students and 40 percent of Latino students attend school in the 20 percent lowest wealth districts in the state. Pennsylvania has funding targets set by the legislature, and the trial court found that the state underfunds its own targets by $2,000 per child on average, a shortfall of $4.6 billion each year.

As the plaintiff coalition reports, "This underfunding isn't some abstract principle. It determines which kids get what they need, and which kids do not. It is teachers and counselors. Nurses and librarians. Computers and STEM labs. Art and music. Smaller class sizes and remedial help for children who are struggling to learn. In Pennsylvania, local wealth shapes everything kids need in school to reach their full potential."[222]

The under-resourced and racially troubled school district where I attended high school in Pennsylvania has a $4,000 per student adequacy funding deficiency, placing it among the worst-funded school districts in the state. The district now has almost six thousand students. Its minority enrollment is 40 percent and poverty remains high. More than 16 percent of the students drop out.[223] Nothing much, it appears, has improved since I finished high school fifty years ago, but the *William Penn* case should help, especially considering the state's response.

The Pennsylvania legislature had until July 2023 to appeal and chose not to. Instead, the Republican-majority legislature embarked on a process involving ten public hearings across the state that resulted in the release of a basic education funding package in January 2024. While the plan is not everything the litigants hoped for, they stated on their website that "[t]he Commission set a measured and meaningful target for what it would cost for every school district to provide the comprehensive, effective, and contemporary public education required by the constitution and affirmed by the Commonwealth Court's decision. The $5.4 billion target for adequate funding statewide would increase total public education funding statewide by 17% over seven years."[224]

The plan, with annual funding infusions for the lowest-wealth districts of approximately $200 million, began immediately. Ironically, the school funding changes were the subject of advocacy by the Republican-led legislature. Democratic Governor Josh Shapiro wasn't a major player in crafting a response to the lawsuit.

Croydon Stands for Its Children

Public support and public engagement for education also can be successful on a smaller scale, as proven in little Croydon, New Hampshire, where Libertarians associated with New Hampshire's Free State experiment tried to stealthily eviscerate the school district's budget. Commitment to public education can rally a town. People everywhere need a cause around which to rally. Croydon is an example of how, after being thrown a curveball, things should work.

Croydon has fewer than eight hundred residents, and is in Sullivan County, one of New Hampshire's poorest counties. Croydon is one of the communities targeted by the libertarian Free State experiment that seeks to have twenty thousand Libertarians move to New Hampshire and take over its government.[225] Free Staters run for local boards and for state rep—and don't always disclose their extreme libertarian bent or affiliation with the experiment. Sometimes they run as Republicans and sometimes as Democrats. There's a bit of a parlor game in parts of New Hampshire focused on outing Free Staters.[226] Matthew Hongoltz-Hetling's book, *A*

Libertarian Walks into a Bear: The Utopian Plot to Liberate an American Town (And Some Bears), provides a very readable description of a predecessor experiment called the "Free Town Movement" that failed, focused on Grafton, New Hampshire, population 1,385.

Croydon engages in New Hampshire's two-centuries-plus experiment in direct democracy. While voters elect school board members to execute policy and run things on a day-to-day basis, they also debate and directly vote on the school district's budget at a district meeting. This exercise in democracy generally works well. Think of lots of flannel shirts, coffee, and cider donuts with children scampering about the meeting place, often a school gym. Usually there is debate about hiring a new teacher, buying new materials, or something similar. The problem is that sometimes more devious or ideological sorts hijack a meeting.

Jody and Ian Underwood are two of the Free Staters who moved to Croydon, in 2007. Both are highly educated. Jody became the chair of the school board. Ian became a member of the board of selectmen. They were, as a result, influential in the management of the town and of the tiny school district that teaches Croydon's fewer than eighty children.

Croydon has one K–4 elementary school. After elementary school, Croydon children have a choice of attending middle school and high school in the neighboring Newport School District or the nearby Sunapee School District. Croydon pays the necessary tuition.

The 2022 school district meeting, with just one substantive vote to adopt or reject the well-vetted school budget for the next year, was to be a "sleeper," except to Ian Underwood.[227]

Underwood considered the school budget to be more of a ransom demand than a proposed plan to meet the town's education needs.[228] The Underwoods don't believe in government, so monies collected in taxes are not freely given, and ways to starve government of resources are always of interest.

After the budget passed, Ian moved to reconsider the budget vote and to cut the school budget from $1.7 million to $800,000. He thought the children in town could be quasi-home-schooled in Prenda pods. Prenda is a tiny company pushing an untested innovation called "microschools," which are run by "guides" who aren't certified teachers. As Prenda touts on its website, you can be a guide if you're a parent, church leader, soccer coach, or businessperson. Teacher training and experience are absolutely unnecessary.[229]

Ian Underwood figured the town could form a handful of Prenda pods and cut the per-pupil spending down to $10,000, less than half the state average. Of course, he hadn't worked out how to split up the children into pods or where those pods would meet or who the eight guides would be. He also hadn't bothered to ask the parents of the eighty children what they thought. He just made the motion and the thirty-four voters still in attendance slashed the school budget. With the new school year beginning in less than four months, everything would change for Croydon children because Ian Underwood resents government.

Jody Underwood knew of her husband's plan but did not inform the people of the school district, who had elected her to watch out for their children's education.[230]

Under New Hampshire law, reconsideration of Croydon's vote required a petition of half the registered voters in the district. The effort to organize the re-vote was undertaken almost immediately. The effort was a strong example of grassroots organizing and democracy in action.

The lead organizer was a resident who taught in another district, Amanda Leslie. Angi Beaulieu, a former school board member, and Hope Damon, a dietitian, were also among the organizers who formed We Stand Up for Croydon Students to support the re-vote. John Tobin provided free legal advice. You can see him smile whenever he talks about consulting with the Croydon group.

The effort to obtain signatures for a re-vote was like a school bake sale on steroids, and a new meeting was called.

Three hundred and seventy-nine people showed up for the re-vote, establishing a quorum. All but two voted to reinstate the budget as it was recommended by the school board, before Ian Underwood's slash-and-burn amendment.

The fallout from the Underwoods' underhanded maneuver was that Hope Damon, one of the We Stand Up for Croydon Students organizers, was elected to the New Hampshire House of Representatives in the next state election. She now sits on the House Education Committee, where she can work to protect school funding. Ian Underwood resigned as a selectman. Jody Underwood was defeated in the next school district election by Angi Beaulieu, another organizer.

I should mention that Jody and Ian Underwood are also big fans of Education Commissioner Frank Edelblut. Both fawned over Edelblut at his 2017 confirmation hearing and used their positions in Croydon as their credentials. Neither disclosed their association with the Free State experiment or Commissioner Edelblut's support for the experiment.

Pittsfield and Money Well Spent

There is also clear, practical evidence that money well spent can and does make a difference. Pittsfield provides our example, but the principle applies anywhere.

John Freeman has shown what well-thought-out, and funded, interventions can accomplish. John had been the principal of Pittsfield Elementary School for nine years when he was promoted to superintendent in 2008. Pittsfield, as previously mentioned, is small, poor, and rural.

As principal, John knew that there was little money for teachers' professional development. The elementary school had poor literacy scores on assessment tests and every teacher appeared to be on their own in battling the problem. With just a little money from the school district, John fashioned a homegrown professional development program that coordinated the efforts of the school's teachers, resulting in remarkable improvement. In June, a year after the coordinated efforts were put in place, one experienced teacher remarked to John, "We were holding them back."

The next year, with a small state grant, John did the same thing by coordinating the grade-to-grade elementary school math curriculum, and again assessment scores improved dramatically.

In 2009, as superintendent, John wrote an application for funds from the US Department of Education's School Improvement Grant (SIG) program, which was focused on each state's five lowest-performing high schools and five lowest-performing middle schools.

Pittsfield won grants for its high school and middle school because both were atrociously bad.

The SIGs had lots of requirements, which included that John fire the principal of the middle-high school and revamp the district's teacher evaluation program. Each SIG was for three years, at $600,000 per year, at a time when Pittsfield's budget was just shy of $10 million. The 6-percent increase in funding for three years resulted in a huge improvement. Student achievement soared so much that an undersecretary of the US Department of Education visited the district to check that its reporting was on the up and up.

In the second year of the School Improvement Grant, John learned of a Nellie Mae Foundation grant program that was open to every high school in New England with at least 40 percent free and reduced-priced lunch participation. Pittsfield won a one-year planning grant for $200,000. If the planning period was successful, Pittsfield would be eligible for a six-year implementation grant focused on personalizing student learning.

The Nellie Mae Foundation, founded in 1998, is the largest New England-based foundation committed to improving education. Its goal is that "[a]ll youth have access to excellent and equitable public education that prepares them to succeed and thrive in the community."[231] At the time of John Freeman's interaction with Nellie Mae, its executive director was Nick Donohue, a former education commissioner in New Hampshire.

Pittsfield won the only planning grant in New Hampshire. In part, John used it to form a community advisory council that was drawn from the greater Pittsfield area, which he stretched to include Concord. The advisory council included students, parents, faculty, staff, local community leaders, the local police and fire chiefs, and Tom Raffio, the CEO of Delta Dental. Delta is a successful insurance company; Tom, its CEO, was a former chair of the New Hampshire State Board of Education. Lynn Kilchenstein was also invited to join the council. She was the president of the local community college. The membership of the council fluctuated between twenty-five and thirty members. Locals called this shadow school board "the Nellies."

The council operated through subcommittees that gathered information about successful schools. They visited charter schools and small high schools in New Hampshire, New York, Maine, and Massachusetts.

The extensive planning effort led to Pittsfield winning one of the four multiyear implementation grants. The other winners were school districts in South Portland and Sanford, Maine, and in Winooski, Vermont. Unfortunately, leadership changes in the other districts undermined their success, but John Freeman remained in Pittsfield for the entire grant period. The first three years of the implementation grant were fully funded, and then funding tailed off for the next three years.

Again, one focus on which John insisted was consistent districtwide professional development. All the educators got on the same page and stayed there. The results were phenomenal. Ninety percent of the grant's benchmarks were met. Assessment scores improved and dropout rates declined.

John knew that academics improve when students are engaged, particularly in school leadership and in extracurricular programming. New student clubs were funded if students could find an advisor. John still considers watching student presentations at national leadership conferences about student empowerment a highlight of his career.

In the ten years that John was superintendent, the school district's budget increased by a total of 3.5 percent, much less than the rate of inflation, while the district achieved remarkably because of the grant funding. The district's results were so remarkable that visitors interested in Pittsfield's "magic sauce" came in order to learn about the district's operations. One group of almost thirty people came from a Chicago charter school. The charter repaid Pittsfield's hospitality by sending enough deep-dish pizza to feed the entire middle-high school. Governor Maggie Hassan and New Hampshire Education Commissioner Virginia Barry also visited, Barry on several occasions.

Although repeatedly invited, Commissioner Frank Edelblut never showed up.

John Freeman's experience shows what good leadership and a small, about 5 percent, sustained increase in funding can do. Unfortunately, the town's school board concluded it could not raise taxes to replace the grant funding when it ended, and again Pittsfield's programs and outcomes declined. There are now few extended learning opportunities. Extracurricular activities were cut. There is no foreign language teacher.[232] Music and art are almost nonexistent. There is, however, a school funding lab that engages with the legislature to advocate for change. The lab is the brainchild of social studies teacher Logan LaRoche.[233]

Chapter 12

Funding Solutions

Before I describe my preferred funding solution, let's identify the best place to triage limited funds. I start here not because New Hampshire has a limited capacity to address school funding but because advocates in other states may face fiscal capacity problems. Better deploying modest funds is also a good way to build credibility and break the hold of the naysayers who, in New Hampshire, support the Pledge.

Early Childhood Education

The best place to start is with little kids, by getting them ready to learn before kindergarten. It makes sense for the children and is a sound investment.

According to New Futures, a not-for-profit advocacy group in New Hampshire, "Ample evidence demonstrates that access to pre-kindergarten, particularly for low-income families, has lasting positive impacts on children beyond the early years, including higher rates of high school graduation, fewer suspensions, and fewer experiences with juvenile incarceration."[234]

Citing the Annie E. Casey Foundation, a leader in the education field, the New Futures report continues, "Early education programs are invaluable in preparing children for elementary school. Such programs are associated with improved academic achievement and emotional and physical health. Preschool also plays a key role in reducing academic and health disparities by socioeconomic status and race. Yet, high-quality early childhood education is inaccessible to many Americans—especially low-income kids and children of color."[235]

Daycare and early childhood education costs are also a burden to every family, even the ones who can afford it. Our three grandchildren and their parents have relevant experience. The costs of daycare and early childhood education for their three young children in 2023 was $4,150 each month. Our youngest grandchild was not yet two and attended a small home-based daycare. Our next youngest grandchild was almost four and attended a traditional, center-based daycare. Their older brother, our eldest grandchild, was in a public bilingual pre-kindergarten, and the city where they lived charged for that schooling on an income-based sliding scale.

In New Hampshire, as the New Hampshire Fiscal Policy Institute notes, "childcare is a major household expense for families with children. For New Hampshire families with both an infant and a four-year-old in center-based care in 2022, the total average annual price of tuition was $28,340. A New Hampshire household with children that earned the median family income of $119,983 in 2022 would have needed to spend approximately 24 percent of their income on childcare."[236]

In 2024, President Biden authorized a tiny pilot program that creates a circuit breaker for childcare expenses that kicks in for lower-income families when daycare and early childhood education hit 7 percent.[237] The pilot program is a good start, but the next president must expand the effort.

The cost of daycare and the cost of early childhood education is worth the investment. A failure to treat these programs as a public good means many families miss out and communities are required to bear later costs that could have been mitigated with early investments. The Maine Chamber of Commerce paper on education previously cited references Nobel Laureate James Heckman as concluding that every dollar invested in early childhood education returns $1.13 in benefits.[238] The RAND Corporation conducted a study in 2017 of the financial benefits of instituting a specific pre-K program in New Hampshire focused on children living in families at up to three times the federal poverty level (at the time, $57,288 for a one-parent, two-child family). Forty-five percent of the four-year-old children in the state would have been eligible for the program. The study concluded that every dollar invested would return two dollars in later cost savings related to better educational and health outcomes and in future earnings.[239]

Funding daycare and early childhood education also has an economic development impact because parents are able to work. The New Hampshire Fiscal Policy Institute estimates 16,000 parents are out of the New Hampshire workforce for lack of childcare.[240] An analysis in 2021 estimated that New Hampshire households collectively lost between

$400 million and $600 million in wages due to unavailable childcare.[241] Another study put the national loss in earnings, productivity, and tax revenues at a post-pandemic $122 billion.[242]

This isn't just a rural or small-state problem. New York City Mayor Eric Adams has caused an uproar by cutting the budget meant to fund universal education for three-year-olds. Former Mayor Bill de Blasio instituted the universal program for four-year-old children, and it was due to expand over time. More than 80 percent of families in New York cannot afford full-time childcare.[243]

In 2021, Congress passed $21 million of pandemic aid for early childcare and education. It made a difference, but as these one-time funds run out, states must figure out how to continue funding streams, even in Republican strongholds. For example, Missouri's Republican Governor Mike Parson has proposed $130 million for childcare for families of modest means.

The New Hampshire Department of Education claims on its website to be "a committed partner supporting statewide efforts for children and schools to promote a seamless system between PreK and K-3 education."[244] The state's financial commitment doesn't match its rhetoric.

New Hampshire is one of only six states in the nation that doesn't fund public preschool programs for four-year-olds with state dollars.[245] Federal monies are used to fund recognized programs like Head Start, but these programs are limited by income guidelines and geographic reach. The income guidelines exclude middle-class families. Head Start does great work, but New Hampshire, unlike other states, does not leverage that work.

In 2019, the federal government awarded $44.3 million for Head Start in Maine, and Maine state government added $3.1 million, enough to serve five thousand children with the combined state and federal funding.[246] Vermont, a state with half of New Hampshire's population, serves almost six thousand children with state and federal funding. Every school district in Vermont has public pre-kindergarten.[247]

New Hampshire serves fewer than two thousand children through its federally funded Head Start program,[248] and there are no state funds added to expand services. Setting a goal of state-funded public pre-kindergarten in every school district in New Hampshire would make a huge difference to New Hampshire families.

Eight states either have or are working toward universal pre-K access for four-year-old children. These are California, Colorado, Hawaii, Illinois, Michigan, New Jersey, Vermont, and New Mexico. New Jersey's leadership in access to early childhood education began with the litigation in the *Abbott* cases that required preschool for the *Abbott* districts as a remedial measure, and its success spread to the rest of the state.[249]

The federal government could also do better. The Biden administration increased Head Start monies by $1 billion in 2023, but half of this money went to cover a 5.6 percent overdue cost-of-living increase for personnel, and the level of staff compensation for Head Start programs remains a recognized concern.[250] Paying Head Start lead teachers the same as their counterparts in public kindergartens is the goal and requiring them to be similarly qualified is the benefit.

The New Hampshire state early childhood education program is led by Deputy Commissioner Christine Brennan. Commissioner Brennan joined the department in 2017. Before that, she spent three and a half years as principal of the Beech Street School in Manchester, where she was previously the assistant principal. The Beech Street School serves a population of about six hundred children in grades K–5.

At the time she left Beech Street, after being passed over for the Manchester superintendency, about 70 percent of Beech Street's enrollment was non-White. Ninety-three percent of its children were eligible for free or reduced-price meals. Thirty-one percent of the students were learning to speak English. Shortly after she left, Beech Street was designated a Comprehensive Support and Improvement school by the US Department of Education because it was in the bottom 5 percent in terms of achievement of the Title I poverty schools in the state. During Brennan's tenure at Beech Street, third- and fourth-grade proficiency in reading and math on state assessments was in the single digits, far from the state's goal of "100% reading proficiency by the end of third grade."[251] Brenann's promotion to deputy commissioner by Governor Sununu and Commissioner Edelblut is more evidence of their lack of commitment to public education.

The road to building a more competent and equitably funded system that also considers economic development concerns should start by expanding pre-K programming to all children regardless of the family's income. New Hampshire should take its Head Start money and leverage it to include benefits for the children of middle-class families.

Funding for Special Education

The next consideration for funding reformation should be the system by which our state pays for special education and related services. We argue in the *Rand* suit that special education services are necessary for some children as a bridge to the general education curriculum, and a constitutionally adequate education and should therefore be funded by the state. The state's inclusion of an increment of adequacy funding for special education costs in state statutes, albeit at an arbitrarily low level, is an admission that we're right.[252]

Special education costs are repeatedly cited as the second-most significant driver of increased school budgets. Again, New Hampshire should do more than just fix funding for special education services, but fixing special education funding is a place to start and fodder for advocates in other states with limited resources.

New Hampshire's special education system creates winners and victims. Too often the victims are children.

About a year after *Claremont* II was decided, a desperate school board in Unity, New Hampshire, where Barack Obama and Hillary Clinton kissed and made up after the 2008 primary, asked Scott Johnson and me to attend their school district meeting to explain how special education funding worked. The school board was afraid the voters would vote down the entire school budget because special education costs had skyrocketed. The personal safety of the school board members and the new family in town with high-needs children was also a concern because the costs of special education were breaking the local school budget.

The key point the voters needed to understand was that the services that were required for the children of this family were mandated by state and federal laws, but state and federal funding left a huge gap to be filled by local monies. Most importantly, the residents needed to understand the town's budget problems weren't the fault of the school board or the family in question. Apparently, Scott and I were successful because the budget passed and the threats of violence subsided.

How do we fix the special education funding problem?

First, when Congress first passed the federal special education laws in 1975 (which became the Individuals with Disabilities Education Act), it committed to funding 40 percent of the cost of compliance. It has never met this standard. Federal funding generally hovers around 20 percent. The $50 million that New Hampshire annually receives from the federal government should be closer to $100 million. The first place for advocacy to start is to instruct our elected members of the US House and Senators to appropriate the missing money. Resolutions by school districts and the state legislature demanding that federal funding promises be kept would be a good first step.

Second, New Hampshire should create a state program analogous to the insurance plan for special education funding proposed by Rep. Cam Kenney. A statewide insurance-style special education funding system would allow local officials to better plan for these expenses, as they'd know roughly what costs to expect year to year. Costs would also be spread across districts, allowing school boards to better focus on other programs and allowing local control to be enhanced.

Additionally, requiring communities without property wealth to raise money in the same way as communities with great property wealth is unfair, and contributes to the scapegoating of the families with high special education needs who often live in the more impoverished communities.

How to Fairly Fund Public Schools

Here's what I believe we should do to fairly fund public schools: diversify revenue sources, rely most heavily on more elastic sources of revenues, and ensure everyone contributes.

An income tax exclusively dedicated to funding public education is the best way to address public policy concerns about taxpayer equity, funding adequacy, and sustainability. Any state income tax should include a healthy exemption for low- and moderate-income families.

The income tax, however, cannot stand on its own.

Clif Below and Liz Hager had it right when they married a flat-rate income tax at 4 percent of adjusted gross income to a state property tax on second homes and business properties. Second homeowners who don't work in New Hampshire won't pay any income tax. Senator Mitt Romney, who owns a $10 million estate in Wolfeboro, New Hampshire, would not contribute to the education of New Hampshire's children if we had only an income tax. He doesn't work in New Hampshire and his Wolfeboro compound is not his primary residence. That's in Utah.

Not to pick on him, but Romney should pay his fair share. He can afford it. Romney's current total education tax bill on that $10 million compound is about $4,000 a year because Wolfeboro has so much expensive lakefront property and the taxes raised only fund local education efforts.

New Hampshire suffers from the same housing crisis as the rest of America. Our state is short twenty thousand housing units. Reducing the burden on property-tax payers in most of the state would encourage housing development to occur more evenly across the state and allow New Hampshire to start to address its housing shortage.

Vermont had school funding litigation in 1997.[253] The Massachusetts school funding case was decided in 1993.[254] Both states quickly responded to the court decisions with funding plans based on income, property, and sales taxes. Their funding plans have been successful, with minor tweaks, for decades.

Both Maine and Vermont use property taxes to raise funds for schools. They also use other funding, but put that aside. Both states recognize the incredibly regressive and inelastic nature of the property tax and use other state funds to lessen the harmful impact of property taxes, particularly on taxpayers with fixed incomes. I'd also follow some of these examples as part of my funding plan.

In 2019, Maine Governor Janet Mills committed more than $40 million to property tax relief programs.[255] The primary relief mechanism is called the Property Tax Fairness Credit program. It protects low- and moderate-income residents from paying more than 6 percent of their income in property taxes or 40 percent of their income in rent. Maine issues credits against the state's income tax or cash refunds to taxpayers who pay more than the designated amount, which is adjusted to inflation.[256]

Maine also has a property tax loan program that allows senior citizens and people with disabilities to avoid losing their homes to taxes. The program lends money to the homeowner and that money is used to pay property taxes to the local municipality. The loans are made from state monies and the "lifeline loans" are recouped when the participant dies or sells the home in question.[257] The loan program was announced by Governor Janet Mills in early 2022, with initial funding of $3.5 million.[258] The program, which has income requirements, is not only humane, but costs less than the nursing homes where elderly folks often move when they lose their homes to taxes.

Vermont's circuit breaker is called an education tax credit, for which lower- and middle-income Vermont homeowners are eligible. The program allows taxpayers with incomes up to about $130,000 to participate. The circuit breaker limits the amount of property taxes that go toward funding education to a certain percent of a taxpayer's home plus up to two acres of land. The state reimburses the local municipality for lost taxes. For low-income taxpayers, there is also a tax credit program against municipal taxes in addition to the typical exemptions.

New Hampshire does not have a meaningful state circuit breaker. Abatement of local property taxes are in the hands of select boards or similar bodies. There is no state circuit breaker to protect renters, and none to provide state help to homeowners with their local property taxes, which make up the huge bulk of property tax payments. The state empowers localities to enact small exemptions or allow abatements, but these then must be funded entirely by the other property owners in the locality, not by state monies.

According to the Institute on Taxation and Economic Policy, the need to use circuit breakers and the benefits derived from their use are clear. "'Circuit breakers' work exactly how they sound: they prevent homeowners and renters from being 'overloaded' by property taxes that go beyond what they can afford to pay. Under most circuit breakers, property taxes above a certain percentage of income are deemed unaffordable and credited back to the taxpayer. . . . Twenty-nine states and the District of Columbia have some form of circuit breaker in effect today, though some are far more robust than others."[259]

Vermont and Maine also offer better examples of current-use taxation than New Hampshire, and this topic should also be revisited in the context of general property tax reform.

Current-use taxation preserves open space and allows for certain limited (or current) uses related to forestry and farming. Right now, large New Hampshire timber corporations take big advantage of this law. Also, in New Hampshire, the local municipality funds the entire cost of the current-use program by forgoing significant property tax revenues, which are not reimbursed by the state. Vermont and Maine provide for state reimbursement to the local communities.

My colleague Natalie Laflamme lives in a community where almost 90 percent of the land is in "current use." This makes for a bucolic community, but one with a very limited tax base and few tax revenues. At the very least, state revenues should be used to reimburse foregone local revenues so that school funding doesn't suffer.

In 2018, Rusty Keith, a Lyme, New Hampshire, selectman, wrote the "estimate[d current-use] program costs property taxpayers some $118 million a year, a burden borne disproportionately by the property taxpayers of small rural municipalities."[260] More than three million acres, half New Hampshire's land area, are enrolled in the current-use program. The owners of this land receive significant discounts on their taxes.

That's my prescription.

- Combine about a 4 percent income tax with a state property tax on second homes and business properties,
- include good exemptions on the income tax and a state-funded circuit breaker for whatever local property tax remains, and
- re-examine current use taxation.

And After We Fund Our Schools

What do we do after we get schools funded?

John Adams's purpose for public education remains. An educated populace is necessary to maintain our democracy. The role of public education has also expanded. A solid public education is necessary to achieve wealth and health, increase life spans, and, dare I say, achieve happiness. Its role couldn't be any more important in this polarized world.

As the New Hampshire Constitution provides, we must "cherish" the interests of education. This doesn't mean that we should enshrine how we currently do education in stone and never examine or change it. There are good innovations that must be considered. These innovations must be evidence-based and not simply adopted to make education cheaper.

Educators must not be targeted in order to scare them away; New Hampshire's education commissioner has done this by creating penalties for teaching topics that concern race that make him feel uncomfortable. Teacher compensation must be fair. And, as we rely more and more heavily on paraprofessionals, their training, compensation, and benefits must be supported and professionalized.

There should be nothing in public education too sacred to avoid fair examination. The 180-day calendar year, for example, was based on agrarian needs. We now know that children regress over the summer. Why haven't we changed our school calendars?

New Hampshire has too many school districts. Which should be consolidated to improve efficiencies and reduce costs? The answer is not always obvious.

Are schools the right place to pilot four-day workweeks throughout the entire year? What happens on the fifth day? When would schools in this model take strategic two-week breaks? The same questions should be asked about school start times now that research makes clear the harm of sleep deprivation to adolescents.

We can include more methodology training in school; more "how" and less "what." Our three children, all of whom have grown up with the *Claremont* litigation, now all work as professionals. Paul Keiner was their middle-school English teacher and taught them how to be organized. To this day, they apply Keiner's principles when they start a new project. They call it being "Keinerized."

Ken Greenbaum, the Moultonborough superintendent, testified at our trial about an Individualized Education Program for every child in his school district, regardless of whether the child had a disability that qualified her for special education services. Moultonborough wanted to meet the needs of every child. The district also wasn't pressed to meet state minimum standards for school approval as the school leaders in Moultonborough considered them to be set too low. Instead, their practices were incorporated in higher-level curricular frameworks, later adopted by the state, that described what children should know when they graduated.

John Freeman proved what a little bit of extra money, well-deployed, could accomplish if it is sustained. Freeman obtained grants equaling about 5 percent of the Pittsfield budget to dramatically improve the school district's performance. He had the district spend the money on professional development that coordinated efforts of teachers within and between grades. He also organized and spent grant funds to better engage a community that extended beyond the arbitrary boundaries of his town to gather input and expertise that was needed by his district. Finally, he funded and encouraged student empowerment and extracurricular activities that created motivation and interest among the students.

Finally, while teachers will invariably have their own books and other resources that they'll bring to school, we should learn from the "red dots" incident, where stickering personally owned items in each of the poorer schools resulted in a sea of red. Supplying materials is a part of the state's duty to provide an adequate education.

We can make education better to preserve what is best about our democracy. But it takes community commitment, leadership, and, yes, a bit of money raised equitably in a manner that doesn't make public schools the cause of resentment. Once we get the basics right, we can devote ourselves to helping public schools flourish for the good of our children and our next generation of leaders.

Good luck to you who work to improve your schools and your communities. Take care of each other. Share your lessons.

Endnotes

1   "Making the Grade 2023," Education Law Center online, https://edlawcenter.org/research/making-the-grade-2023/.

2   Brown v. Board of Education of Topeka, 347 U.S. 483 (1954).

3   Brown at 493.

4   Plessy v. Ferguson, 163 U.S. 537 (1896).

5   Sweatt v. Painter, 339 U.S. 629 (1950) and McLaurin v. Oklahoma State Regents, 629 U.S. 637 (1950).

6   Brennan Center for Justice, State Court Report, October 23, 2023.

7   Brown II, 349 U.S. 294 (1955).

8   "Belton (Bulah) v. Gebhart," National Park Service online, https://www.nps.gov/brvb/learn/historyculture/delaware.htm.

9   "Bolling v. Sharpe," Wikipedia, https://en.wikipedia.org/wiki/Bolling_v._Sharpe.

10   "Vilified in 1940s, Federal Judge is Honored As Civil Rights Hero," US Courts online, April 14, 2014, https://www.uscourts.gov/news/2014/04/14/vilified-1940s-federal-judge-honored-civil-rights-hero.

11   Alexander v. Holmes County Board of Education, 396 U.S. 19 (1969).

12   Valerie J. Nelson, "John Serrano Jr., 69; his lawsuit changed the way state's schools are funded," *LA Times* online, December 6, 2006, https://www.latimes.com/archives/la-xpm-2006-dec-06-me-serrano6-story.html.

13   Wolinsky, "Reflections of a Litigator: Serrano v. Priest Goals and Strategies," *BYU Education and Law Journal* 2021, no. 2, art. 8.

14   McInnis v. Shapiro, 293 F. Supp. 327 (N.D. Ill. 1969) and Burruss v. Wilkerson, 310 F. Supp. 572, 573 (W.D.Va. 1969). "But we do not believe [the school funding statutes] are creatures of discrimination by the State."

15   Christine Rienstra Kiracofe and Spencer Weiler, "Surfing the Waves: An Examination of School Funding Litigation from Serrano v. Priest to Cook v. Raimondo and the Possible Transition of the Fourth Wave," *BYU Education and Law Journal* 2021, no. 2, art. 5.

16   Serrano v. Priest, 5 Cal. 3d at 589.

17   City of Los Angeles v. Alameda Books, Inc., 535 U.S. 425, 455 (2002). "Strict scrutiny leaves few survivors."

18   Serrano, 5 Cal. 3d at 605.

19   Serrano, 5 Cal. 3d at 605.

20   Serrano, 5 Cal. 3d at 607.

21   Serrano, 5 Cal. 3d at 595.

22   Loving v. Virginia, 388 U.S. 1 (1967).

23   Serrano, 5 Cal. 3d at 600.

24   José A. Cárdenas, EdD, *Texas School Finance Reform, An IDRA Perspective,* Intercultural Development Research Association (1997). Hereafter, "Cárdenas."

25   Cárdenas.

26   Michael Eric Taylor, "The African-American community of Richmond, Virginia: 1950–1956," Master's Thesis, University of Richmond (1994), 157.

27   John C. Jeffries, Jr., *Justice Lewis F. Powell, Jr., A Biography,* Fordham University Press (2001). Hereafter, "Jeffries."

28   Linda Greenhouse, "Lewis Powell, Crucial Centrist Justice, Dies at 90," *New York Times* online, August 26, 1998, https://www.nytimes.com/1998/08/26/us/lewis-powell-crucial-centrist-justice-dies-at-90.html.

29   Jeffries at 143-144.

30   "Bar Chief Warns of Crime Rate," San Francisco Chronicle, March 24, 1965.

31   Greenhouse, "Lewis Powell."

32   Jeffries at 174.

33   "Barbara Johns," *Virginia Changemakers,* https://edu.lva.virginia.gov/changemakers/items/show/121.

34   Davis v. County School Board, 103 F. Supp 337, 340 (ED Va 1952).

35   Nancy MacLean, *Democracy in Chains* (Penguin Books, 2017), XV.

36   The author requested information about the legal fees paid to the Hunton firm by PE County from the current superintendent of schools for PE County and from the managing partner of the Hunton firm, Mr. Todd Hayward. Both requests were ignored.

37   "With All Deliberate Speed," *Backstory* (blog), June 15, 2015, https://backstoryradio.org/blog/with-all-deliberate-speed/.

38   Greenhouse, "Lewis Powell."

39   https://www.theusconstitution.org/news/the-right-wing-legacy-of-justice-lewis-powell-and-what-it-means-for-the-supreme-court-today/.

40   FBI memorandum, March 25, 1964, 3, https://vault.fbi.gov/lewis-f.-powell-jr/lewis-f.-powell-jr.-part-08-of/view.

41   Letter from Powell to Hoover, August 28, 1964, 8, https://vault.fbi.gov/lewis-f.-powell-jr/lewis-f.-powell-jr.-part-08-of/view.

42   FBI memorandum, April 1, 1965, 9, https://vault.fbi.gov/lewis-f.-powell-jr/lewis-f.-powell-jr.-part-08-of/view.

43   "The Lewis Powell Memo: A Corporate Blueprint to Dominate Democracy," Greenpeace online, https://www.greenpeace.org/usa/democracy/the-lewis-powell-memo-a-corporate-blueprint-to-dominate-democracy/.

44   Powell Memo.

45   Powell's alma mater, the Washington and Lee School of Law, maintains an online archive of his work, including a section devoted to his papers generated while he was a justice of the Supreme Court. https://law.wlu.edu/powell-archives/. Many of the comments about Powell's thoughts were derived from memos written to Powell by his law clerks and his responses to those memos. Larry Hammond, one of Powell's clerks, wrote in his bench memo for the case, "There is undoubtedly some level of state expenditure at which the parties could agree that an adequate minimum educational package has been offered." Powell responded: "Unlikely—NEA and unions *always* demand more money." (Emphasis in original note.) *San Antonio Independent School District v. Rodriguez.* Supreme Court Case Files Collection. Box 8. Powell Papers. Lewis F. Powell Jr. Archives, Washington and Lee University School of Law, Virginia.

46   James D. Robenalt, "The unknown Supreme Court clerk who single-handedly created the Roe v. Wade viability standard," *Washington Post* online, November 29, 2021. https://www.washingtonpost.com/history/2021/11/29/viability -standard-abortion-supreme-court-hammond/. Hammond is credited with first suggesting the viability analysis used by Justice Blackmun in *Roe v. Wade*, a decision Powell supported. For two decades prior to his death in 2020, Hammond was also president of the Arizona version of the Innocence Project, working to exonerate death row inmates.

47   Jeffries at 55-56. Wilkinson became a law professor and judge, ultimately serving on the US Court of Appeals for the 4th Circuit, which includes Virginia.

48   Thomas Jefferson, "Memoir, correspondence, and miscellanies from the papers of T. Jefferson," (1829).

49   George Washington, Farewell Address, in Allen, ed, George Washington at 521-22 (1988) and Charles R. Kesler, Education and Politics: Lessons from the Founding, 1991 U of Chicago Legal Forum.

50   "Charles Alan Wright," Wikipedia, https://en.wikipedia.org/wiki/Charles_Alan _Wright; John H. Cushman Jr., "Charles A. Wright, 72, Legal Consultant to Nixon, Dies," *New York Times* online, July 9, 2000, https://www.nytimes.com/2000/07/09 /us/charles-a-wright-72-legal-consultant-to-nixon-dies.html.

51   Memo, Powell to Larry Hammond, August 31, 1972, Supreme Court Case Files Collection. Box 8. Powell Papers. Lewis F. Powell Jr. Archives, Washington and Lee University School of Law, Virginia.

52   Letter, Charles Alan Wright to Powell, April 25, 1973, Supreme Court Case Files Collection. Box 8. Powell Papers. Lewis F. Powell Jr. Archives, Washington and Lee University School of Law, Virginia.

53   San Antonio Independent School District v. Rodriguez, 411 U.S. at 28.

54   Brown v. Board of Education of Topeka, 347 U.S. at 493.

55   San Antonio Independent School District v. Rodriguez, 411 U.S. at 71.

56   Danny Adelman explained at the ELC-sponsored litigators' conference in 2023 that the awful conditions of school buildings cause students to suffer health problems, including hypertension, that plague students for the rest of their lives.

57   Matt Barnum, "The racist idea that changed American education," February 27, 2023, Chalkbeat, https://www.chalkbeat.org/2023/2/27/23612851/school-funding-rodriguez-racist-supreme-court.

58   Barnum, "The racist idea."

59   Wilkinson, "The Supreme Court, The Equal Protection Clause, and the Three Faces of Constitutional Equality," *Virginia Law Review* 61, no. 5 (June 1975): 945, 949.

60   Supreme Court Case Files Collection. Box 8, 246-247. Powell Papers. Lewis F. Powell Jr. Archives, Washington and Lee University School of Law, Virginia.

61   San Antonio Independent School District v. Rodriguez, 411 U.S. 677, 691 (1973).

62   Erika M. Kitzmiller, *The Roots of Educational Inequality* (University of Pennsylvania Press 2022), 140.

63   Cárdenas, 45.

64   Professor Kauffman was kind enough to share *pan dulce* with my wife, Amy, and me at Marisa Bono's home in January 2023. Marisa Bono is the executive director of "Every Texan," a strong and accomplished advocacy group headquartered in San Antonio. Bono was previously a lawyer with MALDEF who worked on education litigation in the Southwest.

65   See IDRA Newsletter L, no. 4 (April 2023), https://files.eric.ed.gov/fulltext/ED628666.pdf.

66   Cárdenas, 5.

67   "Edgewood ISD v. Kirby," The Texas Politics Project at the University of Texas at Austin, https://texaspolitics.utexas.edu/educational-resources/edgewood-isd-v-kirby.

68   Cárdenas, 220-21.

69   Edgewood Independent School District v. Kirby, 777 SW 2d at 391 (Tx.1989)

70   Edgewood Independent School District v. Kirby, 777 SW 2d at 393.

71   Cárdenas, 339–43.

72   Cárdenas, 361–62.

73   "West Orange Cove Ruling," IDRA, https://www.idra.org/resource-center/west-orange-cove-ruling/.

74   See "Yazzie/Martinez v. State of New Mexico Decision," University of New Mexico, https://race.unm.edu/assets/documents/yazzie-martinez-english.pdf.

75   Serrano I, 5 Cal. 3d at 596, fn. 11.

76   Serrano II, 18 Cal. 3d at 747.

77   Serrano II, 18 Cal. 3d at 748.

78   Serrano II, 18 Cal. 3d at 768.

79   Serrano III, 20 Cal. 3d 31 (1977).

80   William Fischel, "Did Serrano Cause Proposition 13?" *National Tax Journal* 42, no. 4 (December 1989).

81   Josh Mound, "Stirrings of Revolt: Regressive Levies, the Pocketbook Squeeze, and the 1960s Roots of the 1970s Tax Revolt," *Journal of Policy History* 32, no.2 (April 2020): 105; Isaac Martin, "Does School Finance Litigation Cause Taxpayer Revolt? Serrano and Proposition 13," *Law & Society Review* 40, no. 3 (September 2006): 525.

82   Skeen v. State of Minnesota, 505 N.W. 2d 299 (MN 1993).

83   "Massachusetts Passes First Education Law," Mass Moments, https://www.massmoments.org/moment-details/massachusetts-passes-first-education-law.html.

84   See "Massachusetts Passes First Education Law."

85   "Horace Mann (1796–1859)," *Only a Teacher* series, PBS online, https://www.pbs.org/onlyateacher/horace.html.

86   Alexandria Azzar, "History of Literacy Laws in America and the Fight in 2022," Black Organizing Project, https://blackorganizingproject.org/the-power-of-books-and-the-fight-in-2022/.

87   NH RSA 186:5 (1919).

88   "Extension of education, 1914–39," UK Parliament online, https://www.parliament.uk/about/living-heritage/transformingsociety/livinglearning/school/overview/1914-39/.

89   Douglas E. Hall, "Lessons from New Hampshire: What we can learn from the History of the State's role in School Finance 1642-1998," *New Hampshire Center for Public Policy Studies*, April 1998, unpublished article maintained in author's collection.

90   See Ross Gittell and Timothy Lord, "Profile of New Hampshire's Foreign-born Population," University of New Hampshire Carsey Institute, no. 8 (Spring 2008).

91   Gittell and Lord, "Profile of New Hampshire's Foreign-born Population."

92   91st Biennial Report, NH State Board of Education (1983–85).

93   "From the Archives; State-Wide Kindergarten Seemed Far-Fetched in 1990," New Hampshire Public Radio online, August 20, 2015, https://www.nhpr.org/nhpr-blogs/2015-08-20/from-the-archives-state-wide-kindergarten-seemed-far-fetched-in-1990.

94   See, e.g., Ro Khanna, *Dignity in a Digital Age* (Simon and Schuster 2022).

95   Sarah Gibson, "'We're Trying to Just Survive': How State Cuts Fueled Berlin's School Funding Crisis," New Hampshire Public Radio online, March 28, 2019, https://www.nhpr.org/nh-news/2019-03-28/were-trying-to-just-survive-how-state-cuts-fueled-berlins-school-funding-crisis.

96   Jackie Harris and Rick Ganley, "Berlin's mayor-elect Robert Cone says Burgess biomass plant is here to stay," New Hampshire Public Radio

online, November 20, 2023, https://www.nhpr.org/nh-news/2023-11-20/berlins-mayor-elect-robert-cone-says-burgess-biopower-plant-is-here-to-stay.

97   "Joy workers vote for pay cut," United Press International, October 24, 1983, https://www.upi.com/Archives/1983/10/24/Joy-workers-vote-for-pay-cut/9813435816000/.

98   "Things are so tough in Claremont, NH that the city literally can't give away commercial land. The city launched a competition in May called the 'Perfect Place Challenge' to give away a lot for a buck in their new industrial park to the most promising business to apply. Unfortunately, despite clever advertising, the city hasn't found a single taker. . . ." https://archboston.com/community/threads/claremont-nh.1212/.

99   Khari Thompson and Carrie Jung, "How racism shows up in Boston sports culture," WBUR online, updated July 15, 2023, https://www.wbur.org/radioboston/2023/04/28/celtics-bill-russell-adam-jones-weei.

100 John Gfroerer, "Powerful as Truth, William Loeb and 35 Years of New Hampshire," Accompany Video Production, 2001 and aired on NH PBS February 20, 2014.

101 Gfroerer, "Powerful as Truth."

102 Meg Heckman, *Political Godmother: Nackey Scripps Loeb and the Newspaper that Shook the Republican Party* (Potomac Books, 2020).

103 Gabrielle Emanuel, "The Cruel Story Behind the 'Reverse Freedom Rides,'" NPR online, February 29, 2020, https://www.npr.org/sections/codeswitch/2020/02/29/809740346/the-cruel-story-behind-the-reverse-freedom-rides.

104 See also, Arnie Alpert, "Nackey Loeb and the Spread of Right-Wing Populism," InDepthNH.org, July 26, 2020, https://indepthnh.org/2020/07/26/nackey-loeb-and-the-spread-of-right-wing-populism/.

105 "The 15 Year Battle for Martin Luther King, Jr. Day," Smithsonian National Museum of African American History and Culture online, https://nmaahc.si.edu/explore/stories/15-year-battle-martin-luther-king-jr-day.

106 "The 15 Year Battle."

107 Michael Brindley, "NH's Martin Luther King Jr. Day Didn't Happen Without a Fight," New Hampshire Public Radio online, August 27, 2013, https://www.nhpr.org/nh-news/2013-08-27/n-h-s-martin-luther-king-jr-day-didnt-happen-without-a-fight.

108 *Individual Income Tax: Year of Adoption by State*, digital image of a map, Tax Foundation, https://files.taxfoundation.org/legacy/docs/Income%20Tax%20Adoption%20Year%20by%20State%20UPDATED.png.

109 "State income tax," Wikipedia, https://en.wikipedia.org/wiki/State_income_tax.

110 "The Progressive Era: 1895–1925, A Short History of Wisconsin," Wisconsin Historical Society online, https://www.wisconsinhistory.org/Records/Article/CS3588; "Wisconsin Income Tax is 100 Years Old," Wisconsin Historical Society online, https://www.wisconsinhistory.org/Records/Article/.

111 Tax Foundation map.

112 Mark Luscombe, "Historical income tax rates," Wolters Kluwer online, December 30, 2022, https://www.wolterskluwer.com/en/expert-insights/whole-ball-of-tax-historical-income-tax-rates.

113 Sacha Dray, Camille Landais, and Stefanie Stantcheva, "Wealth and Property Taxation in the United States," NBER Working Paper 31080, National Bureau of Economic Research, March 2023, https://econ.lse.ac.uk/staff/clandais/cgi-bin/Articles/DLS_wealth_property_tax.pdf.

114 Conversation between Craig Benson and the author on November 29, 2023.

115 Benson and author conversation.

116 Michaela Towfighi, "Feeling Taxed Out," *Concord Monitor*, December 3, 2023.

117 "Facts & Figures 2024: How Does Your State Compare?" Tax Foundation online, April 3, 2024, https://taxfoundation.org/data/all/state/2024-state-tax-data/.

118 "State and Local Tax Burdens, Calendar Year 2022," Tax Foundation online, April 7, 2022, https://taxfoundation.org/data/all/state/tax-burden-by-state-2022/.

119 Jared Walczak, "How High Are State and Local Tax Collections in Your State?" Tax Foundation online, November 21, 2023, https://taxfoundation.org/data/all/state/state-local-tax-collections-per-capita-fy-2021/.

120 "2022 Making the Grade," Education Law Center online, https://edlawcenter.org/research/making-the-grade-2022.html .

121 Laconia Board of Education v. Laconia, 111 N.H. 389 (1971).

122 Laconia Board.

123 Paul Snow, "Spending and Taxation for Public School Education in New Hampshire," expert report, June 6, 1983.

124 91st Biennial Report of the NH State Board of Education, (1983-1985).

125 Jeff Feingold, "Getting Our Money's Worth," *The Spectator*, October 1990.

126 Feingold, "Getting Our Money's Worth."

127 Feingold, "Getting Our Money's Worth."

128 *New Hampshire: My Responsibility, Final Report* (Governor's Commission on New Hampshire in the 21st Century, 1991), 7, https://www.nh.gov/water-sustainability/publications/documents/nh-my-responsibility-1991.pdf.

129 Rule 38, NH Supreme Court Rules, Canon 3C (1).

130 See Molly McUsic, "The Use of Education Clauses in School Finance Reform Litigation," *Harvard Journal on Legislation* 28, no. 2 (Summer 1991): 307.

131 Claremont v. Governor, 138 N.H. 183 (1993).

132 Structuring Order of December 27, 1995 at 2.

133 Rick Broussard, "The Man Who Changed the Rules," *New Hampshire Editions 14, no.3* (March 1999): 20.

134 Associated Press, "Bakesale to Aid Education Funding Foes," *Union Leader*, March 10, 1994.

135 Broussard, "Man Who Changed the Rules."

136 Jo Becker, "Claremont Suit Destined for Appeal," *Concord Monitor*, May 12, 1996.

137 Becker, "Claremont Suit."

138 Tresa Baldas, "Judge Inspects Districts' Schools," *Concord Monitor*, April 27, 1996.

139 Trial Transcript, Vol. I at 42.

140 Transcript at 55–56.

141 Trial Transcript, Vol III at 19.

142 Transcript at 35.

143 Trial Transcript, Vol IV at 20.

144 Transcript at 42.

145 Transcript at 44–45.

146 Transcript at 216.

147 John Distaso, "Ex-Supt.: Claremont Lacks Funds," *Union Leader*, May 11, 1996.

148 Trial Transcript, Vol. V at 119.

149 John Distaso, "State Moves to Exclude Testimony by Ex-Officials," *Union Leader*, May 14, 1996.

150 Trial Transcript, Vol. V at 161.

151 Transcript at 188–89.

152 Distaso, "Claremont Lacks Funds."

153 See trial transcript, Vol. 23 at 186–187.

154 Becker, "Claremont Suit."

155 John Distaso, "Plaintiffs Show How Rich Live, *Union Leader*, May 21, 1996, at A-4.

156 Associated Press, "Official: 'Pittsfield Schools, Teachers Battle for Basics," *Union Leader*, May 22, 1996.

157 Jo Becker, "Allenstown Official Paints a Bleak Picture," *Concord Monitor*, May 24, 1996.

158 Kent Fischer, "A Have-Not High School," *Concord Monitor*, May 5, 1996.

159 Fischer, "A Have-Not High School."

160 Trial Transcript, Vol. 21 at 203.

161 Transcript at 209.

162 Trial Transcript, Vol. 22 at 43–44.

163   William M. Stevens, "Nixon School Report a Challenge; It Denies Direct Link Between Funds and Pupils' Progress," *New York Times*, March 3, 1970:

164 C. Kirabo Jackson and Claire Mackevicius, "The Distribution of School Spending Impacts," NBER Working Paper 28517, National Bureau of Economic Research, rev. July 2021, https://www.nber.org/system/files/working_papers/w28517/w28517.pdf.

165 Matt Barnum, "The racist idea that changed American education," February 27, 2023, Chalkbeat, www.chalkbeat.org/2023/2/27/23612851/school-funding-rodriguez-racist-supreme-court.

166 Andrew Merton, "State's Witnesses Self-Destruct," *Boston Globe*, June 23, 1996 at NH-2.

167 Merton, State's Witnesses.

168 Merton, State's Witnesses.

169 Claremont School Dist. v. Governor, 138 N.H. 183, 192 (N.H. 1993).

170 Order on the Merits, November 2, 1992, at 133.

171 Claremont v. Governor, 142 N.H. 462 (1997).

172 Jim Graham, "For Lawyers, Sweet Victory," *Concord Monitor*, December 18, 1997, at 1.

173 Graham, For Lawyers.

174 Graham, For Lawyers.

175 Matthew T. Hall, "For Volinsky, Few Obstacles Too Large, *Concord Monitor*, January 4, 1998.

176 "Oral History Project," NH Supreme Court Society online, https://www.nhsupremecourtsociety.org/special-projects/oral-histories/.

177 Sarah Schweitzer, "Let's See If They Follow Through," *Concord Monitor*, December 18, 1997.

178 Schweitzer, "Follow Through."

179 Editorial, "A Statist Decision, 'Claremont' Ruling a Boon to Broad-Basers," *Union Leader*, December 18, 1997.

180 William Siroty, "Letter to the Editor," *Union Leader*, January 4, 1998.

181 Matthew T. Hall, "Court Sweeps Out School Tax System, State is Ordered to Fix It," *Concord Monitor*, December 18, 1997.

182 Hall, "Fix It."

183 There are two accolades that we received of which I am very proud. First, the New Hampshire branch of the ACLU honored all eighteen of us plaintiff lawyers with the Bill of Rights Award. The award was for making the Constitution a living, breathing document with enforceable rights. Second, I shared the NEA's Friend of Education Award with Charlie Marston in 1996, a very high honor indeed.

184 Dan Balz, "School v. Property-Tax Dilemma Testing New Hampshire Communities," *Washington Post,* January 10, 1997.

185 Balz, "School v. Property-Tax Dilemma."

186 John DiStaso, "Shaheen's Education Fund Plan Challenged," *Union Leader*, January 29, 1998.

187 Dan Billin, "Shaheen's School Plan Would Leave Disparities in Tax Rates," *Valley News*, January 29, 1998.

188 Billin, "Shaheen's School Plan."

189 Editorial, "School Finance, III," *Valley News*, January 31, 1998.

190 Editorial, "School Finance, III."

191 Matthew T. Hall, "ABC's Constitutionality Challenged," *Concord Monitor*, March 21, 1998.

192 Sarah Koenig, "Republicans rally behind amendment," *Concord Monitor*, February 1, 1998.

193 Opinion of the Justices, 142 N.H. 892 (1998).

194 CPI Inflation Calculator, online tool, https://www.in2013dollars.com/us/inflation/1998?amount=28000.

195 "New Hampshire: 2000, Summary Social, Economic, and Housing Characteristics," US Census, April 2003, https://www2.census.gov/library/publications/2003/dec/phc-2-31.pdf.

196 Connair, "Question: Is New Hampshire Raising Enough for School Spending?" *Wall Street Journal*, August 11, 1999.

197 Claremont School District v. Governor, 144 N.H. 210 (1999).

198 NHRSA 189:14-a.

199 Editorial, "Coming Together," *Concord Monitor*, February 29, 2000.

200 "Coming Together," *Concord Monitor*.

201 "Coming Together," *Concord Monitor*.

202 "David Brock Impeachment Trial: 2000," Encyclopedia.com, https://www.encyclopedia.com/law/law-magazines/david-brock-impeachment-trial-2000. See also Carey Goldberg, "New Hampshire Supreme Court Justice Is Acquitted in His Impeachment Trial," *New York Times*, October 11, 2000, https://www.nytimes.com/2000/10/11/us/new-hampshire-supreme-court-justice-is-acquitted-in-his-impeachment-trial.html.

203 Opinion of the Justices (Reformed Public School Financing System), 145 N.H. 474, 476 (2000).

204 Opinion of the Justices (Tax Plan Referendum), 143 N.H. 429 (1999).

205 Claremont Sch. Dist. & a.v. Governor & a., 147 N.H. 499, 508–9 (N.H. 2002) citing Fish v. Homestead Woolen Mills, 134 N.H. 361, 365 (1991).

206 *Union Leader* editorial, January 4, 2002.

207 "Governor Lynch Calls For Education Funding Amendment," New Hampshire Public Radio online, October 21, 2011, https://www.nhpr.org/nh-news/2011-10-21/governor-lynch-calls-for-education-funding-amendment.

208 "Chuck Douglas," Wikipedia, https://en.wikipedia.org/wiki/Chuck_Douglas.

209 Ken Ringle, "A Splitting Headache," *Washington Post*, March 14, 1999. https://www.washingtonpost.com/archive/lifestyle/1999/03/15/a-splitting-headache/671f88ec-cce0-4ed0-b622-653d34ef9eeb/.

210 Bailey Ludlam, "Gov. Lynch's education amendment defeated by the House, another proposal remains pending," Ballotpedia, December 5, 2011, https://ballotpedia.org /Gov._Lynch%27s_education_amendment_defeated_by_the_House,_another _proposal_remains_pending.

211 Sirrell v. State, 146 N.H. 364 (2001).

212 Londonderry School District v. State, 154 N.H. 153 (2006).

213 Londonderry.

214 Londonderry at 162.

215 Londonderry at 163.

216 Phil Ochs, "Love Me, I'm a Liberal," side two, track 5 on *Phil Ochs in Concert*, Elektra, 1966.

217 https://carsey.unh.edu/sites/default/files/media/2020/12/final_report _forcommission_v5_12012020.pdf.

218 Oyebola Olabisi, "New Hampshire's Quest for a Constitutionally Adequate Education," New England Public Policy Center, Discussion Paper 06-2, October 2006.

219 See also Paul Wellstone, *The Conscience of a Liberal* (University of Minnesota Press, 2001).

220 Contoocook Valley School District v. State, 174 N.H. 154 (2021).

221 See Amanda Gokee, "NH school funding and education tax scheme found unconstitutional," *Boston Globe*, November 20, 2023 and Michael Kitch, "Judge: NH school funding is inadequate, unconstitutional," *NH Business Review*, November 21, 2023.

222 "William Penn School District et al. v. Pennsylvania Department of Education et al.," Fund Our Schools PA online, https://www.fundourschoolspa.org /students-vs-pennsylvania-department-of-education.

223 "Bristol Township School District," *US News and World Report* online, https://www. usnews.com/education/k12/ristolania/districts/ristol-township-sd-103473.

224 "School Funding Lawsuit Update, Basic Education Funding Commission Releases a Proposal that Could Make a Life-Changing Difference for Pennsylvania Students," Public Interest Law Center online, January 11, 2024, https://pubintlaw.org /cases-and-projects/basic-education-funding-commission-releases-a-proposal -that-could-make-a-life-changing-difference-for-pennsylvania-students/.

225 Nancy West, "Slashed Croydon School Budget Restored on New Vote Saturday," InDepthNH.org, May 7, 2022, https://indepthnh.org/2022/05/07 /slashed-croydon-school-budget-restored-on-new-vote-saturday/.

226 "Free State Project Update," Granite State Matters online, July 2023, https://us16 .campaign-archive.com/?u=6c680615e217a5e85c70827b9&id=ca05a1e211.

227 See Dan Barry, "One Small Step for Democracy in a 'Live Free or Die' Town," *New York Times*, July 10, 2022, https://www.nytimes.com/2022/07/10/us/croydon -free-state-politics.html.

228 Ian Underwood, "Ian Underwood on What Free Staters Believe," InDepthNH.org, July 25, 2022, https://indepthnh.org/2022/07/25/op-ed-ian -underwood-on-what-free-staters-believe/.

229 "Prenda in New Hampshire," Prenda (microschool company) online, https://www. prenda.com/states/new-hampshire.

230 Barry, "One Small Step for Democracy."

231 nmefoundation.org.

232 Eric Rynston-Lobel, "Cuts Soften Budget Blow," *Concord Monitor*, February 10, 2024.

233 For more information about Pittsfield's successful experiment in providing sufficient resources, the district's master planning document may be found here: https://www. sau51.org/sau/wp-content/uploads/2013/03/263-DLSC-II-Pittsfield-NMEF -Revised-Logic-Model-5.15.17.pdf.

234 "Early Education/Pre-K," New Futures online, https://new-futures.org/issues /early-education.

235 "Low Preschool Enrollment Rates Threaten to Worsen Student Achievement," Annie E. Casey Foundation online, October 24, 2023, https://www.aecf.org/blog /low-preschool-enrollment-rates-threaten-to-worsen-student-achievement.

236 "The State of Child Care in New Hampshire: End of One-Time Federal Invest-ments May Reduce Industry Stability," NH Fiscal Policy Institute online, February 2, 2024, https://nhfpi.org/resource/the-state-of-child-care-in-new-hampshire-end -of-one-time-federal-investments-may-reduce-industry-stability/.

237 "Fact Sheet: Vice President Harris Announces Action to Lower Child Care costs for More than 100,000 Families," press statement available at WhiteHouse.gov, February 29, 2024.

238 Funding-Public-Education-in-Maine-2020_Final.pdf, https://www.educatemaine .org/docs/Funding-Public-Education-in-Maine-2020_Final.pdf.

239 Lynn A. Karoly, "The Economic Returns from Investing in Early Childhood Pro-grams in the Granite State," RAND research organization online, https://www. rand.org/pubs/research_briefs/RB9952.html.

240 "The State of Child Care in New Hampshire: End of One-Time Federal Invest-ments May Reduce Industry Stability," issue brief available at NHFPI.org .

241 NHFPI, "The State of Child Care."

242 "$122 Billion: The Growing, Annual Cost of the Infant-Toddler Child Care Crisis," Council for a Strong America online, February 2, 2023, https://www.strongnation .org/articles/2038-122-billion-the-growing-annual-cost-of-the-infant-toddler -child-care-crisis.

243 Troy Closson, "A $30,000 Question: Who Will Get a Free Preschool Seat in New York City?" *New York Times*, February 8, 2024, https://www.nytimes .com/2024/02/27/nyregion/nyc-free-3k-preschool.html?searchResultPosition=1.

244 "Early Childhood Education," NH Department of Education online, https://www.education.nh.gov/who-we-are/deputy-commissioner/early-childhood-education.

245 "Early Education/Pre-K," New Futures.

246 Funding Public Education in Maine.

247 "Head Start Policy and Regulations," Head Start online, https://eclkc.ohs.acf.hhs.gov/policy/pi/acf-pi-hs-23-02.

248 "Head Start Policy and Regulations."

249 See *State of Preschool 2022 Yearbook*, National Institute for Early Education Research, Rutgers University.

250 "Head Start Policy and Regulations."

251 "Early Childhood Education," NH Dept. of Ed.

252 See NHRSA 198:40-a.

253 Brigham v. Vermont Department of Education, 166 Vt. 246 (1997).

254 McDuffy v. Secretary of Education, 615 N.E.2d 516 (MA 1993).

255 https://www.mecep.org/blog/maines-budget-provides-historic-supports-and-fortifies-the-foundation-for-a-strong-economy/.

256 "Get a Refund on Your Property Taxes or Rent," Pine Tree Legal Assistance online, 2014, https://www.ptla.org/maine-property-tax-fairness-credit.

257 "The State Property Tax Deferral Program: 2024 Guide for Applicants," Maine.gov, https://www.maine.gov/revenue/sites/maine.gov.revenue/files/inline-files/DeferralApplicantGuide.pdf.

258 "Governor Mills Announces $3.5 Million in Lifeline Loans to Cover the Property Tax Bills of Older or Disabled Maine People," Maine.gov, January 5, 2022, https://www.maine.gov/governor/mills/news/governor-mills-announces-35-million-lifeline-loans-cover-property-tax-bills-older-or-disabled.

259 "Preventing an Overload: How Property Tax Circuit Breakers Promote Housing Affordability," ITEP online, 2023, https://itep.org/property-tax-affordability-circuit-breaker-credits/.

260 Michael Kitch, "Current use system raises questions on fairness, cost," *NH Business Review*, March 1, 2018, https://www.nhbr.com/current-use-system-raises-questions-on-fairness-cost/.

Index

Acknowledgments

Thanks to Tom Connair and Arpy Saunders for starting me on this school funding journey and trusting my judgment along the way. And to Steve Bright for first suggesting that lawyers could and should do good. Thanks to Jeff Deck for whipping my writing into shape and to Jeff, Eric, Michael, and Caitlin, my first readers. Thanks also to Becky for recommending Peter E. Randall Publisher. And finally, a very big thank you to Mike Marland for the generous artistic contributions he made over many years to the cause and to me.

About the Author

AUTHOR ANDRU VOLINSKY is an attorney, a former NH Executive Councilor and 2020 candidate for governor who is currently flunking retirement by writing his first book, teaching a graduate course in public policy and practicing law on a limited basis. He was the lead lawyer in the Claremont School Funding case for twenty years. Andru earned his BA from the University of Miami in psychology in

1976 and a Certificate in Conflicts Resolution Studies from the University of Pittsburgh in 1975. He earned his law degree from George Washington University in 1980. He lives with his wife, Amy, in East Concord, NH. Follow him on his Substack, https://substack.com/@andruvolinsky.